The Complete

CUSTOMER SERVICE MODEL LETTER & MEMO BOOK

MICHAEL RAMUNDO

PRENTICE HALL
Englewood Cliffs, New Jersey 07632

Prentice-Hall International, Inc., *London*
Prentice-Hall of Australia Pty., Ltd., *Sydney*
Prentice-Hall Canada, Inc., *Toronto*
Prentice-Hall Hispanoamericana, S.A., *Mexico*
Prentice-Hall of India Private Ltd., *New Delhi*
Prentice-Hall of Japan, Inc., *Tokyo*
Prentice-Hall of Southeast Asia Pte., Ltd., *Singapore*
Editora Prentice-Hall do Brasil, Ltda., *Rio de Janeiro*

© 1995 by
PRENTICE HALL

10   9   8   7   6   5   4   3   2   1

This publication is designed to provide accurate and authoritative information in regard to the subject matter covered. It is sold with the understanding that the publisher is not engaged in rendering legal, accounting, or other professional service. If legal advice or other expert assistance is required, the services of a competent professional person should be sought.

From a Declaration of Principles Jointly Adopted by
a Committee of the American Bar Association
and a Committee of Publishers and Associations.

Library of Congress Cataloging-in-Publication Data

Ramundo, Michael.
    The complete customer service model letter & memo book / Michael Ramundo.
       p.   cm.
    Includes index.
    ISBN 0–13–335803–8
    1. Commercial correspondence. 2. Customer service. 3. Business communication. 4. Memorandums.   I. Title.
HF5726.R35 1995
a651.7'5—dc20
                                            94–29915
                                              CIP

ISBN 0-13-335803-8

PRENTICE HALL
Career and Personal Development
Englewood Cliffs, NJ 07632

Simon & Schuster, A Paramount Communications Company

PRINTED IN THE UNITED STATES OF AMERICA

Contents

Part One:
COMMUNICATING *with* CURRENT CUSTOMERS—*1*

Chapter *1*: THE ORDER—*3*

Chapter *2*: FULFILLMENT AND DELIVERY—*13*

Chapter *3*: BILLING CLARIFICATIONS AND DISPUTES—*31*

Chapter *4*: CUSTOMER-DEALER ISSUES—*41*

HOW TO DO IT *41*

Chapter *5*: THANKS FOR THE PURCHASE—*53*

HOW TO DO IT *53*

Chapter *6*: MAXIMIZING PRODUCT BENEFITS—*61*

HOW TO DO IT *61*

Chapter 7: CUSTOMER SUPPORT AND TRAINING—70

Chapter *8*: WARRANTY AND REPAIR ISSUES—*86*

Chapter *9*: PRODUCT COMPLAINTS—*100*

Chapter *IO*: SERVICE COMPLAINTS—*116*

Chapter *II*: PRODUCT RECALLS AND SAFETY ISSUES—*124*

Chapter *12*: SERVICE AS SALES: RECOMMENDING ACCESSORIES AND ADDITIONAL PRODUCTS—*132*

Chapter *13*: SERVICE AS SALES: SECURING CUSTOMER REFERRALS, RECOMMENDATIONS, AND TESTIMONIALS—*146*

Part Two:

REACHING PROSPECTIVE CUSTOMERS—*159*

Chapter *14*: SELLING THE SERVICE ADVANTAGE—*161*

Chapter *15*: THE WARRANTY AS PRODUCT FEATURE—*167*

Chapter *16*: SELLING COMPANY PRIDE, PERFORMANCE, AND CHARACTER—*170*

Part Three:

INTRADEPARTMENTAL *and* DEALER COMMUNICATIONS—*175*

Chapter *17*: EXPLAINING AND IMPLEMENTING PROCEDURES AND POLICIES—*177*

Chapter *18*: SCHEDULES AND WORK ASSIGNMENTS—*183*

Chapter *19*: UPDATES AND ADVISORIES: NEW PRODUCTS—*189*

Chapter *20*: UPDATES AND ADVISORIES: PRODUCT MODIFICATIONS AND WARRANTY CHANGES—*199*

Chapter $2\,I$: UPDATES AND ADVISORIES: SHIPPING, BILLING, AND DELIVERY CHANGES—*210*

Chapter $2\,2$: UPDATES AND ADVISORIES: HANDLING SPECIAL PROBLEMS—*213*

Chapter 2 3: UPDATES AND ADVISORIES: NOTIFICATION OF RECALL—*218*

Chapter 2 4: REPORTING RECURRING PROBLEMS—*222*

Chapter 2 5: DEPARTMENTAL EVALUATION—*229*

Chapter 33: COMMUNICATING WITH SALES: TRANSMITTING LEADS AND ADVISING OF PROBLEMS—*286*

Chapter 34: INTERDEPARTMENTAL POSITIVE REINFORCEMENT—*292*

Chapter 35: THE CORPORATE CUSTOMER SERVICE NEWSLETTER—*301*

Part Five:
Public Relations—*309*

Chapter 36: Safety Issues—*311*

Chapter 37: Product Recalls—*323*

Chapter 38: Environmental Issues—*333*

Chapter *39*: CONSUMER ADVICE AND PRODUCT-RELATED EDUCATION—*345*

Index—*357*

Foreword

How This Book *Will* Help You Profit
from Customer Service

Have you noticed how many companies are out there right now making personal computers? I can't give you an exact count, because the companies come and go almost overnight, but in a recent issue of a popular national computer magazine, I counted advertisements for 126 computer manufacturers. This does not include the untold numbers of firms that did not advertise in this particular issue or do not generally advertise in the magazine. Nor does it include those that do not advertise at all. In this same computer magazine, the CEO of one of the more successful mail-order computer manufacturers summed up the situation with great candor. These days, he said, "any idiot with a screwdriver can make a personal computer."

What he could have said is that, these days, any idiot with a screwdriver can make a personal computer that actually works!

He could also have said—and I hear this lament from attendees in my workshops from Sidney, Australia to Cincinnati, Ohio—that, since the seventies, technical advantage with any product is rapidly disappearing. He could have said, and should have said, that the playing field has leveled for all products. Today, competitors everywhere are capable of duplicating your high quality. Sure, there are product differences, but the fact is that just about all technical products now have high quality. Further, high quality has become the expected norm. This being the case, you'd think that most consumers would simply find the screwdriver-wielding idiot who charged the least and buy from him.

But that is not the case.

What, then, separates an army of idiots from the handful of truly successful manufacturers? The answer is in the ability of the very sharp few to make themselves unique, to make themselves stand above the crowd. The answer is in customer service or, more correctly, value-added customer service.

The big money in the future is not in technical expertise, which can be easily copied. The big profits are going to be in value-added service. Profits will flow to those who can make their presentation to the market unique, special, and customer-oriented—in short, to those who can sell the company behind the product.

Service and Support: The Quality that Separates You from the Competition

From the highest-technology computers and software to the lowest-technology commodity, such as gravel or asphalt, your ability to command higher profit will be dependent upon your ability to make yourself uniquely customer-oriented. Customer service is about accountability. It's about trust. It's about finding better ways to make your customer make money or save money. It's about confidence. It's about assuring your customer and proving to your customer that you are the folks that provide the most comfort and security. Customer service is the public but personal voice of your company. How you support your customer during and after the sale—and throughout the entire lifespan of the product or service—tells customers virtually everything they will ever know about you. It also tells them virtually everything they will tell their friends about you.

Customer service is a tradition of communication. In *The Complete Customer Service Model Letter & Memo Book,* you will find 700 ready-to-use tools for effective communication. In addition, the model letters and memos in this book will give you two bonuses:

1. They will eloquently demonstrate to your customers that you are willing to invest the time necessary to look after them to see that they get the most out of their investment in you.

2. They will save you a great deal of that very necessary and very valuable commodity: time.

Drawing on more than two decades of experience in customer service, I have put *my* time into these model letters and memos so that you can invest *your* time in other equally necessary things. In purchasing *The Complete Customer Service Model Letter and Memo Book,* you are buying time—both mine and your own.

Making a Profit Out of Necessity

There are four inescapable truths concerning customer service:

1. It is a necessity. You have to do it if you want to survive.
2. It takes time to do it well.
3. Because it takes time, it takes money.
4. Done well, it creates fantastic additional value for your company.

The letters included here cover every phase of serving current customers, and of reaching potential customers. But effective customer service communications are also required *within* the company for "internal customers." So this book includes a variety of intradepartmental and interdepartmental memos, advisories, and newsletters to help customer service personnel and other departments provide all of your customers optimal service all of the time.

This book will improve your customer service operation by helping you do most effectively what you have to do. Therefore, it will improve your bottom line. Take care of your customers, add value to the relationship, and they will take care of you.

Because this book will save you time, it will, invariably, save you money.

But the best news of all is that *The Complete Customer Service Model Letter and Memo Book* will do even more. It will help you turn a necessity into a virtue.

Yes, customer service is a necessity. And, yes, happy customers always mean lower cost and greater profits *eventually*.

Many a business has gone bust waiting for "eventual" profits.

I could tell you just to relax, that good customer service is bound to pay off sooner or later. But why settle for later when you can have sooner? You *have* to have customer service, so why not make it pay *right now*. Why not transform it from a necessary support operation to a bona fide profit center?

Whenever possible, the letters and memos in this book are aimed at increasing sales directly through customer service. This is accomplished in part through letters that educate customers; that show them how to maximize product benefits; that recruit customers as grassroots, word-of-mouth salespeople. Moreover, while the traditional approach to customer service deals only with current customers, *The Complete Customer Service Model Letter & Memo Book* includes an entire section on how customer service can serve *potential* customers as well: by selling the service advantage, by promoting the warranty as a very special product feature, and by making potential customers aware of your company's pride, performance, and character.

Transforming customer service into a center of profit requires help from other internal departments. The memos, advisories, and departmental newsletters are intended to strengthen the internal network that exists (or should exist) among research and development, marketing, sales, and customer service. Customer service can and should serve as a link between each department and the consumer. This book will show how effective communications can forge this most desirable and profitable link.

MAKING THE BEST USE OF THIS BOOK

Most letter books are tools, useful only *as* needed and used only when needed. There is nothing wrong with this arrangement. However, I suggest that you take some time to leaf through these pages now. Get an idea of what's here, of which letters and memos you can use just as they are and which letters and memos will serve to spark your own ideas to meet your own specific needs and situations. Even in the most specialized of circumstances, you can borrow phrases, sentences, and paragraphs—taking and combining whatever you need from more than one letter or memo, if necessary. In any case, you will want to look through this book at your earliest convenience and then keep it within easy reach for frequent reference.

HOW THIS BOOK IS ORGANIZED

The Complete Customer Service Model Letter & Memo Book is divided into five major sections:

Part One: Communicating with Current Customers

Part Two: Reaching Prospective Customers

Part Three: Intradepartmental and Dealer Communications

Part Four: Interdepartmental Communications

Part Five: Public Relations

Within these sections, letters and memos are grouped into logical chapters according to type of communication. Each chapter is introduced by a concise "How to Do It" overview, which outlines the steps you should take to create effective communications in the area under consideration.

Acknowledgments

Nobody writes a book alone. If it were not for Porter Henry, Bert Holtje, Ellen Coleman, and Alan Axelrod this book would not exist.

Thanks to my wife Beverly Thomas for never-ending support, confidence, inspiration, comfort, and love.

T/J, tomorrow is yours; seize it, forge ahead, and enjoy your quest.

Part One

COMMUNICATING *with* CURRENT CUSTOMERS

Chapter
I

The Order

How to Do It

Dealing with orders can be done in two ways: as an impersonal, proforma chore or as an opportunity for a businesslike but friendly and considerate exchange. Both methods can convey the necessary basic information concerning the order, but both methods offer additional information as well. An impersonal note or annotation on an invoice tells the customer that she is just one of many customers. A personalized letter communicates special regard for the customer, letting her know that she is dealing not only with a company, but with fellow human beings. Moreover, she is made aware that you feel you are dealing with a person, not just a repository of dollars and cents.

Sell Your Service Advantage

Every necessary business communication—even something as mundane as confirming an order—is an opportunity to sell. It is not an occasion for selling a particular product, but for selling service, which is the same as selling your company. Each communication is an opportunity to build a relationship that, over the short or longer term, is likely to result in the kind of customer or client loyalty that generates revenue.

3

This does not mean that you should turn an essentially utilitarian, informational communication into a long, rambling letter. First and foremost, make certain that you convey the essential information concisely and clearly. Then add the personal touch: "It is a pleasure to confirm," "Thank you for your order," "We appreciate," and so on. The very fact that you send a letter rather than an impersonal postcard is in itself a big step toward selling your firm's support advantage. Also take the time in a sentence or two to stress your desire for a lifelong relationship. Mention your 800 number for the help desk or other information. *Encourage* the customer to call with technical questions. Be certain customers know you will follow up with *them* on order status. If you take the additional measure of addressing even the most routine communication to an individual ("Dear Ms. Smith" instead of "Dear Customer"), you have made another significant leap into personal service. And in these days where a PC can be found on every desk, tracking a customer and printing out a letter that addresses her personally is no great chore. Indeed, with the general availability of database technology, such personal service has become the state of the art and is expected.

— Confirming Order —

Dear *(Name)*:

It is a pleasure to confirm your order of *(date)* for the following:

   (items)   *(quantities)*

We plan to ship the order on *(date)*, and we will notify you if there is any change.

If you have any questions about your order, please call us at *(telephone number)* and mention order number *(number)*.

Sincerely,

———————

Dear (Name):

Thanks for your order.

To confirm: We are shipping *(quantity)* *(item 1)* to *(destination 1)* and *(quantity)* *(item 2)* to *(destination 2)*.

All items will be shipped via *(carrier)* by *(date)*. You should expect the *(destination 1)* shipment to arrive by *(date)*, and the *(destination 2)* shipment to arrive by *(date)*. Please call Customer Service at *(phone number)* if your merchandise has not reached you by these dates.

Sincerely,

— Clarifying Order: Item —

Dear *(Name)*:

Thank you for your order of *(date)*.

Your purchase order specifies *(item)*. The fact is we offer *(number)* *(items)*: *(list models)*.

I am enclosing leaflets on each of these models. You should find them helpful in deciding which *(item[s])* will best serve your needs. Then just give me a call at *(phone number)*. I also invite you to call *(Name)*, who is our service specialist in *(item)*. He'll be very glad to help you make a choice you'll be pleased with.

Sincerely,

Dear *(Name)*:

We have received your order for *(product)*, but the order form is incomplete. No color or engine type are specified.

I am enclosing a copy of your order form, together with a copy of our descriptive brochure, which lists the range of colors and engine types available. Please make your choices and return the completed form to me, *(Name)* at *(address)*. I will see that processing is expedited. If I may be of any assistance in choosing color or engine type, just give me a call at *(phone number)*.

Sincerely,

— Clarifying Order: Quantity —

Dear *(Name)*:

Many thanks for your order of *(date)*.

Your purchase order does not specify a quantity for *(item)*. Am I correct in assuming that you'll be needing *(quantity)*, as usual?

Please give me a confirming call at *(phone number)*, or fax at *(fax number)*.

Sincerely yours,

———————

Dear *(Name)*:

Thanks so much for your order of *(date)*. Please note, however, that your purchase order does not specify quantity. I am therefore returning the purchase order. Please specify the quantity desired, and return the completed purchase order directly to my attention—*(Name)* at *(address)*—and I will ensure that it is given top priority.

Sincerely,

— Confirming Revised Order —

Dear *(Name)*:

Thanks for your revised order of *(date)*.

This will confirm your new instructions to us:

> Ship *(quantity)* *(item)* to *(destination)*
> Ship *(quantity)* *(item)* to *(destination)*
> Ship *(quantity)* *(item)* to *(destination)*
> Ship *(quantity)* *(item)* to *(destination)*

Please call me at *(phone number)* by *(date)* if any of the above is incorrect. If we do not hear from you by *(date)*, the scheduled ship date, we will assume that the order is correct as revised here.

Sincerely yours,

Dear *(Name)*:

We have received your revised order and plan to ship as follows:

    Ship *(quantity)* *(item)* to *(destination)*

    Ship *(quantity)* *(item)* to *(destination)*

    Ship *(quantity)* *(item)* to *(destination)*

    Ship *(quantity)* *(item)* to *(destination)*

Ship date is *(date)*. If any of the above is incorrect, please call *(phone number)* before *(date)*. Refer to order number *(number)*. If the above is correct, there is no need to call. Your order will be shipped on the date promised.

Sincerely,

— Clarifying Revised Order —

Dear *(Name)*:

As you know, your recent order *(order number)* has been subject to a number of changes and revisions. Since our greatest concern is serving you efficiently and correctly, I ask that you review the following to ensure that we have understood your instructions fully:

    Ship *(quantity)* *(item)* to *(destination)*

    Ship *(quantity)* *(item)* to *(destination)*

    Ship *(quantity)* *(item)* to *(destination)*

    Ship *(quantity)* *(item)* to *(destination)*

The scheduled ship date is *(date)*. There is no need to call if the above is correct. If we do not hear from you by the ship date, we will ship the items and quantities to the aforementioned destinations.

We appreciate your business!

Sincerely,

Dear *(Name)*:

On *(date)*, we received two versions of a revised order for *(product)*. One specified *(quantity)* of *(model 1)*, and the other specified *(quantity)* *(model 2)*. Please call *(phone number)* or fax *(fax number)* us for clarification.

We will have both models in stock and can ship as soon as we receive your confirmation.

Sincerely,

— Item Temporarily Out of Stock —

Dear *(Name)*:

We're sorry to tell you that *(item)* is out of stock temporarily. We expect to receive more by *(date)*, and we will ship your order just as soon as we are restocked.

Have you given any thought to *(alternate item)*? Our customers have been very happy with it, and many actually prefer it to *(item ordered)*. We have these in stock and can ship one to you immediately. I'm enclosing a brochure that describes *(alternate item)*, and I invite you to call if you have any questions.

If we do not hear from you, we will ship your originally ordered item as noted above. In the meantime, we apologize for any inconvenience, and we appreciate your understanding.

Sincerely,

Insert with partial shipment

Dear *(Name)*:

We're sorry, but *(product 1)* is out of stock temporarily. We expect that it will be available by *(date)*. In the meantime, we have made this partial shipment.

(Product 2) is the specification and price equivalent of *(product 1)*. If you would like, we can ship that immediately. Just call *(phone number)* before *(date)*.

We apologize for any inconvenience the unavailability of *(product 1)* may have caused.

Sincerely,

— Item Discontinued —

Dear *(Name)*:

As the old saying goes, I've got bad news and good news for you.

The bad news is that we no longer carry *(item and model)*, which you ordered on *(date)*. It is discontinued.

The good news is that it has been replaced by an updated and improved version, *(alternate item and model)*, which we do have in stock. It meets or exceeds all the specifications of *(ordered item and model)* for the comparable price of *($ amount)*. I am enclosing some literature on *(alternate item and model)*, and if you'll call me at *(phone number)*, I'll be happy to revise your order for you.

Sincerely,

Insert with partial shipment

Dear Customer:

We are very sorry, but one of the items you ordered, *(product)*, has been discontinued and is out of stock permanently.

We have shipped the balance of your order, together with a copy of our latest catalog. We invite you to consult the catalog on pages *(page numbers)* for improved replacements.

Your account will be credited *($ amount)* for the unavailable item.

Sincerely,

— Advice of Item Substitution: Same Price —
Notice enclosed with shipped order

Dear Customer:

Please note that *(Manufacturer)* has replaced *(ordered item and model)* with *(shipped item and model)*. Because the new model meets or exceeds all of the specifications of the item you ordered, we have substituted it in this shipment.

The cost to you is the same.

If you have any questions, please call Customer Service at *(phone number)*. We'll be glad to help.

Thanks for your order.

Sincerely,

Insert with order shipped

Dear Customer:

The item you ordered, *(item/item number)*, has been replaced by a new model, *(new item/new item number)*, which meets or exceeds the features and performance specifications of the older model. We have substituted *(new item/new item number)* at no additional cost to you. We encourage your feedback regarding the new product.

Sincerely,

— Advice of Item Substitution: Higher Price —

Dear *(Name)*:

Thanks for your recent order of *(item and model)*. We have replaced that model with the significantly improved model, *(model name)*, which is now available. The cost of the new model is slightly higher, by *($ amount)*, and while we believe the new model represents significantly greater value, we don't want to ship and bill you for the substitution without your approval.

I have enclosed a copy of the *(model name)* brochure, which details the additional benefits and improvements. Please take a few moments to review the specifications and call me at *(phone number)* to authorize the substitution.

Sincerely,

Dear *(Name)*:

Thank you for your recent order. *(Product 1)* is no longer available and has been replaced by *(product 2)*, a greatly enhanced product, which offers higher value. A leaflet describing it is enclosed.

Since *(product 2)* is priced at *($ amount)*, slightly higher than *(product 1)*, we will need your approval before shipping. Please contact us at *(phone number)*. You may also call this number if you have any questions about specifications or performance.

Sincerely,

— Confirmation of Item Substitution —
Notice enclosed with shipped order

Dear Customer:

Many thanks for your order!

As you instructed, due to the unavailability of *(item and model)*, we have substituted *(alternate item and model)* in this shipment.

If you have any questions, please call Customer Service at *(phone number)*.

Sincerely,

Notice enclosed with shipped order

Dear Customer:

As per your telephone instructions of *(date)*, your original order was changed to substitute *(product 1)* for *(product 2)*. The enclosed invoice reflects this alteration.

Sincerely,

— Product Superseded by New Model: Same Price —
Notice enclosed with shipped order

Dear Customer:

Thank you for your order.

Please note that we have replaced *(item and model)* with an upgraded version, *(new model)*. We have substituted the new version—at the same price—for the item you ordered.

At *(Store)*, we sell only the latest versions of the product, to ensure that you benefit from each improvement and all support. If you have any questions, please call me at *(phone number)*.

Sincerely yours,

— Product Superseded by New Model: Higher Price —

Dear *(Name)*:

As you know, we are a company dedicated to keeping our customers on the leading edge of technology. Our *(item and model)*, which you ordered on *(date)*, has been replaced by the new *(new model)*, which incorporates the following improvements and benefits, making it the best value in the industry:

> *(list new benefits)*

We know that total value received is important to you and all our customers. Therefore, *(new model)* has been very competitively priced at *(new price)*. Considering the much greater benefits, I am sure you agree the *(new model)* will produce greater value for you.

(New model) is ready to ship now. I will call you after you have had time to review the benefits *(new model)* offers. With your authorization, I can ship immediately.

Sincerely yours,

Chapter 2

FULFILLMENT *and* DELIVERY

HOW TO DO IT

Communications relating to fulfillment and delivery include requests to customers for shipping instructions and clarification or confirmation of same; advice of shipping dates and any changes in same; instructions to customers on how to prepare for delivery (for example, of large, temperature-sensitive, or perishable goods); apologies for shipping and fulfillment errors, lateness, and so on; and instructions concerning the return of goods.

Why Write?

Don't forget the most important customer service rule of all: Once the customer contacts you with an order, problem, or anything else, he should never have to take the initiative of contacting you again. You should grab and you should retain the driver's seat. Lifelong customer retention through effective service means all status reports needed to build a proactive and permanent relationship should be initiated by you. Modern computer communications makes this goal achievable and very affordable. Offering all these necessary reports in writing is far more effective than using the telephone. Even when the telephone is used, send the written report as a back-up.

What must be borne in mind when preparing these communications is that, at every stage of shipping and fulfillment, the customer is depending on your firm. Your customer is counting on you, quite literally, to deliver. While much of the kind of information the letters in this chapter convey might be communicated by a simple telephone call just as easily, letters written at this stage in the supplier-customer relationship have three advantages:

1. They provide a written record of types, quantities, dates, and charges. They clarify the contract and make procedures and promises crystal clear. In the case of an apology or adjustment, they give your customer the feeling that you are willing to stand by your work and own up to your mistakes by going "on record" with them.

2. They convey to your customer a sense of procedural orderliness. Unlike a mere phone call, a letter is a physical "product," that you deliver to your customer. He is, therefore, given the message that he is being served and his needs are being carefully and systematically looked after.

3. Finally, as always in business correspondence, the fulfillment and delivery letter is an opportunity to deliver more than a particular product or service. It is a vehicle for "delivering"—personally—the resources of your entire company. It builds a bond between the customer and the writer of the letter, who is a human being representing your firm.

Explain? Apologize? Excuse?

Devote particular attention to the letters in this chapter that deal with changes in expectation or deviation from schedule. At minimum, what you owe your customer in such cases is an explanation for the change or deviation—even if that change is an improvement (for example, an earlier than anticipated shipping date). Not only does the explanation help the customer make whatever changes in his plans may be necessary to accommodate a revised delivery date, it also conveys your high regard for his needs. A dictator explains nothing. In contrast, a business partner—and that is precisely how you want your customer to view you—is forthcoming with information and explanations. Also, whereas the dictator is removed and aloof, the business partner is readily accessible and responsive. To this end, always encourage your customer to contact you if he has any questions. It is a good idea to accompany this invitation with your direct toll-free phone number, even if it is simply printed on your letterhead.

Be careful to distinguish among explanation, apology, and excuse. Simple changes in schedule rarely require an apology; an explanation is sufficient. Where an error has occurred, explain and apologize. If the error is serious enough, you may offer some reparation in addition to the apology—for example, a modest discount, free freight, and so on. The apology should state your culpability forthrightly, but should not emphasize it. Don't put yourself in the position of persuading your customer that you have committed a felony when you are guilty of nothing more than a misdemeanor. Avoid telling your customer how he should feel about you. Instead, underscore your gratitude for your customer's patience and understanding. This empowers your customer, making him feel less like the victim of your oversight or carelessness. It also strengthens the business partner bond between you.

As for excuses, there is only one thing to say: Don't make them. Errors are your problem. You own them, and your customer doesn't want them. Explain, apologize, and tell your customer how you will rectify the situation.

— Request for Shipping Instructions —

FAX TO: *(Name)*
FROM: *(Name)*
RE: Shipping Instructions

Dear *(Name)*:

Many thanks for your order of *(date)*.

As you know, we have a set of standing shipping instructions on file for you, but *(Name)* of your office recently told me that you have moved your main warehouse. It occurred to me that our standing instructions might be out of date.

Please call *(phone number)* or fax me *(fax number)* with your current shipping address.

Best regards,

FAX TO: *(Name)*
FROM: *(Name)*
SUBJECT: Shipping Instructions

Thanks for your order, number *(number)*, dated *(date)*.

Please note that the order did not specify the following information:

> *(date due)*
>
> *(destination)*
>
> *(quantity)*
>
> *(etc.)*

Please call me at *(phone number)* with instructions, or if you prefer fax me at *(fax number)*.

We have the product in stock and, depending on quantity, we are prepared to ship just as soon as we have this information.

— Clarifying Shipping Instructions —

FAX TO: *(Name)*
FROM: *(Name)*
RE: Shipping Instructions for Order *(number)*

Thanks for your order, number *(number)*, dated *(date)*. Please note that page 3 of the order specified expedited air freight, and page 6 specifies ground delivery.

Expedited air will reach you by *(date)* at a surcharge of *($ amount)*. Ground delivery will reach you by *(date)* and is included in our price.

Please call me at *(phone number)* or fax me at *(fax number)* to let me know whether to use air or ground shipping.

We're ready to go as soon as we hear from you.

———————

Dear *(Name)*:

Recently, we discussed changing your standing shipping instructions. You were contemplating changing your regular shipping mode from standard ground to expedited air.

If you would like me to put this change into effect in your standing shipping instructions, please complete the enclosed form and return it to me by *(date)*. If you do not want to change shipping mode at this time, no response is necessary.

Thanks.

Sincerely,

— Confirming Shipping Instructions —

Dear *(Name)*:

Thank you for your order of *(date)*.

We will ship

> *(quantity) (item)* to *(destination)*
>
> *(quantity) (item)* to *(destination)*
>
> *(quantity) (item)* to *(destination)*
>
> *(quantity) (item)* to *(destination)*

If any of the above is incorrect, please call the Shipping Department at *(phone number)* no later than the scheduled ship date of *(date)*. If the above order is correct, there is no need to call, and you may expect delivery by *(date)*.

Sincerely yours,

———

Dear Customer:

Your order has been received. Thanks!

To confirm: We will ship

> *(quantity) (item)* to *(destination)*
>
> *(quantity) (item)* to *(destination)*
>
> *(quantity) (item)* to *(destination)*
>
> *(quantity) (item)* to *(destination)*

If any of the above has changed or is incorrect, please call *(phone number)* before the ship date: *(date)*. You need not call if this information is correct.

Sincerely,

— Confirming Revised Shipping Instructions —

FAX TO: *(Name)*
FROM: *(Name)*
SUBJECT: Revised Shipping Instructions *(date)*

This confirms our understanding that you now want us to ship

> *(quantity) (item)* to *(destination)*
>
> *(quantity) (item)* to *(destination)*
>
> *(quantity) (item)* to *(destination)*
>
> *(quantity) (item)* to *(destination)*

If this is correct, no further action is needed. If any of the above is incorrect, please call the Shipping Department at *(phone number)* or fax us at *(fax number)*.

Thank you for your order!

Dear *(Name)*:

As per your instructions of *(date)*, we are changing your standing shipping instructions so that all shipments to you will be made by *two-day air freight* unless you specify otherwise.

Sincerely,

— Shipping Date —

Dear Customer:

Thanks for your order!

Order number *(number)* will be shipped by *(date)* via *(carrier)*. Please expect delivery at *(Name)* warehouse after *(hour)* A.M. between *(date)* and *(date)*.

If you have any questions concerning this shipment, please call our Shipping Department at *(phone number)* and refer to order number *(number)*.

FAX TO:
FROM: Customer Service, *(Name of company)*
SUBJECT: Ship date for order number *(number)*

Your order *(number)* will be shipped on *(date)*, complete, to your *(Name of place)* warehouse via *(carrier)*.

If you would like to alter any of these instructions, please call *(phone number)* or fax *(fax number)* no later than *(date)*.

— Shipping Dates: Split Shipment —

Dear Customer:

Thank you for your order!

(Item) is, unfortunately, out of stock temporarily, but we expect to ship it to you by *(date)*. In order to avoid delaying the balance of your order, we will ship everything except *(item)* by *(date)* to *(Name)* warehouse via *(carrier)*.

Sincerely,

FAX TO:
FROM: Customer Service, *(Name of company)*
SUBJECT: Split shipment of order *(number)*

One of the items you ordered, *(product)*, will not be available until *(date)*. We will ship the balance of your order as promised on *(date 1)* and *(product)* by *(date 2)*.

— On-Time Shipment —

Dear Customer:

Many thanks for your recent order.

As promised, the order will be shipped by *(date)* to your *(Name)* warehouse via *(carrier)*.

Sincerely,

FAX TO:
FROM: Customer Service, *(Name of company)*
SUBJECT: Confirmation of ship date, order *(number)*

As you have been advised, your order, order number *(number)*, will ship from our *(Name of place)* warehouse on *(date)*. Expect arrival at your facility by *(date)*.

— Early Shipment —

Dear *(Name)*:

I thought you would want to know that we will be able to ship your order of *(date)* a full week *(or other time period)* earlier than promised. If this is unsatisfactory, please call at *(phone number)*. If you can accept the earlier date, you need do nothing.

Thanks for your order.

Sincerely,

FAX TO:
FROM: Customer Service, *(Name of company)*
SUBJECT: Order number *(number)* to be shipped early

We thought you'd like to know that your order number *(number)* will ship on *(date 1)* rather than *(date 2)* as originally scheduled. You should expect to receive it by *(date 3)*. If this is unsatisfactory, please call me at *(phone number)*. If the earlier ship date is okay, you need do nothing.

— Late Shipment —

Dear *(Name)*:

Confirming our phone conversation, because of manufacturing delays *(or other cause)*, your order number *(number)* of *(date)* will be shipped on *(date)* instead of *(date)*, as scheduled originally.

I am sorry for this delay, which is unavoidable. If you have any questions, please call me at *(telephone number)* and mention order number *(number)*.

I hope, *(Name)*, this delay does not greatly inconvenience you.

Sincerely yours,

FAX TO:
FROM: Customer Service, *(Name of company)*
SUBJECT: Ship date for order number *(number)* rescheduled

Due to manufacturing delays *(or other cause)*, your order number *(number)*, scheduled to ship on *(date 1)* originally, will be shipped on *(date 2)*. You should expect to receive it by *(date 3)*.

We apologize for any inconvenience this unavoidable change in schedule may cause. If you have any questions, please call *(phone number)*.

— Partial Shipment —

FAX TO:
FROM: Customer Service, *(Name of company)*
SUBJECT: Partial shipment, order number *(number)*

Due to manufacturing delays *(or other cause)*, we are unable to ship *(product)* with the other items in your order *(number)*, which is scheduled to ship on *(date)*. We expect to ship *(product)* by *(date)*.

We apologize for any inconvenience this split shipment may cause. If you have any questions, please call *(phone number)*.

Enclosure with shipment

Dear Customer:

This is a partial shipment of your order.

We are sorry that the following items are out of stock temporarily:

(quantity) (item)
(quantity) (item)
(quantity) (item)
(quantity) (item)

We expect to be able to ship all of the above to you by *(date)*. In the meantime, we thought it best to avoid a delay in shipping the balance of your order.

Thanks for your order, and we greatly appreciate your understanding.

Sincerely,

— How to Prepare for Delivery —

Dear Customer:

The *(item)* that you ordered on *(date)* will be shipped on *(date)* via *(carrier)*. You should receive it at your office on *(date)* or *(date)*.

Please note that many of the electronic components of the *(item)* are highly sensitive to excessive heat, cold, and moisture. When you take delivery of *(item)*, please store it indoors at a temperature above 45 degrees F but below 95 degrees F, avoiding direct sunlight. Relative humidity should not exceed 60 percent. Please keep *(item)* at least six feet away from any strong magnetic field, such as that generated by large motors or television/video imaging equipment.

If you have any questions, please don't hesitate to call Technical Support at *(phone number)*.

Thanks for your order.

Sincerely,

FAX TO:
FROM: Customer Service, *(Name of company)*
SUBJECT: Preparation to receive *(product)*

(Product) is temperature-sensitive. While it will be shipped to you in a specially insulated container, it is important that the unopened shipping carton NOT be stored at temperatures lower than *(temperature 1)* or exceeding *(temperature 2)* for more than *(time period)*. The unopened carton should not be exposed to direct sunlight.

Please prepare to receive the shipment accordingly.

Dear *(Name)*:

Your fine new *(product)* will be coming to you soon. Our scheduled ship date is *(date)*. You should plan for an arrival on *(date)*.

The following items must be completed in advance:

> *(list)*

To save you cost, these site preparation items must be completed prior to the scheduled arrival date. Please understand that the rigging crew can set the *(product)* in place only if the *(preparation)* is complete. If, for some reason, the site cannot be ready in time, give me a call at *(phone)* to discuss a delayed shipment until the site preparation is complete.

Sincerely,

Dear *(Name)*:

Your new *(product)* will be arriving on *(date)*. It was shipped via *(carrier)*.

The site preparation should now be complete. Please advise if there are any difficulties. It is very advantageous if your maintenance crews work with our engineers during the installation process. However, for them to get maximum benefit, they should participate in training first. We are currently holding *(number of seats)* for you in our *(class)* scheduled for *(date)*. Please call our *(training manager)* at *(phone)* and confirm this very important training.

At that time, we also recommend that you discuss the following training classes with our manager:

> *(list)*

Having a well-trained crew is the best way to ensure that you receive maximum value from your new *(product)*.

Sincerely,

— Apologies for Late Shipment —

Dear *(Name)*:

I trust that you are making good use of the *(item)* you ordered from us.

I just wanted to take this opportunity to apologize to you for the delay in shipping your order and to thank you for enduring the delay with patience.

As I mentioned to you, demand for *(item)* has been overwhelming, and we have really had to scramble to get orders out!

Thanks for being so understanding.

Sincerely yours,

––––––––––

Dear *(Name)*:

I was relieved and happy to receive confirmation from our Shipping Department that your *(product)* has been shipped. Please accept my apologies for the delay in shipping, which, as we explained, was due to shortages and unusually heavy demand.

Thank you for your patience and understanding.

Sincerely,

— Apologies for Partial Shipment —

Dear *(Name)*:

(Name), to whom you spoke in our Shipping Department, tells me that our having to make a partial shipment to you on *(date)* has caused you some inconvenience.

I am truly sorry for that, and I want to take this opportunity to apologize.

We try our best to fill orders fully and promptly, but, ours is a volatile business, and it is not always possible to anticipate customer demand perfectly. Please know that we will make every effort to prevent this from happening again. You can help me anticipate demand by ordering early. With sufficient lead time we can, in most cases ensure that we have sufficient stock on hand to ship all orders fully.

Sincerely yours,

Insert with balance of partial shipment

Dear *(Name)*:

We are pleased to deliver the balance of your shipment for order number *(number)*.

I am sorry we had to split the shipment, and hope this has not caused you any inconvenience.

Sincerely,

— Apologies for Shipping/Fulfillment Error: Wrong Item —

Dear *(Name)*:

I wanted to write you personally with my apologies for our having shipped the wrong item to you on *(date)*. It was an unfortunate mistake.

I have no excuse to offer, but I can promise that we will do our utmost to see that we never inconvenience you again by shipping the wrong item.

I am very grateful for your order, your understanding, and your patience.

Sincerely,

———————

Dear *(Name)*:

Here's a quick bit of history. On *(date)*, you ordered *(quantity)* of *(product)*. On *(date)*, we shipped *(quantity)* of *(wrong product)*. When you called us about the error, we responded by expediting to you another *(quantity)* of the *(wrong product)*.

By *(date)*, we finally shipped you what you wanted.

You have every right to be angry, and for that reason, I am very grateful for your patience and understanding.

We won't let it happen again. Just test us again, and please accept a *(percent amount)* discount off your next order.

Sincerely,

— Apologies for Shipping/Fulfillment Error: Wrong Quantity —

I am sorry we shipped the wrong quantity and caused your receiving department such inconvenience. I sincerely appreciate all the extra effort you incurred in returning the over-shipment to us.

In gratitude, we have credited your account for the total shipping cost, including the shipping expenses you would have incurred normally. Further, please accept a *(percent amount)* discount on your next order.

Thank you for your understanding and support. We are determined to continually improve our operations.

Sincerely,

Dear *(Name)*:

Please accept my apologies for having shorted you so drastically on your last order. I trust our expedited shipment of the balance of your order helped minimize any inconvenience.

I am in the process of investigating just where the slip-up occurred. When I locate the weakness in our system, you can be certain I will eliminate it.

Thank you for your understanding.

Sincerely,

— Apologies for Shipping/Fulfillment Error: Delivery to Wrong Location —

Dear *(Name)*:

Thank you for your order and your understanding. I apologize for shipping to the wrong address.

As you are aware, we did expedite on short notice an additional partial shipment to you in order to minimize the inconvenience.

Your original order has been located and transhipped to you. We have credited your account for all shipping expenses, including those you would have normally incurred. Further, please accept the partial extra shipment at no charge as our way of apologizing for the error.

Thank you for your consideration, and we appreciate your continuing support.

Sincerely,

Dear *(Name)*:

Thank you for advising that our shipment arrived at the wrong address. We apologize for the error.

The error has been located in our system, and we have updated your address file.

We appreciate your taking the time to contact us thereby helping us improve our quality of service.

— Apologies/Adjustments: Damaged Shipment —

Dear *(Name)*:

I was very sorry to hear that your new *(item)* arrived damaged.

I understand that you returned the damaged item and that we shipped you a replacement on *(date)*. I trust that it arrived safe and sound. If you have any problems or questions, please call me at *(phone number)*.

Again, I apologize for any inconvenience.

Sincerely,

Enclosed with replacement shipment

Dear *(Name)*:

I am very sorry that your new *(product)* arrived damaged in shipment. We do our very best to keep such things from happening, but sometimes . . . .

I trust the enclosed has arrived safe and sound.

Thank you for your patience and understanding.

Sincerely,

— How to Return Goods —

Dear *(Name)*:

To return products, please call *(Name of company)* Customer Service at *(phone number)* to receive a Credit Return Authorization Number. To minimize possibility of loss, we suggest you ship the products to us in the original packaging, prepay shipping charges, and insure the shipment. Please understand that we cannot be responsible for loss or damage during shipment.

Returned products must be in as-new condition, complete with all manuals, parts, and accessories as sold originally.

Sincerely,

Dear Customer:

I am sorry you have had difficulty with *(product)*.

To return defective goods, please:

1. Include a cover letter with your name, daytime phone number, and address. Describe the problem/defect as fully as possible.

2. Pack the unit in its original carton with all original shipping material. This material is specially designed to prevent shipping damage.

3. Call customer service at *(phone number)*, and they will send a carrier to pick up the defective merchandise.

We apologize for the inconvenience and will either repair the *(product)* or replace it quickly.

Thank you for your understanding.

Sincerely,

— How to Return Goods for Exchange/Replacement —

Dear Customer:

To return products, please call *(name of company)* Customer Service at *(phone number)* to receive a Credit Return Authorization Number. To ensure compliance with warranty provisions, you must ship the products to *(Name of company)* in the original packaging. Please call *(phone number)*, and we will send a carrier to pick up the package.

Sincerely,

Dear Customer:

We are sorry you have had difficulty with your new *(product)*. To return your unit for warranty repair or replacement, please repack the unit in its original carton with all original shipping material and *all* accessories supplied originally. Please include a cover note with your:

Customer Number *(see your warranty)*

Name

Address

Daytime phone

Brief description of the problem or defect

Allow *(time period)* for the repair or replacement.

Sincerely,

— How to Return Goods for Exchange/Replacement: Cross Shipment —

Dear Customer:

We are sorry you have had difficulty with our *(product)*.

To return products, please call *(Name of company)* Customer Service at *(phone number)* to receive a Credit Return Authorization Number. Please inform the Customer Service Representative that you would like to take advantage of our cross-shipment policy. We will ship a replacement unit immediately.

Please return the defective unit within five days after the new unit arrives to avoid being billed for the trans-shipped replacement. Use the shipping carton from the replacement unit to return the defective unit to us. A return shipping label is supplied with the replacement unit.

Please be certain to include all manuals, parts, and accessories as sold originally.

We apologize for any inconvenience problems with our product may have caused you.

Sincerely,

Chapter 3

BILLING CLARIFICATIONS
and DISPUTES

HOW TO DO IT

Written communication is particularly important in the case of billing clarifications and disputes since memories get hazy—and tempers inflamed—where dollars and cents are involved. But writing "for the record" is only half the purpose of the letters in this chapter. All of the letters here are aimed at humanizing money transactions. Think of them as the language equivalent of the handshake that accompanies a deal.

Clarifications

When a customer requests clarification of the amount or terms of a payment due or an invoice, you might handle the request in one of three ways:

1. A phone call

2. Sending a duplicate invoice

3. A letter

In some simple cases, a phone call may be sufficient, but then you have no written record of the exchange. Even if a phone call is used, sending a follow-up letter confirming what was said is good business practice, effective customer service, and effective future selling. Sending a duplicate invoice is helpful only if the customer asks for one, perhaps having misplaced the one you had sent her previously. In most cases, a letter—or fax—is the safest, most efficient, and most effective means of clarifying charges and resolving disputes.

In providing a clarification, be careful not to demean or patronize the customer. If possible, identify with her problem: "I can understand the reason for your confusion . . .," "I see where the problem is . . .," "I appreciate your concern . . .," and so on. Do not scold or admonish the customer. Do not refer menacingly to an agreement she may have signed. Instead of writing something like, "The agreement you signed clearly states . . .," include both your customer and your firm in any reference to an agreement or sales document: "As you will recall, our agreement . . . ." Never use language that risks having a discussion regarding clarification escalate into a dispute. Such inflammatory language includes anything that comes down to "we" versus "you." Use language that emphasizes agreement, consensus, and collaboration, such as "our mutual objective" or "our common goal" and so on.

Cover Letters, Invoice Inserts, and Incentives

It is a good customer service strategy to include a cover letter or an insert with an invoice. Such documents serve to explain terms or various charges, humanize a financial transaction, or even provide a means for announcing an incentive to prompt payment (for example, a 2 percent discount for payment within ten days). Cover letters are also excellent ways to cross-sell, up-sell, seek testimonials, and secure new leads.

Disputes

Much of what has been said about billing clarification also applies to resolving disputes. Avoid "get tough" language that draws lines and defines adversarial roles. Approach the task of resolving a dispute by first defining—and then starting from—some common ground. Express your understanding and appreciation of the customer's position. Do not defend your firm's position; explain it. If the customer is in error, gently but unmistakably point that error out and show him how correcting the error resolves the dispute.

There are at least two ways of determining your goals in resolving a dispute. One is simply to determine that you are right and then to insist on your position as the only satisfactory resolution of the dispute. The other is to decide just how cost effective it is to be absolutely and unyieldingly right. Resolving a dispute with flexibility offers a valuable opportunity for rendering effective customer service. For example, your customer delays payment to you beyond your thirty-day net terms. You send him a second invoice, which incorporates a finance charge. He disputes the charge. You can explain the charge, refer to the invoice terms, and, in effect, demand payment with the finance charge. Or you can remind the customer of the invoice terms and then offer to waive or modify the finance charge, say, in exchange for immediate payment of the balance due. Such flexibility develops long-term relationships. It compels the customer to make an investment in your company.

Finally, if there is one cardinal rule for resolving disputes, it is to approach the task with the assumption that the customer is being honest and sincere in disputing the charges. Remember: Many studies suggest customers are right more often than the company. Make certain that your correspondence conveys your sense of the customer's honesty.

Apologies

The best way to apologize for a billing error is to correct the error immediately, providing an immediate credit or refund. Any letter of apology you write should be accompanied by such an adjustment, in the form of a credit memo, a corrected invoice, or a check.

The other key ingredient in an apology for a billing error is an explanation. Your customer is not interested in hearing a long, detailed rehearsal of your accounting procedures, but a sentence or two that explains the source of the error will be welcome.

— Requests for Billing Address —
Reply card

Dear Customer:

In order to speed the processing of your credit request, we need to have your complete billing address. Please provide this in the following section, detach, and return as soon as possible.

Company Name _____

Department _____

Street _____

Floor/suite _____

City _____

State _____ Zip _____

Attn: _____

Title _____

———————

FAX TO:

FROM: Customer Service, *(Name of company)*

SUBJECT: Request for billing information

We are trying to expedite your order. Kindly supply the billing information requested. You may fax this form directly to *(fax number)*. Thanks!

Company Name _____

Department _____

Street _____

Floor/suite _____

City _____

State _____ Zip _____

Attn: _____

Title _____

— Responses to Request for Clarification: Amount —

Dear *(Name)*:

Thank you for your recent correspondence concerning the amount due on your account *(number)* for the month of *(month)*.

I understand your confusion about the total due. Please note that *two* different discount rates apply. You have calculated the total using only one rate. If you take both into account, you will see that our figure is correct. Thanks for asking us to clarify.

Please give me a call if you have any further questions about this matter.

Sincerely yours,

———————

Dear *(Name)*:

We have received your letter questioning the amount of time billed for *(service)* from *(date)* to *(date)*. I am currently reviewing the time logs for the project with the consultant team assigned to it, and will respond to your letter by *(date)*.

Sincerely,

— Responses to Request for Clarification: Terms —

Dear *(Name)*:

I wanted to confirm our telephone conversation this morning regarding the payment terms we propose for completing *(name of project)*.

The total fee agreed upon is *($ amount)*, payable as follows:

On signing agreement	*($ amount)*
On completion of Phase I	*($ amount)*
On completion of Phase II	*($ amount)*
On completion of Phases III–V	*($ amount)*
On final approval	*($ amount)*

All reasonable expenses will be documented and invoiced at the conclusion of Phases II and V.

Please return one signed copy, and I will proceed to draw up the agreement.

Thank you, and we look forward to a great project.

Sincerely,

Agreed:

_____

Signature

——————

Dear *(Name)*:

Thank you for returning the purchase agreements so promptly.

You asked for clarification on our Early Bird Discount Program mentioned in paragraph *(number)*. The discounts apply to each specific monthly invoice and must be taken each month. Each invoice will identify the date range and applicable discount allowed if payment is postmarked within the noted range.

If you have any other questions, please don't hesitate to call me at *(phone number)*. Thank you again and we are looking forward to a mutually beneficial relationship.

Sincerely,

— Cover Letters: Explanation of Terms —

Dear *(Name)*:

Thank you for choosing *(Name of company)* as your supplier of *(product or service)*. For your convenience and ease of reference, I have enclosed a brochure that details the range of terms and payment options we offer. These options have been formulated based upon many customer requests over the years, and we believe that you will find a plan tailored precisely to your needs.

I will give you a call after you have had time to review in order to help you select a payment plan best suited to your needs.

Sincerely yours,

———————

Dear *(Name)*:

One of the great things about working with us is that we make every effort to put you in the driver's seat, not only by offering you a great range of custom options on our products, but by making available a range of payment plans. In fact, we consider the terms we offer one of the greatest benefits you receive from us. Please review the enclosed brochure. If you like, give me a call at *(phone number)*. I will be happy to help you choose the plan that's best for you.

Sincerely,

— Invoice Inserts: Explanation of Terms —

Dear Customer:

At *(Name of company)*, we have only two goals: To give you the best possible price, and to create 100 percent customer satisfaction. So that we can continue to achieve both these goals, we ask that you take note of our 30-day net payment terms and help us by adhering to them.

Thank you for your order and your consideration.

Sincerely,

— Cover Letters: Incentive for Prompt Payment —

Dear *(Name)*:

It has been a great pleasure serving you. Our invoice for professional services rendered is enclosed, together with a very special offer. Return payment in full no later than *(date)*, and you will receive a *($ amount)* credit on your next service appointment.

Please call me at *(phone number)* if you have any questions.

Sincerely,

— Invoice Inserts: Incentive for Prompt Payment —

Dear Customer:

Thanks for your order!

Please remember that you are invited to subtract *(percent amount)* from the total due on the enclosed invoice if you make payment within 10 days of the invoice date.

It's our way of thanking you for your prompt payment.

Sincerely,

———

Dear Customer:

Please remember—you are invited to subtract *(percent amount)* from the total due if your payment is postmarked within *(number)* days of our invoice date.

Sincerely,

P. S. Want to save more?

Pay this invoice within *(number)* days of the invoice date, and you may subtract an additional *(percent amount)* from the total due.

It's our way of saying thanks for prompt payment!

— Responses to Disputed Amount —

Dear *(Name)*:

Thank you for your letter of *(date)*.

I understand and appreciate the questions you raise concerning the number of hours for which you have been billed. I have reviewed your account representative's time sheets. We have performed all of the services you requested and in a timely and efficient manner. Please review copies of the time sheets enclosed.

Accordingly, I ask that you check our itemized invoice once again and render payment in accordance with our agreed terms. If you still have questions concerning the amount billed, give me a call at *(phone number)*.

Sincerely yours,

Dear *(Name)*:

We have received your note regarding the total due on our invoice number *(number)*. Please note that we have carried over *($ amount)* from the previous billing. Adding to this month's invoice total, this comes to a grand total of *($ amount)*.

Our math, then, is correct, and as of *(date)* we have not received the balance due on the previous invoice. If you have any further questions, please call *(phone number)*.

We would appreciate payment in full by *(date)* in compliance with our net terms.

Sincerely,

— Responses to Disputed Terms —

Dear *(Name)*:

Thank you for your note of *(date)* concerning the payment schedule for *(name of project)*.

Our invoice for this billing period, *(date to date)*, covers the following items as specified in our letter of agreement of *(date)*: *(list items)*.

We billed strictly according to the schedule set out in our agreement. Certainly, we are willing to modify the remainder of the work and billing schedule if your needs have changed. If you would like to discuss this, please give *(Name)* in our *(department)* a call at *(phone number)*. She will be happy to work out such a modification with you.

As to the present invoice, which reflects work completed according to the schedule we created in consultation with you, we ask that you make payment at your earliest possible convenience.

Sincerely yours,

————————

Dear *(Name)*:

Thank you for your note of *(date)* in reference to the terms of our latest invoice to you, dated *(date)*.

Please note that the finance charge applies to the unpaid balance due at *(number)* days past our invoice date. As of *(date)*, *($ amount)* was outstanding and, therefore, subject to the finance charge.

I hope this answers your question. If I can be of further assistance, please call me at *(phone number)*.

Sincerely,

— Apologies for Billing Errors —

Dear *(Name)*:

If you're angry with us, you certainly don't show it. We made a billing error that put you to the time and trouble of checking your records and writing us a letter, and on behalf of *(Name of company)*, please let me apologize for the error.

The payment that you recalculated and rendered is correct, and I thank you for it. I also greatly appreciate your patience and understanding in this matter.

Sincerely yours,

————————

Dear *(Name)*:

Thank you for directing our attention to the error in our invoice to you of *(date)*. Please accept our sincere apologies. A corrected invoice is enclosed.

We appreciate your business.

Sincerely yours,

Chapter 4

Customer-Dealer Issues

How to Do It

Customer service is a veritable minefield of adversarial traps, threatening to pit the firm against the customer. Throw customer-dealer relations into the fray, and you have the potential for a three-way dispute among the company, the customer, and the dealer. Your communications with the customer need to convey that both you and your authorized dealers are committed to serving the customer. That is all your customer really cares about.

In handling customer–dealer situations, remember the most important customer consideration: The independent dealer is not independent in the customer's eyes; he is only an extension of the company. If positive relationships are not maintained between the dealer and the customer, it is the supplier as well as the dealer who typically pays the price. The customer sees you both as members of the same team.

Introducing Dealers

Always introduce dealers with a personal letter and convey that they are part of the total service team. Your communication should suggest your firm's confidence and pride in its network of dealers. Promote them not as necessary middlemen, but as a valuable product benefit, a means through which your customer can obtain the highest level of service possible. Think of these informational letters as effective sales tools.

Responding to Complaints

The customer may go around the dealer directly to the customer service department. Today, manufacturers promote direct customer contact by listing a "hot line" 800 number on all packaging. Installing a 800 direct response system is an excellent idea. It tells your customer you are interested in his concerns, gives you another data stream covering how the customer feels about your product, and gives you critical feedback on your dealer network.

If the customer is complaining about the dealer in a general way, it is a bad idea to side with the customer against the dealer; you will be perceived as being critical of your own organization. It is far better just to resolve the issue without taking sides.

Encourage dealer training in your company, too. If the dealer is doing his job perfectly, there is no reason why the customer should ever have to "go around" him.

If it was the customer that contacted you, begin by thanking him for doing so. Let him know that he has done absolutely the right thing. This helps to define your customer's ongoing relationship with your company.

If the dealer brought you into the dispute, the dealer should handle the continuing relationship with the customer, and you should be guiding the dealer on the range of options available. The dealer should be sufficiently empowered and capable of generating enough confidence so that the customer does not feel the need to involve you directly.

If things are completely out of hand, and the customer and dealer are no longer communicating, just resolve the issue with the customer. Tilt toward the customer even if she is wrong. Appeasement to save the relationship with the customer is certainly cheaper than court action or bad advertising caused by dissatisfied customers. However, after things cool down, look hard at the individual dealer involved. Companies cannot survive long using dealers who destroy communication links to customers.

Sample letters to handle disputes when the company is forced to go around the dealer are included because I recognize this is an imperfect world filled with imperfect dealers. These letters at best support recovery programs. Again, the customer should not feel the need to go around the dealer in the first place. The dealer should be acting as an extension of the company.

In all cases, emphasize communication, not policy or procedure. In fact, it is best to avoid the words *Policy* and *Procedure* completely. Arrive at some course of action, and state it clearly, together with your reasons for taking that course of action. State specifically what you can do. If this still does not work, just ask the customer what she wants to resolve the issue. Her demand may be less costly than it first appears. Automaker Saturn, for example, received many millions of dollars in free positive advertising from all three major networks by replacing thousands of faulty cars.

If the dealer or the company is in any way at fault, offer an apology. As with other apologies, do not dwell on culpability, but emphasize your appreciation of the customer's patience and understanding. Concessions or incentives as partial reparation for inconvenience caused by the error create positive word-of-mouth advertising value.

Always be certain the dealer receives all copies of the correspondence when you must communicate directly with the customer.

— Letter Introducing Dealers in the Area —

Dear *(Name)*:

You've been such a great direct-order customer over the past *(number)* years that I take special pleasure in introducing to you a brand-new way of doing business with us.

(Name of company) now has a franchised, authorized, and specially trained dealer in your area. He is *(Name and location)*.

(Name) is a graduate of our new Dealer Development Program and is a longtime resident of your area. Before joining our team he was *(name of position)* with *(Name of company)*. Formidable as his professional qualifications are, he's one heck of a nice guy, and he and I invite you to drop by the dealership on *(date)* or *(date)*, any time from *(time)* to *(time)* for a cup of coffee, some dynamite sweetrolls, and a little conversation. I'll be there, and I look forward to seeing you.

What does the new dealership mean to you?

1. Faster, more personal, face-to-face service.

2. A person willing to put himself on the line, each and every day, to meet your needs.

3. A nearby, quick, and convenient *authorized* service center.

4. A catalog showroom that allows you to see the latest in our full line of *(type of merchandise)* any time you want.

Best of all is what the new dealership does *not* mean:

It does *not* mean higher prices, premiums, or surcharges.

What you get is better service and greater convenience at the same great prices you've been paying ever since we started doing business together in *(year)*.

Copies of all your service and merchandise records have been sent to *(Name)*. You don't have to do a thing.

I hope to see you on *(date)* or *(date)*.

Sincerely yours,

— Letter Listing Dealers in the Area —

Dear *(Name)*:

I am pleased to send the information you requested about *(Name of company)* dealers in your area.

Our company is represented by the following dealers in *(Name of area)*:

> *(list)*

All of these factory-trained and factory-authorized dealers are eager to serve your needs.

Sincerely,

— Responses to Complaint: Dealer Misinformation —

Dear *(Name)*:

Thank you for contacting *(Name of company)* Customer Relations regarding what seems to have been an unfortunate miscommunication between yourself and *(Name)*, our dealer in your area.

After discussing the incident with you, I contacted *(Name of dealer)*, and we concluded that the source of the miscommunication was the dealer's assumption that the *(part)* you ordered was meant to be used in our updated model *(Name of equipment)*. While your order form did not specify the type of model—and the model you own has been out of production for several years now—*(Name of dealer)* and I agreed that he should have questioned you on this before filling your order. Therefore, *(Name of dealer)* will send you an appropriate replacement for *(part)*, and we ask that you ship the part you now have back to the dealer within ten days via *(carrier)*. We will reimburse you for the cost of shipping.

We intend to take the following steps to ensure that such a miscommunication is not repeated:

1. We have asked our dealers to doublecheck and confirm all potentially ambiguous orders.

2. We will advise customers through our order forms to specify model types and numbers in full.

I regret any inconvenience you may have had, and I thank you for your understanding.

Sincerely,

Dear *(Name)*:

(Name), our authorized dealer in *(place)*, has forwarded to me a copy of your letter to her. I know that she has responded to you with a personal apology for having misquoted the price on *(product)*, but she has also asked me to extend apologies on behalf of the company and to assure you that the misquote was an honest error.

If I can be of any assistance in this matter—or any other matter relating to *(Name of company)*—please call me at *(phone number)*.

Sincerely,

— Responses to Complaint: Dealer Unresponsive —

Dear *(Name)*:

Your letter concerning your recent unsatisfactory experience with one of our dealers, *(Name of dealer)*, was forwarded to me.

I have discussed the matter with *(Name of dealer)*, who agrees with you that he was not as responsive as he would like to have been. *(Name)* explained to me that the recent bad weather and flu epidemic left him critically shorthanded at a very busy time. He told me that he would be contacting you personally with an apology and, better yet, a free *(item or service)* to help make up for what was a frustrating experience.

Ms. *(Name)*, I thank you for taking the trouble to write, and please be assured that we at *(Name of company)* are always trying to improve the level of service we offer. Thank you for helping us improve.

Sincerely,

———————

Dear *(Name)*:

Thank you for taking the time to write to us concerning the difficulty you've been experiencing with *(Name of dealer)*.

I have spoken to *(Name of dealer)*, who has explained that she has been operating with a greatly reduced staff and has been unable to return all of her calls. His staffing problems have been corrected, and, by the time you receive this letter, she will have contacted you.

(Name of dealer) and *(Name of company)* apologize for these service difficulties.

Sincerely yours,

— Responses to Complaint: Stock in Poor Condition —

Dear *(Name)*:

Thank you for your observations concerning the condition of merchandise at our dealership in *(City)*. Our records indicate a healthy and fast-paced merchandise turnover in *(City)*, and your communication is the only such comment we have ever received concerning that dealership. However, I have asked our district manager, *(Name)*, to visit the dealership and assess the condition of the merchandise. He will report his findings to me within a few days, and I will contact you shortly thereafter with an update.

Sincerely yours,

Dear *(Name)*:

I am sorry to hear that you find the condition of *(Name of dealer's)* stock less than satisfactory. Our district manager will be paying a call next week.

I would like to note for the record, however, that yours is the first complaint we have had about the condition of this dealer's stock. Perhaps it is worth a second look?

Sincerely,

— Responses to Complaint: Dealer Out of Stock —

Dear *(Name)*:

I can well appreciate your frustration over the repeated unavailability of *(item)* at *(Name of dealer)*. The shortage of this item is not the fault of the dealer, however, but is a result of *(Name of company)* having suspended production of the *(item)* informally. A new and enhanced model is in final development, scheduled to be made available to our dealers by *(date)*.

You are a highly valued customer, and to resolve your immediate problem, I have tracked down one of the very few *(items)* available in the region and have arranged for its shipment to *(Name of dealer)*. You may purchase the unit or, if you prefer, lease it for a nominal fee to serve you in the interim period before the new model becomes available. To help make up for the frustration and inconvenience you have suffered, *(Name of dealer)* has agreed to apply *(percent amount)* of the lease fee toward purchase of the new model *(item)*.

Please contact *(Name of dealer)* at your earliest convenience, your dealer, as well as *(Name of company)*. Thank you for your understanding and patience.

Sincerely yours,

———

Dear *(Name)*:

We make every effort to keep our dealers well supplied, but sometimes unusually high customer demand gets ahead of us. This has been particularly true of *(product)*, which we have been forced to ration to dealers.

We have stepped up production of *(product)* and expect to be meeting demand fully by *(date)*. In the meantime, you have been placed on a regional priority list to receive shipment of *(product)* as soon as stocks become available at *any* dealer in your area.

We are very sorry for the delay and are doing our best to correct the situation. We appreciate your patience.

Sincerely,

— Responses to Complaint: Dealer Uncooperative —

Dear *(Name):*

We are a service-intensive company, which is why we take comments like yours concerning *(Name of dealer)* very seriously. Your letter details the incident clearly, and I have thoroughly discussed it with *(Name of dealer)*. She explained that, based on your current financial statement, it is not possible for her to extend to you the credit terms you have requested, but she would like to emphasize her willingness to cooperate with you in arriving at terms that you both can live with.

Mr. *(Name)*, I cannot dictate terms to our independent dealers, but, based on my conversation with *(Name of dealer)*, I can assure you that she values you as a customer and is most eager to negotiate further.

I suggest you call her at *(phone number)*.

Sincerely yours,

———

Dear *(Name)*:

(Name of dealer) has sent me a copy of your letter of *(date)* and has asked me to reply.

I can understand how you would characterize *(Name of dealer)* as "uncooperative" because he declined your application for credit. These situations are always difficult. Your financial data has been reviewed by our financial supporters and, unfortunately, they are unable to extend credit at this time.

Both *(Name of dealer)* and I urge you to reapply at some future time. In the meantime, *(Name of dealer)* and *(Name of company)* will be delighted to serve you on a cash-with-order basis.

Sincerely,

— Responses to Complaint: Disputed Charge —

Dear *(Name)*:

I am very sorry about the confusion over a charge in the amount of *($ amount)* you have had with *(Name of dealer)*. However, I am pleased that you have taken the time to contact Customer Service about the matter.

As I understand the situation, you ordered *(item 1)* without being aware that it is always sold as a package with *(item 2)*, and *(Name of dealer)* shipped that item to you automatically. I have contacted *(Name of dealer)* and have asked him to break our package and sell you *(item 1)* only for the price of *($ amount)*. If this is agreeable to you, please return *(item 2)* directly to *(Name of dealer)* via *(carrier)*. You will be issued a new invoice for *(item 1)* less a shipping and handling allowance of *($ amount)*.

We at *(Name of company)* value your business, and I thank you again for contacting us in this matter.

Sincerely,

———————

Dear *(Name)*:

I was sorry to learn that you and *(Name of dealer)* have not resolved your differences over the *($ amount)* charged for *(service)*.

Please allow those of us at Customer Service *(time period)* to review the matter in order to reach an equitable solution to the matter.

Your business is very important to us, and I promise that we will work diligently to arrive at an equitable solution.

Sincerely yours,

— Response to Complaint: Promised Price Not Given —

Dear *(Name)*:

Nothing is more frustrating than the feeling of being lied to or cheated. As soon as I received your letter of *(date)*, I contacted *(Name)* at the dealership, who discussed the matter of the original price quotation with the sales associate to whom you spoke. Our sales associates always make an immediate memorandum of prices and terms extended verbally. *(Name of sales associate)* consulted his memorandum book, which clearly notes a price of *($ amount 1)* rather than the price of *($ amount 2)* that you understood he offered. I enclose a photocopy of the relevant page from the memorandum book.

The worst thing about misunderstandings like this is that they can be destructive to otherwise sound business relationships. While it is not feasible economically for us to extend a below-cost price of *($ amount 2)* to you, we would like to offer *(item)* to you at *($ amount 3)* as a goodwill gesture.

We hope you will find this a fair price, and that you will accept our apologies for this misunderstanding. If the new price is agreeable to you, just contact *(Name of dealer)* at *(phone number)*, and your order will be shipped promptly.

Sincerely yours,

— Responses to Complaint: Unacceptable Substitute Item —

Dear *(Name)*:

Thank you for your letter of *(date)* concerning our substitution of *(item 1)* for *(item 2)* in filling your recent order.

Because most of our customers would rather accept timely delivery of an equivalent substitute item than wait for the original item ordered, we specify on our order forms that equivalent substitutes will be shipped when necessary.

Mr. *(Name)*, I have polled all of our dealers, and none currently stock *(item 2)*. At this point, our suppliers are unable to tell us when the item will become available. I regret that I cannot give you more precise information, and please be assured that, if I could obtain the item for you, I would.

At this time, I can offer you two options. Either retain *(item 1)*, or return it to *(Name of dealer)* for a full refund. To assist you in this decision, I have enclosed a brochure describing and listing the specifications of *(item 1)*.

I hope this is of help to you.

Sincerely,

———————

Dear *(Name)*:

I am very sorry that you find unacceptable the substitute item *(Name of dealer)* furnished in response to your order number *(number)*. The substitute item is our current replacement for the item you ordered—a product that has been discontinued. And that is something we must stress: We cannot obtain the item you ordered. It is no longer being manufactured.

As *(Name of dealer)* has offered, we can exchange the item for another, we can give you full credit toward a later purchase, or we can make a cash refund. I'm afraid these are the only alternatives we have.

Please call *(Name of dealer)* to advise on how you would like to proceed.

Sincerely,

— Responses to Complaint: Return/Refund/Exchange Dispute —

Dear *(Name)*:

We try—to the extent that we can—to create customer satisfaction in all situations.

Now, Ms. *(Name)*, while it is true that the sales agreement we both signed specifies no cash refunds, I have reviewed the matter with the dealer, *(Name of dealer)*, who has agreed to waive the Agreement and will make a cash refund *provided that* the merchandise is returned in its original packaging, complete with all manuals, and is in as-new condition.

If this is agreeable to you, please drop by the store at *(address)* and present the merchandise to *(Name)* or *(Name)*, who will give you an immediate refund.

Thank you for your business.

Sincerely yours,

Dear *(Name)*:

Thank you for writing to Customer Service concerning *(Name of dealer's)* declining to make a cash refund for the *(product)* you returned on *(date)*.

Our dealers are independent business people, with independent return, refund, and exchange guidelines.

I have spoken at length to *(Name of dealer)*, who agrees that he would rather make a customer happy than adhere to his policy. If you still want a cash refund, please call *(Name of dealer)* at *(phone number)* and he will make the necessary arrangements.

Thank you for taking the time to bring this matter to our attention.

Sincerely,

Chapter 5

THANKS *for* THE PURCHASE

HOW TO DO IT

The ancient Salesman's Maxim goes: "Once you have made the sale, shut up." This is true enough—if all you are interested in is a single sale. In that case, you might as well make the sale, shut up, pack up, and get out of town, too. But customer service exists on the assumption that making a sale is not enough to keep a company going, let alone growing. Lifetime customers are needed, customers who will create positive word-of-mouth advertising for you. Any given sale is just one transaction among the many that make up a lifetime relationship, and each sale should be an experience that strengthens the ongoing relationship. This is where letters thanking the customer for her purchase come in.

New Customer

It used to be common practice for manufacturing companies to include a little prefatory note in such documentation as instruction manuals congratulating the purchaser on having bought the finest this or that available. Unfortunately, this practice seems to have waned. Perhaps manufacturers find it corny. In fact, positive reinforcement of the purchase decision is highly effective.

1. It helps the customer feel that he has made the right decision. If you don't believe your product was the best value available, then don't sell it.

2. It conveys that those who build and service the product have a sense of pride.

3. It demonstrates an "attitude-of-service," telling the customer you appreciate his support and confidence in your company.

A letter expressing thanks for purchasing a product or using a service adds a strong positive element to the sale, which helps turn that sale into the foundation of a longer-term relationship—the goal of all sales.

Repeat Customer

The letter of thanks to a repeat customer should acknowledge loyalty. Your firm really does owe a debt of gratitude to repeat customers. A great asset, they are your most promising pool of future business. Customers will do business with a firm that is a known quantity and has a large following of repeat customers.

— Thanks for Purchase —

Dear *(Name)*:

Don't worry. Now that you've taken the terrific step of purchasing *(item)*, we're not going to bury you in junk mail. But we did want to take this opportunity to thank you for your purchase and to congratulate you on buying the finest *(item)* on the market today.

Remember, in buying the *(item)* you've not only bought a fine piece of hardware, you've also bought the expertise of our Technical Support staff. They're available at *(phone number)* to assist you and answer any questions you may have.

Sincerely,

Dear *(Name)*:

Thank you for buying our product, which we take great pride in being able to offer you. We guarantee you'll be happy with it, and we guarantee that you'll be happy with the service that goes along with it.

We at Customer Service not only stand behind our products should anything go wrong, but we're here to help you get the most out of your *(product)* when things are going just fine too! Please give us a call any time you have a question that the *User's Manual* doesn't answer to your satisfaction. And when it comes time to explore the range of accessories and related products available to complement your *(product)*, well, just give us a call.

Congratulations on a very wise purchase.

Sincerely,

— Congratulations on Purchase —

Dear *(Name)*:

Life involves one decision after another, many difficult and confusing. Whatever other decisions you made on *(date of purchase)*, you can at least be certain that you made one you will never forget. Congratulations on owning the finest *(item)* available anywhere.

Sincerely,

———————

Dear *(Name)*:

Sit back and relax. You've made the right choice.

Not only is your new *(product)* the finest *(product)* available today, it is backed by a great warranty and technical support that will protect your investment for years to come.

If you have any questions concerning your new *(product)*, just call our Customer Answer Line at *(phone number)*.

Sincerely yours,

— Thanks for Using Our Service —

Dear *(Name)*:

Thanks! Thanks for trusting us with your *(type of service)* needs.

We know you have a choice when it comes to *(providers of type of service)*, and we not only appreciate your having chosen us, but we will do our best to ensure that you are happy with your choice.

We look forward to working with you.

Sincerely,

———————

Dear *(Name)*:

It has been such a pleasure serving you that, on behalf of *(Name of company)*, I just wanted to say thanks.

We invite your comments on our service. You may write us at *(address)*, call at *(phone number)*, or fax us at *(fax number)*.

We hope you'll think of us again whenever you need a *(service)* company.

Sincerely yours,

— Welcome to Our Family of Customers —

Dear *(Name)*:

Welcome to a very big and very special family!

You're now one of the *(number)* people who own *(brand name item)*. Chances are you made your purchase on the recommendation of one of these folks. We're a word-of-mouth company, and that's why we like to think of our customers as family.

And because you're family, we won't let you down, and in fact we'd like to make you a very special offer. For every new "family member" you send our way, we'll award you *($ amount)* toward your next purchase from *(Name of company)*.

Hey, what's a family for?

Sincerely yours,

————

Dear *(Name)*:

Welcome to our family of customers.

A lot of companies say things like that. At *(Name of company)*, we really mean it. We'll treat you like family by giving you our best—our best technology, materials, prices, and our best service. We intend to offer the best total value.

Our relationship doesn't end with the sale. It begins with it. We have a large and knowledgeable staff of Customer Service Representatives and Technical Support Agents to assist you with your *(product)* for as long as you own it. We'll also make certain that you are kept up to date on upgrades, accessories, and related products.

So, as we said, welcome to the family!

Sincerely,

— Thanks for Accepting Special Offer —

Dear *(Name)*:

Thank you for taking advantage of our special offer on *(product)*. We are pleased you have joined our customer family, and we invite your comments and questions. You may contact us at *(phone number)* or *(address)*.

We know that you will enjoy using your *(product)*.

Sincerely yours,

Dear Customer:

Thank you for taking advantage of our special offer on *(product)*. We are confident that you'll be pleased with it, and we invite your questions and comments. Just give us a call at *(phone number)*.

Sincerely,

— Thanks for Accepting Trial Offer —

Dear *(Name)*:

Thanks for giving us a try! We're confident that you'll be glad you did, and that when the trial period ends, you will decide to purchase the *(product)*.

Of course, we want you to have the full advantage of *(product)* right away. So if you have any questions, just dial our Customer Hot Line at *(phone number)*. We're here to help.

Sincerely yours,

Dear Customer:

Thank you for accepting this opportunity to try *(product)* for *(number)* days.

We are so confident that you'll be sold on our product, that if you would like to purchase it, you need do nothing. We'll send a bill out to you.

Should you not want to purchase *(product)*, just return it in its original carton no later than *(date)*.

Enjoy!

Sincerely,

— Thanks for Purchase: Repeat Customer —

Dear *(Name)*:

It is always a delight to thank a good customer for doing business with us again. Please be assured that we don't take your confidence in us lightly, and we are available at your convenience to make your experience with our product as rewarding and trouble-free as possible.

As always, if you have questions or need technical assistance, call us at *(telephone number)* weekdays from *(time)* to *(time)*.

Sincerely,

———————

Dear *(Name)*:

Thanks for purchasing your second *(third, fourth, etc.) (product)*. We certainly appreciate your loyalty and continued support.

We've made some important improvements, such as *(list)*. Maybe most important of all is our new warranty and customer support policy. If you haven't looked over the User's Manual yet, we invite you to turn to the warranty page *(number)*. We've doubled your coverage!

As always, give us a call if you have any questions.

Sincerely yours,

— Thanks for Loyalty —

Dear *(Name)*:

We've been doing business together for *(number)* years now. There aren't all that many relationships that last so long, and that makes ours special. I just wanted to let you know we at *(Name of company)* appreciate your confidence in us and your loyalty, and we consider your business something to be treated as the precious commodity it is.

Sincerely yours,

———————

Dear *(Name)*:

It's our anniversary! As of *(date)*, you've been a *(Name of company)* customer for *(number)* years.

To celebrate—and thank you for your loyal patronage—please accept the enclosed certificate, which entitles you to *($ amount)* off your next order.

It's our way of saying thanks for *(number)* great years together.

Sincerely,

Chapter 6

MAXIMIZING PRODUCT BENEFITS

HOW TO DO IT

No one will deny that good advertising and marketing are essential to the success of a product. But a firm's best advertising does not come from Madison Avenue. It is generated by the customers and clients who use and are satisfied with your products and services. Studies are clear: Every satisifed customer has the potential to produce positive comments about your product. Unfortunately, every dissatisfied customer has the potential to produce negative comments about your product. One of the most important functions of the customer service department is to ensure that users of the company's products get the maximum benefit from those products. A satisfied customer becomes a strong advertisement, even a convincing salesperson.

Product Inserts

Many of the letters in this section can be "delivered" as inserts accompanying products. However, they should not be printed as anonymous cards, but in letter form in a way that speaks to the user of the product directly.

Three messages are of primary importance in such product inserts:

1. *Read the manual.* Few owner's manuals are read with any kind of thoroughness. The result is trouble, which is wrongly blamed on the product, or unnecessary calls to the customer service center.

2. *Troubleshooting guidelines.* These can be handled in a user's manual, of course, but including a list of troubleshooting procedures in a separate letter may help avert unnecessary calls to busy technical support personnel.

3. *Benefits of product registration.* Only a small percentage of product users ever return the registration forms. A separate insert letter outlining the benefits of product registration can help.

Other Letters

Users of many products, especially professional products and those requiring a substantial investment, enjoy receiving mail related to their purchase. Customer service professionals can take advantage of this by sending a mix of product enhancement advice, including lists of free bulletins and so on, as well as offers for fee-based product-related publications. It is very important to send instructional correspondence designed to help the customer receive greater value from the product or service. It also pays to create and send reminders concerning preventive maintenance, and care and storage procedures.

— Read *Owner's Manual* —
Insert with product

Dear Customer:

We know you're in a hurry to get started . . . but please take some time to read through the enclosed *Owner's Manual*. It is very "user friendly" and was written to allow you to get the very most and the very best from your new *(product)*. We believe it will answer all of your questions about *(product)*, but if you still have questions after consulting the manual, give our Technical Service Department a call at *(phone number)*. They will be happy to help.

Sincerely,

Insert with product

We're here to help—and just a phone call away at *(phone number)*. But before you call Technical Support, save time by consulting the *User's Manual*. Chances are, the answer to your question is right there. It's your *first* resort.

— Troubleshooting Guidelines —

Insert with product

Dear Customer:

If you are experiencing a problem with your *(product)*, please refer first to *(chapter[s] and/or page number[s])* of your *Owner's Manual*. In the vast majority of cases, you can solve the problem on your own.

If difficulty persists, call Customer Service at *(telephone number)* for assistance.

To facilitate your call and to obtain the most accurate information, please prepare for the call as follows:

1. Have your product serial number ready. It will be found on *(location)*.

2. Have a list of accessories ready.

3. Be prepared to explain the problem as fully and as precisely as possible. It will help to jot down the "symptoms" before you make the call.

But, please, above all: Do consult your *Owner's Manual* first. There are many sketches and diagrams which might lead you directly to and quickly to a solution.

Sincerely,

Insert with product

Troubleshooting *(Product)*

First: Consult the *User's Manual*. It has most of the answers to most problems you are likely to encounter.

Second: Call Technical Support at *(phone number)*. Please be prepared to describe the problem—and all the symptoms—fully.

— Benefits of Product Registration —
Insert with product

Dear *(Product)* User:

You've just spent good money on a great product. Now why not take the next step to really get your money's worth?

Fill out the enclosed registration form and mail it to us in the postage-paid envelope provided.

Why?

To take advantage of all product benefits, including:

> Technical support
> News of upgrades and special offers
> Special bulletins, tips, and advisories
> News of related products

So go ahead. Dig the registration form out of the package. It's yellow. It's short. It won't take more than three minutes of your time.

Thanks,

— Product Registration Instructions —
Insert with product

Dear Customer:

Registering your *(product)* is easy. Just fill out the enclosed card as fully as you can. You will find the product serial number affixed to the rear chassis. Remove one of the self-adhesive labels and apply it to the registration card.

When you have completed the registration card, drop it into any mailbox

No postage is necessary.

It is essential that you register *(product)* to ensure we can contact you about the full benefits of our Customer Assistance Program.

Sincerely,

Insert with product

(Percent amount) of our customers are cheated.

That's right. *(Percent amount)* of people who buy our products fail to fill out and return the enclosed registration form. That means that *(percent amount)* of our customers do NOT get notified if we need them.

To get full value from us and confirm your warranty is on file, please mail your registration today.

Thanks,

— Sign Up for Free Product Bulletins —

Insert with product

Dear *(Product)* User:

We hate junk mail, and we refuse to burden you with it. But we're sure you'll agree that late-breaking news about your *(product)* and *(Name of company's)* other related products is mail well worth receiving. So we invite you to complete and mail us the enclosed Registration to receive bulletins, updates, and product information.

Sincerely,

Dear *(Name)*:

Would you like to get more out of your *(product)*? We can help.

(Name of company) has a full range of technical bulletins available on such topics as:

> *(list)*

The enclosed brochure lists them all, and they're free for the asking. Just call *(phone number)* and use our automated literature ordering system. A brochure describing how to use *(product)* is enclosed. It's really simple to get more value.

This is another service from *(Name of company)*, which wants you to get the very best we can offer.

Sincerely,

— Order Product Bulletins (Fee Service) —

Dear *(Name)*:

At *(Name of company)*, we take great pride in the comprehensive authority and clarity of our user's manuals and the high level of our customer technical support. But *(product)* is so rich a product that, if you are like most of our customers, your needs—and your creative imagination—will soon send you looking for more information on applications.

That's where our Product Application Bulletin Series can help.

For *($ amount)* per month, you can subscribe to an up-to-the-minute journal filled with the answers to your technical and creative questions and offering a wealth of ideas from our in-house experts, consultants, and users like you.

It will cost you nothing to find out if the Product Bulletin Series is right for you. Just return the enclosed coupon for your free trial issue. If you would like to continue the subscription, no response is required. You will be billed for a one year subscription. If you decide that the Product Bulletin Series does not meet your needs, just write "cancel" on your subscription invoice.

Sincerely,

Dear *(Name)*:

Would you like to get more out of your *(product)*? We can help.

(Name of company) has a full range of technical applications bulletins available on such topics as:

> *(list)*

A complete catalogue and price list of applications bulletins is just a phone call away at *(phone number)*. The catalogue is free.

Sincerely,

— Recommended Literature —

Insert with product

Dear Customer:

The technical documentation included with *(product)* is ample and extensive, but the potential uses of *(product)* are limited only by the user's knowledge and imagination. To help stimulate these, we recommend the following books:

   (list)

Those marked with an asterisk may be ordered from *(Name of company)* Customer Service Department directly. Call us at *(phone number)* or write to: *(address)*.

Sincerely,

Dear *(Name)*:

Thank you for your recent inquiry concerning *(subject)* and how it relates to *(product)*. After consulting with our technical staff, I can recommend the following *(number)* books to you:

   (list)

The first one seems to be the most comprehensive.

I hope you find this helpful.

Sincerely,

— Importance of Maintenance —

Insert with product

Dear Customer:

Your new *(product)* is designed to give you years of trouble-free service, if you provide an important *minimal* level of maintenance. You will find instructions for routine maintenance in pages *(number–number)* of the *User's Manual.* If you have any questions about performing routine maintenance, please call our Customer Support Hot Line at *(phone number).*

Approximately *(percent amount)* of the customer service on-site calls we make are necessary because simple routine maintenance is not practiced. Save yourself money, downtime, and aggravation by acquainting yourself now with routine maintenance requirements and practices. Get maximum life from your *(product).*

Sincerely,

— Advice on Preventive Maintenance —
Insert with product

Dear Customer:

Sure, we trust you to plow through all *(number)* pages of our *Technical Support Manual*—but, just in case you miss a few pages, allow us to direct your attention here and now to preventive maintenance.

Please read pages *(number-number)* of the Technical Support Manual to learn how to use the self-test features of your new *(product).* These self-tests should be run every *(number)* *(weeks, months, etc.)* to detect any problems before they become serious. Please, if you read nothing else in the Technical Support Manual, examine pages *(number–number).*

Sincerely,

Insert with product

Dear Customer:

PLEASE READ THIS FIRST!

More than half of the calls we get for technical service concern problems caused by failure to perform simple preventive maintenance. Avoid downtime by taking the following steps:

BEFORE USING *(PRODUCT)* FOR THE FIRST TIME

   (list steps)

AFTER EACH SHUTDOWN

(list steps)

AFTER EVERY *(NUMBER)* HOURS OF OPERATION

(list steps)

Preventive maintenance should consume approximately *(number)* minutes each day—a small price to pay to ensure flawless operation and a maximum lifespan with a minimum of downtime.

Sincerely,

— Importance of Proper Storage —
Insert with product

Dear Customer:

The consumable components of your *(product)*—*(list consumables)*—must be stored under the proper conditions to achieve optimum results. Please take the time to examine the Storage Notice on the inside front cover of your *User's Manual*.

Sincerely,

Insert with product

PLEASE READ THIS BEFORE UNPACKING INNER CARTON

This unit contains components that are shock sensitive. Please store the unit in its inner carton until you are ready to install it. The inner carton affords the best protection for storing your *(product)* until it is ready for use.

Insert with product

This envelope contains highly sensitive electronic components. Be certain to wear a static bracelet before handling!

Chapter 7

CUSTOMER SUPPORT
and TRAINING

HOW TO DO IT

Increasingly, the most visible—and bankable—customer service asset is follow-up customer support. This is particularly true in high-technology industries such as computers, medical diagnostic equipment, programmable manufacturing equipment, robotics, special manufacturing machinery, and so on. The list grows daily and, in many cases, the sale today is exclusively dependent upon the amount and availability of after-sale support. Product support is rapidly becoming a major product differentiator. On many types of high tech-products, product support training is required and included in the initial purchase price. In many cases, the customer must attend training even before the product is installed.

Increasing Awareness of Customer Support

Letters describing and promoting the range of customer support services offered may be written in response to a particular inquiry or may be sent to customers unsolicited. In either case, these are essentially sales letters and, as such, follow this basic formula:

1. Establish the need for the service or support.

2. Offer to satisfy this need or solve the support problem.

If the support program requires a fee, follow the previous steps with these:

3. Overcome your customer's anticipated objections to your offer.

4. Reinforce the need for the support or service.

5. Urge the customer to act.

Response to Problems

Delivering on the promise of customer support also requires accountability for service that falls short of customer expectation. Begin your response to such problems with an apology combined with thanks for bringing the problem to your attention. Express your concern for and your sympathetic understanding of the customer's feelings. Outline a course of action. If possible, offer the customer more than one alternative. Finally, provide the customer with an accountable party—usually yourself—complete with phone number.

Thanks for Using Customer Support

Among the most effective expressions of a company's service ethic and commitment to its customers is a thank you letter to acknowledge the customer's having used customer support. Such a letter is a virtual must when the support (or training) is provided on a fee basis, but it is also a great relationship builder when support is provided without charge. A special thank you note is in order to acknowledge kind words and praise from satisfied customers.

— Services Available —

Dear *(Name)*:

Thank you for your inquiry about our Customer Training Program. We have *(number)* exciting programs to offer, including in-person seminars, correspondence programs, and video training programs. I invite you to examine the enclosed brochure, and I am confident that you will find programs that are just right for you. If you don't see what you need, why not give me a call at *(phone number)*? Perhaps we can custom design a training program for you.

Sincerely,

Dear *(Name)*:

I'm writing to tell you about an exciting new program of *(product)* training seminars. We have designed a series of courses for users of *(product)* at every level, from beginner through intermediate and advanced. The seminars are tailored to fit your particular area of interest, including:

> *(list)*

The seminars are offered at times most convenient for business professionals.

Our seminars are taught by our own industry experts, who understand theory *and* application. Sure, our seminars will help you get the most out of *(product)*, but, even more importantly, they are intended to develop your company's greatest asset: its people.

We'll be happy to send you a full catalogue of seminars, together with our video training series. Just call *(phone number)* and ask for the *Seminar Catalogue.*

Sincerely,

Dear *(Name)*:

Congratulations on your purchase of *(product)*. It has proved over time to be one of the most successful *(products)* of its type. Our purpose is to ensure that you, like all our other customers, receive maximum benefit and value from your new *(product)*.

Training is essential for successful installation and application. Different types of training should occur before and after installation. Our recommended training sequence is:

> *(describe)*

(Number) of training seats are included, tuition-free, with the purchase of your *(product)*. To take full advantage of this tuition-free training, the program must be completed within our recommended guidelines. Of course, additional training is always available. Our tuition fee is *($ amount)* per *(week/class/person)*.

Our classes book well in advance. Please make your reservations at minimum 90 days before your needed date.

Sincerely,

— How to Get Help —
Insert with product

Dear Customer:

Need help? Don't panic and don't get mad. We're here for you.

Customer assistance is available *(day)* through *(day)* from *(hour)* to *(hour)* and can be accessed by:

> Phone, at *(phone number)*
>
> Fax, at *(fax number)*
>
> Electronic bulletin board, at *(BBS number)*
>
> Mail, at *(address)*

All we ask is that you consult your *User's Manual* before calling us. We find that a high percentage of customer issues can be resolved quickly and easily by consulting the "Troubleshooting" section of the manual.

Sincerely,

Insert with product

Dear Customer:

Why not take advantage of us? We like it.

We're here to provide you with expert assistance on such *(product)* issues as:

> *(list)*

(number) days a week, *(hours)* a day. Just call *(phone number)* and have your serial number ready—you'll find it on the upper righthand corner of the rear chassis.

Sincerely,

— How to Get Installation Assistance —

Dear *(Name)*:

Your *(product)* will be shipped on *(date)*, so I thought I would take this opportunity to advise you of our Installation Assistance Program.

As you know, you should be able to install your new *(product)* without assistance. However, many of our customers find it more convenient to use our Installation Assistance Program. At your option, we can provide the following services:

> Predelivery consultation
>
> Complete installation service
>
> Installation assistance via our special hotline

The last service is included at no charge during the warranty period, while the first two options are subject to the following fees:

> *(list fees)*

Many of our customers opt for the predelivery consultation. If, after conferring with the consultant, you decide to use our complete installation service, the cost of the predelivery consultation will be deducted from the installation fee.

If you have any questions about these services, please contact me at *(phone number)*.

Sincerely yours,

<u>Insert with product</u>

Dear *(Name)*:

Please read this first!

Your *(product)* is designed for ease of installation. However, certain special circumstances may present some challenges, such as:

(list)

Help is available.

By phone: For installation help by telephone, just call *(phone number)*.

On site: Installation specialists are available on an hourly basis. Please call *(phone number)* for information.

Sincerely,

— Introducing Customer Support —

Dear *(Name)*:

Welcome to our family of *(product)* users!

We're a close-knit family, and we *will* be here for you if you need us.

Our Customer Support Program is your Customer Support Program, and it is available to you *(hours)* a day, *(number)* days a week. We can answer such questions as:

> How do I *(item)*?
> How do I *(item)*?
> How do I *(item)*?
> How do I *(item)*?

And more.

So, if you ever have a question about your *(product)*, just give us a call at *(phone number)*. We'll be here.

Sincerely,

Dear *(Product)* User:

Now that your *(product)* is in your hands, you are in the hands of experts.

(Name of company) Technical Support Staff is available to answer all of your technical questions, such as:

> *(list typical questions)*

And we're ready to advise you on techniques and accessories to enhance your experience with *(product)*.

Our special phone line for billing- or sales-related questions is *(phone number)*.

Sincerely,

— Responses to Customer Support Problems: —
Technician Unresponsive

Dear *(Name)*:

Your comments concerning the handling of your recent call to Customer Support were referred to me for action.

First of all, I am very sorry that you had a problem with the *(product)*, and I regret even more that your experience with Customer Support did not resolve the problem.

I have discussed the issue with the Technical Service Representative to whom you spoke. He explained to me that the problem you reported was such that it could not be handled over the telephone and required a service call. He reports that you were unwilling to accept that evaluation.

Mr. *(Name)*, I can certainly appreciate your frustration over not receiving an instant answer to a vexing problem. However, nobody knows our product better than our Technical Service staff. I am convinced that our Technical Service Representative made his evaluation of the problem thoroughly and accurately. Accordingly, I can only concur with him that your *(product)* requires on-site evaluation.

Because the warranty period has elapsed, a service call is subject to a minimum fee of *($ amount)*. Our hourly rate is *($ amount)*. I can dispatch a technician to your site with your authorization and am confident that we will resolve your problem within a reasonable time. You can reach me at *(phone number)*.

Sincerely,

Dear *(Name)*:

You're right. Getting through to Customer Service can be a problem.

However, it's not the fault of *(Name)*, your Customer Service Representative. Let me be frank with you. Our company has expanded so rapidly that our recruitment and hiring of people with the "right stuff" to be a *(Name of company)* Customer Service Representative has lagged behind our growth in sales.

We're doing our best to catch up, but it will take time—more time than both you and I would like.

I can promise that we are here to assist you, and we will do our best to assist you promptly. However, because we are still understaffed, I suggest that you try to confine your calls to *(time)* or *(time)* and *avoid* peak hours: *(time)*.

We appreciate your patience and understanding in this frustrating matter.

Sincerely,

— Responses to Customer Support Problems: —
Problem Unresolved

Dear *(Name)*:

I am very sorry to learn that our Technical Representative has been unable to resolve your difficulty with *(product)* through telephone support. After we received your letter about this, I discussed the matter with the representative, who indicated that she advised you to return the *(product)* for evaluation and repair or replacement as necessary.

I understand that you would like us to replace the unit immediately. This, however, is not a decision that can be made without careful evaluation, and since the steps our representative advised over the telephone did not resolve the problem, the only choice, other than your purchasing a new unit, is for you to return the *(product)* for evaluation.

I realize that this is an inconvenience, but I can promise you a turnaround time no longer than *(time period)*; it may well be briefer than that. I can also make available to you a "loaner" unit at a nominal fee of *($ amount)* per *(time period)*, if that would be of assistance to you.

Please give me a call at *(phone number)* when you have reached a decision.

Sincerely yours,

––––––––––

Dear *(Name)*:

I am very sorry to learn that our Technical Representative has been unable to resolve your difficulty with *(product)* through telephone support.

I understand that you would like us to replace the unit immediately. Please be advised that we do have available our advance exchange program for the nominal fee of *($ amount)*.

If you would like us to activate this program, just call me at *(phone number)*. With your authorization of charges, we will immediately ship a rebuilt unit. You can return your present unit in the same packaging you receive with our rebuilt replacement.

We hope you find this arrangement satisfactory and I thank you for your continued support.

Sincerely,

––––––––––

Dear *(Name)*:

I was very sorry to hear that your problem with *(product)* remains unresolved after several calls to Customer Service.

I have reviewed the matter with our technical service representatives, and I am convinced that all the appropriate procedures were attempted.

At this point, I ask that you return the unit to your nearest authorized dealer (a list of dealers in your area is enclosed). Please call the dealer before you bring the unit in. We will arrange for the dealer to give you a "loaner" unit for your use while your unit is inspected, tested, and repaired or, if necessary, replaced.

I am sorry, and I hope the "loaner" will help you in the interim.

Sincerely yours,

— Responses to Customer Support Problems: —
Inaccurate Information Supplied

Dear *(Name)*:

I just thought that I would write personally to express the apology of the Customer Service Department for the error made concerning troubleshooting the *(product)*.

As you know, the *(product)* is a productive and, therefore, complex system. Please be assured that we have taken steps to ensure that such an error will not be repeated. I apologize for any inconvenience you may have experienced, and I thank you for your understanding.

Sincerely,

––––––––––

Dear *(Name)*:

To confirm our telephone conversation of this morning: Our Customer Service Representative was in error when she explained *(procedure)* to you.

The correct procedure to follow is

1. *(procedure)*

2. *(procedure)*

3. *(procedure)*

We apologize for the misinformation.

Sincerely,

— Responses to Customer Support Problems: —
Phone Support Line Always Busy

Dear *(Name)*:

Few things in life are more frustrating than making an important call and then being put on hold—except when you make an important call and don't even get beyond the busy signal.

At *(Name of company)*, we are working as quickly as possible to provide more Customer Support. Unfortunately, doing so is not just a matter of putting in more telephone lines—though we *are* doing just that. To give you the best, most thorough, and most knowledgeable support, we must carefully select and train our technical representatives. And that takes time.

Please be assured that we are working to improve the situation. In the meantime, I have one suggestion and one promise.

My suggestion is that you try to call between *(hour)* and *(hour)*, when our call volume is at its lowest.

My promise is that we will not forget you. Although you may get some busy signals, we *are* here, serving other customers just like you, and we *will* answer your call just as quickly as we can.

Sincerely yours,

———————

Dear *(Name)*:

Yes, Ms. *(Name)*, you *are* right. Our phones are often busy—and we're working to correct the situation.

By *(date)* we will have *(number)* additional lines installed. By *(date)*, we will have installed an automated Answer Line to handle routine calls for literature. And, finally, we have an ongoing program in place to recruit additional customer support staff.

In the meantime, I apologize for your having to endure busy signals, and I ask for your patience and understanding.

Sincerely,

— Acknowledging Praise for Customer Support: — *Thanks for Kind Words*

Dear *(Name)*:

Too often, customers think of the Customer Service Department as the Complaint Department. Sometimes even we start thinking of ourselves that way.

Then we get a wonderful letter like yours—a compliment to the "Complaint Department"—that really makes our day!

On behalf of all of us here at Customer Service, please accept my thanks for your kind words and be assured that we will make every effort to continue to live up to them.

Sincerely yours,

———————

Dear *(Name)*:

Wow!

Thanks for the kind words. I've put your letter up on the bulletin board. It sure makes a welcome contrast to all the technical bulletins and announcements that are up there, and it's brought us a lot of smiles and satisfaction.

Sincerely,

— Customer Support Use Questionnaire —

HELP US HELP YOU
BETTER

We think we're doing an effective job in Customer Service to answer your questions and to resolve any problems you may have with our products. Now we'd like to know what you think. It will help us to help you better.

Your name: _____

Your company: _____

Date you called us: _____

Reason you called: _____

Please return this questionnaire in the enclosed self-addressed postage-paid envelope.

And thanks!

	How well did we do?			How Important is this to you?		
	Good	OK	Needs improvement	Very important	Somewhat important	Low importance
Ease of reaching us. Consider how we responded as well as the information available on how to reach us.						
Attitude and courtesy of our phone technicians.						
Helpfulness of the customer service technician.						
Demonstrated skills of our technician.						
Time frame required to resolve your problem.						
Assistance from our technician with additional training or information						

Other Comments: _____

_____

_____

_____

_____

_____

_____

— **Customer Support Letters to Promote Training Program:** —
Benefits of Training

Dear *(Name)*:

Wouldn't it be great to have a *(product/service)* guru available right on staff, whenever and wherever you wanted?

A luxury? Something only the biggest corporations can afford?

Not anymore.

(Name of company) now offers a full range of training programs in *(product/service)* taught by our own experts: the same technical staff you have been relying on to serve all of your *(product/service)* installation and maintenance needs.

Now, at *(Name of company)*, we pride ourselves on delivering prompt, efficient installation and maintenance service to you. But the fact is, we are not a part of your organization. And the fact is that nothing can substitute for an on-staff expert when you're dealing with mission-critical issues.

Now you can have that on-staff expert.

Why not read the enclosed brochure to discover the range of training programs *(Name of company)* offers? Save out-of-pocket costs, and save time—so that you can serve more customers more effectively.

Sincerely,

———

Dear *(Name)*:

We charge you darn good money to keep your *(product)* running. Do you really want to keep paying us?

Or maybe you'd rather FIX IT YOURSELF: In-house maintenance increases uptime, too.

If more uptime is what you want, we can show you how with our *(number)*-day Technical Training Course. This program will fully qualify a member of your staff to perform all routine maintenance on *(products)* and to diagnose problems that require more extensive work. Maintenance work done by graduates of the course is fully compliant with all warranty provisions, and having a graduate on your staff entitles your firm to purchase all parts at wholesale.

For more information regarding the Technical Training Course, please call *(Name)* at *(phone number)*. He'll be glad to help.

Sincerely,

— Customer Support Letters: Training Programs Offered —

Dear Customer:

Congratulations on having purchased the finest *(product)* system available.

We have devoted a great deal of time and effort to create user documentation to get you up and running quickly and effectively. We have also developed a series of training programs meant to get both you and your personnel up and running in even less time, giving you the opportunity to explore the full potential of your new product.

We offer courses at the Start-up, Intermediate, and Advanced Levels in addition to our Comprehensive Course, which takes you through all three stages quickly.

If you would like more information on our *(product)* training courses and seminars, please give me a call at *(phone number)*. We can set something up that's just right for you.

Sincerely,

Dear *(Name)*:

Here is the information you requested on the training programs we offer. As you will see, the programs range from two-day intensive seminars to *(number)*-week comprehensive courses that cover all phases of maintaining and operating *(product)*.

If you have any questions, just give us a call at *(phone number)*.

Sincerely,

— Program Enrollment —

Dear *(Name)*:

Thank you for your inquiry about our training programs in *(product/service)*. We offer *(number)* programs. Most of our customers find the *(name 1)* program the best introduction to the *(product/service)*, while customers with some experience in *(product/service)* usually enroll in our *(name 2)* program.

Signing up is easy. Just decide which level of course is right for you, consult the enclosed schedule, then fill out the addressed, postage-paid reply card.

Please take note of the enrollment deadlines. We cannot guarantee an opening for enrollment we receive after the deadline date.

Sincerely,

————————

Dear *(Name)*:

To enroll in one of our training programs, simply make your selection from the enclosed list and specify which session you prefer. We'll do the rest.

All of your course reading material will be supplied and is included in the application fee.

Sincerely,

Chapter
8

WARRANTY
and REPAIR ISSUES

HOW TO DO IT

Letters in this area fall into four categories:

1. Informational (for example, how to confirm a product warranty)

2. Sales (for example, recommending and promoting warranty extensions)

3. Dispute resolution

4. Breaking the bad news: you're not covered

Informational Letters

As with the kind of correspondence that accompanies orders, informational letters relating to warranty issues should be, first and foremost, clear, concise, and straightforward. However, do take advantage of an opportunity to be friendly and, in a word, *human*. You might also use the occasion to underscore the value of the warranty, and you should always take every advantage to develop lifelong relationships with customers.

Sales

Good sales letters begin by establishing a need for the product. Promoting a warranty extension is no exception, but the need should not be established at the expense of the value of the existing warranty. Promoting a warranty extension should be based on the assumption that, if the existing warranty is excellent, it is well worth extending that excellence. Present the extension as an opportunity, not as just another item you're trying to sell your customer.

Dispute Resolution

A warranty is both a contract and an implied promise. Your customer perceives it not only as a protection for her investment, but as an expression of the values of your company. For this reason, it is critically important to handle warranty disputes effectively.

1. Begin by thanking the customer for contacting you.

2. Express concern about the problem and be understanding of the customer's point of view.

3. Assume the customer's honesty, and convey this assumption.

4. Tell the customer what steps you have taken to resolve the dispute.

5. Render your decision or propose a course of action.

6. If the outcome is not favorable to the customer, propose an alternative.

Bad News Letters

There are situations in which you must inform a customer that his warranty has expired, does not cover a particular defect or part, or has even been voided by customer action (for example, an unauthorized modification or misuse). The difficult task in this case is to be firm and unmistakable in the "no" without alienating the customer. The first three steps toward this end are identical to those for resolving a warranty dispute:

1. Begin with thanks.

2. Express concern and understanding.

3. Assume honesty.

From here, render your decision, explaining the reasons for it. In providing this explanation, it is best to avoid the "woulda-shoulda-coulda" approach ("If only you had acted sooner," "Had you maintained the unit properly, your warranty would not have been voided," and so on). Such an approach rubs the customer's nose in his own error, misjudgment, or misfortune.

Finally—and this is the most critical step toward averting alienation—offer *alternatives:* "Although we cannot repair the unit under warranty, we can overhaul and repair it at a factory-authorized facility for a fee. I will ensure that the work is expedited properly."

— How to Confirm Warranty —

Insert with product

Dear Customer:

Congratulations on having bought a great product backed by a terrific warranty.

But that warranty begins with you.

To confirm warranty coverage in case you misplace your original receipt, please fill out and return the attached card, making sure to specify the name and address of the dealer from whom you purchased your *(product)*. This also ensures we will be able to reach you if the need arises.

If you have any questions about your warranty coverage, please call us at *(phone number)*.

Sincerely,

Insert with product

Dear Customer:

Your *(product)* is guaranteed fully for *(time period)* from date of purchase.

To confirm your warranty you may wish to call *(phone number)* from a touchtone telephone and answer a few simple questions on our automated registration system, OR you may mail in the enclosed warranty card.

Sincerely,

— Part/Defect Not Covered by Warranty —

Dear *(Name)*:

We have received your service claim for repair or replacement of *(part)* Please note that your warranty covers durable parts only, not consumable parts, which includes *(part)* which must routinely be replaced on your *(product)*.

Based on your date of purchase, you might note that the part in question has actually outlasted its specified duty life.

We have a replacement *(part)* in stock and ready to ship at a cost to you of *($ amount)* Since you have an account with us, all you need do is call us at *(phone number)* to authorize shipment and we will expedite delivery of the part to you. Full installation instructions are enclosed with the part.

Sincerely,

————————

Dear *(Name)*:

We have received your *(product)* for warranty repair. The unit has three defective parts, *(list)*. Two of these, *(part 1)* and *(part 2)*, are covered by your warranty fully. *(Part 3)*, however, is a "consumable part" and, therefore, is not covered.

The cost of replacing *(part 3)* is *($ amount)* inclusive of labor.

Please call *(phone number)* to authorize the repair.

Sincerely,

— Warranty Expired —

Dear *(Name)*:

We have received your *(product)* which you returned for warranty repair.

Please note that your warranty expired on *(date)*. We will be pleased to repair your *(product)* at a reasonable cost. Please call us at *(phone)* to discuss estimate.

Sincerely,

––––––––

Dear *(Name)*:

We have received your *(product)* for repair. Please note that the warranty on this unit expired on *(date)*. We need your authorization to proceed with repair work at our standard service rate of *($ amount)* per hour, exclusive of parts. We can estimate past costs after an investigation.

You may give your authorization over the phone by dialing *(phone number)*.

Sincerely,

— Warranty Voided —

Dear *(Name)*:

We have received your *(product)*, which you returned to us for warranty repair. Our technician noted that the factory-sealed protective cover has been opened, which, unfortunately, voids the warranty.

We will, if you would like, repair the unit at our usual rate of *($ amount)* per hour. If you would like a free estimate of the total repair costs, please call us at *(phone number)*.

Sincerely,

––––––––

Dear *(Name)*:

We have received your *(product)* for warranty repair.

The following modifications were made to the unit:

   (list)

These modifications using third-party components, a number of which were installed permanently, unfortunately voided the warranty.

If you like, we can proceed with repairs, which will be charged at our standard rate of *($ amount)* per hour, plus parts. However, we cannot guarantee how the repairs will work, because of the third-party modifications.

Please call Customer Service at *(phone number)* and tell us as to how you would like to proceed.

Sincerely,

— Warranty Disputes —

Dear *(Name)*:

Thank you for your letter explaining your dissatisfaction with our decision regarding warranty coverage of your *(product)*, which you returned for repair on *(date)*.

I have asked two additional members of our technical staff to examine the *(product)*, and both agree that its failure is due not to defect but to impact damage, specifically: *(describe)*.

Our units are built tough, but even they cannot be expected to take a heavy impact. Mr. *(Name)*, it would not be fair to ask us to bear the cost of repairing what is clearly accident-caused damage. What I can offer is to furnish a full technical statement, which may be useful if you plan to file an insurance claim. I can also offer to repair the unit at a reasonable price. Once the unit is repaired, we are willing to continue your warranty on its present terms—which will cover expenses should some part fail in the course of normal use.

Please telephone me at *(phone number)* with your instructions.

Sincerely,

———————

Dear *(Name)*:

I understand and appreciate your frustration at learning that third-party modifications made to your *(product)* voided your warranty. I also appreciate your position that you were not aware that the modifications would void the warranty. However, this is clearly stated in your warranty contract, paragraph number *(number)*.

Because of the modifications, we cannot honor the original warranty. We are, however, willing to make the necessary repairs on the unit at our most favorable rate of *($ amount)* per hour, plus the cost of any necessary parts. This is a rate generally reserved for our high-volume customers, but given the circumstances of your situation, we will extend it to you as well.

I hope this is helpful. Please call me at *(phone number)* to advise me on how you would like to proceed.

Sincerely,

— Warranty Extension: Full Product —

Dear *(Name)*:

We don't like it either, but, unfortunately, sometimes products do not perform up to our exacting standards. We are terribly sorry you have been having difficulty with our *(product)*, and we appreciate your patience. I, however, do want to assure you that we will stand behind the *(product)*.

This letter is to confirm that the warranty on your *(product)* is extended until *(date)*, doubling the standard warranty. We at *(Name of company)* are not perfect; however, we fully support our products and customers.

Please file this letter with your original warranty. Thank you again for your understanding.

Sincerely,

— Partial Warranty Extension —

Dear *(Name)*:

The *(part)* on your *(product)* has been replaced under warranty. The *(product)* has been fully tested and is now meeting all our expected standards.

However, as you know, this is the second *(part)* we have had to replace on this *(product)*. To us, this is an unacceptable performance level, and we are extending the warranty on this *(part)* until *(date)*. Please understand that this warranty extension relates to the *(part)* and not the total *(product)*.

Thank you for your support, and we are sorry for the inconvenience. Please save this letter with your original warranty documentation for the *(product)*.

Sincerely,

— Warranty Extension as a Sales Incentive —

Dear *(name)*:

Our sales agent, *(Name)*, informs us you are giving serious thought to purchase of our new *(product 1)*, which will triple your capacity when it is placed in production with your *(product 2)*, purchased from us on *(date)*.

We believe *(product 1)* is the finest *(product type)* on the market, and we are very proud of the current customer interest in its outstanding value. We want to be a part of your expansion plans. By purchasing the new *(product type)* from us, you will have less training cost because operations between *(product 1)* and *(product 2)* are similar. Further, preventive maintenance procedures between the different systems are similar, and many consumables are interchangeable.

Additionally—and this is the big advantage—if you keep us as your partners as you expand and purchase *(product 1)* from us now, we will extend the warranty on the existing *(product 2)* to match the new warranty you will receive on *(product 1)*. In short, grow your business with us by purchasing *(product 1)* and we will throw a new warranty blanket over your existing equipment.

As I said, we want to help you grow your business.

Sincerely,

— Recommendation to Purchase Warranty Extension —
Insert with product

Dear Customer:

Experience has taught us that your *(product)* will long outlive its factory warranty, and what is even more important, its advanced design ensures that it will not become obsolete. It's a durable product, which you will be able to use for a long time.

Durable though it is, things can go wrong, and for that reason, we recommend strongly that you purchase a warranty extension. The cost now is nominal, only *($ amount)* for *(number) (months, years)* of coverage, guaranteeing that your *(product)* will be maintained and repaired by factory-trained and factory-authorized experts.

Our warranty extension plan has two other advantages as well:

1. It entitles you to annual preventive maintenance inspections by one of our factory-trained and factory-authorized technical representatives. This is a great way to detect minor problems before they become work-stopping catastrophes.

2. It is transferable. If you sell your *(product)*, the extended warranty goes with it, greatly enhancing the product's value. This is NOT the case with the standard factory warranty.

Why not use the attached reply card to enroll in our Warranty Extension Program today?

Sincerely,

Dear *(Product)* Owner:

(Name of manufacturer) gives you one of the best guarantees in the business.

But it isn't as good as we'd like it to be.

It covers:

   (list)

But not:

   (list)

And the standard guarantee covers parts and labor for *(time period)*, with an additional *(time period)* for parts alone.

What we'd like to do is give you coverage on each and every component of your system, and give you that coverage—parts *and* labor—for a full *(time period)*.

That is a comprehensive warranty designed to produce complete security.

This extended coverage can be yours for a *($ amount)* payable in *(number)* installments of *($ amount)* each. Sound reasonable? We think so.

Just complete and tear off the bottom portion of this letter and return to us in the envelope provided.

Then sit back, relax, and enjoy. We've got you covered.

Sincerely,

— How to Purchase Warranty Extension —

Dear *(Name)*:

Thank you for your inquiry concerning the availability of an extended warranty for your *(product)*. We have three plans available:

(list)

Enrolling in the program is simple. Just complete the enclosed card and return it to us with a check for the amount indicated. Please note that if you enroll by *(date)* you can take advantage of our early-enrollment pricing, which represents a *(percent amount)* discount on the full cost of the program.

If you have any questions concerning the Warranty Extension Program, please call me at *(phone number)*, and I'll be glad to help.

Sincerely,

Dear *(Name)*:

Yes, we do offer several extended warranty plans. You may purchase *(time period)* protection for *($ amount)*, *(time period)* protection for *($ amount)*, or *(time period)* protection for *($ amount)*.

Just check out the normal cost of some of these out-of-warranty repairs, and you'll see just how reasonable coverage is:

(repair)   (cost)

(repair)   (cost)

(repair)   (cost)

(repair)   (cost)

(repair)   (cost)

To purchase coverage, just give me a call at *(phone number)*, and I'll do the rest. Your extended coverage will begin immediately after the expiration of your manufacturer's warranty.

Sincerely,

— Location of Repair Service —

Dear *(Name)*:

Here is a list of factory-authorized repair centers in your area. Please note that they are independent businesses, so it pays to compare by phone the value they offer before making a trip with your *(product)*.

(list)

Sincerely yours,

————————

Dear *(Name)*:

There are many fully authorized repair shops in your area. A list is enclosed.

All of these repair facilities charge a standard price for labor—*($ amount per hour)*—and for parts, and they are staffed by factory-trained technicians.

Sincerely,

— How to Return Item for Repair (Warranty) —

Dear *(Name)*:

Returning an item for warranty service is quick and simple.

1. Call *(phone number)* to obtain a Return Authorization Number.

2. Carefully pack the unit in its original box and with its original packing material. Be sure to include a piece of paper listing

   Your name

   Your phone number

   Your shipping address

   Your Return Authorization Number

3. Send the unit to the Warranty Center at *(address)* via *(carrier)*.

Most repairs are completed within *(time period)*.

Sincerely yours,

— How to Return Item for Repair (Nonwarranty) —

Dear *(Name)*:

You may return your *(product)* directly to our *(Name of place)* repair facility or to any of our authorized independent outlets.

If you are returning the item directly to our facility, please carefully pack the unit in its original box with its original packing material. If the original materials are no longer available, be certain your packaging will withstand dropping or impact. Be sure to include a piece of paper listing

   Your name

   Your phone number

   Your shipping address

We will call you, at the number you specify, with our repair estimate.

If you plan to bring the unit into an authorized independent repair outlet, we advise you to call a number of those located near you, and note that their service fees and turnaround times may vary.

I have enclosed a list of authorized independent repair outlets in your region.

Sincerely yours,

— Obtaining Replacement Parts (Warranty) —
Insert with product

Dear Customer:

Should you require a replacement part, please take the following steps:

1. Call Warranty Parts Service at *(phone number)* to obtain a Replacement Authorization Number.

2. Pack the damaged or defective part carefully and ship via *(carrier)*, to Warranty Parts Service Department, *(address)*. Be sure to include the following information with the returned part:

   Your name

   Your shipping address

   Your daytime telephone number

   The Replacement Authorization Number

Subject to availability, we make every effort to ship replacement parts within *(number)* days of our receiving the defective or damaged part you returned.

Sincerely,

— Obtaining Replacement Parts (Nonwarranty) —

Dear *(Name)*:

Thank you for your inquiry regarding how to obtain replacement parts for your *(product)*.

The process is very simple.

Please use the Parts List that came with your *(product)* (or the one I have enclosed with this letter), and clearly check off those items you would like to order. Prices listed on either form are valid through *(date)*. Please be certain to provide your name, address, and daytime telephone number.

Mail the Parts List form directly to the Replacement Parts Department, *(address)*.

Subject to availability, we make every effort to ship ordered parts within *(number)* days of receiving your order.

Sincerely,

— Obtaining "Loaner" —

Dear *(Name)*:

Thank you for your inquiry concerning our Loaner Program.

One of the best things about our Customer Protection Policy is that we won't leave you stranded. If your unit requires warranty repair, you will be asked, when you call Customer Service, whether you would like to receive a loaner unit. These units are available at a nominal fee of *($ amount)* per *(time period)* and are shipped via *(carrier)* directly to you as soon as you place your warranty repair order.

Loaners are also available for customers receiving out-of-warranty and non-warranty repairs. The *(time period)* fee is *($ amount)* and, as with loaners for warranty repair units, shipping is immediate.

Sincerely,

Chapter
9

PRODUCT COMPLAINTS

HOW TO DO IT

Nobody wants things to go wrong. But they do. When the widget your company sold to Jane Smith falls apart, Ms. Smith becomes angry. She will get a lot angrier, however, if she calls or writes to your company and no one is there to help her. Yet responding to complaints is more than a necessary evil. Sure, it's bad for Jane Smith and your firm if something goes wrong. But if she then turns to you and you are forthcoming with a helpful response, if you demonstrate your company's willingness to stand behind the product or service and make things right again, Ms. Smith may become one of your most loyal customers. In fact, some studies suggest that customers who have had problems effectively handled can be more loyal than customers who have never had a problem with your product.

Responding to complaints is more than mere damage control. It is an opportunity to build and strengthen a positive relationship with your customer. The hoary adage of sales professionals—"You don't sell a product, you sell yourself"—got so hoary by being so true. Responding effectively to a complaint is an opportunity to sell yourself—and your company—to a customer who, at the moment, may be more than merely disappointed with your product. It is a chance not merely to keep a negative situation from getting worse, but even to turn it around.

A Plan for Response

Your response must unmistakably communicate three principal things:

1. Your commitment to help
2. Your competence to help
3. Your commitment to the relationship

Bearing these goals in mind as you:

1. Acknowledge receipt of the complaint or the returned product.
2. Express sympathy, understanding, and concern for the customer.
3. Tell the customer what you propose to do.
4. Advise him of any steps he must take to make the repair, replacement, or adjustment possible (for example, take the product to the nearest authorized dealer).
5. Explain all procedures—both your own and those you ask your customer to carry out.
6. Provide any information the customer needs (for example, a list of authorized repair facilities in her area).
7. Apologize. Do not dwell on your company's culpability, but instead emphasize your gratitude for the customer's patience and understanding.

In cases where there is no quick fix, provide the customer with your best advice and the most attractive alternatives: "We are aware of the problem, and we are working to correct it. We do not anticipate a solution before *(date)*. We will advise you of our progress by *(date)*. In the meantime, I suggest . . ."

Disputing Claims

Of course, many customer complaints are unjustified or without basis. As with the "bad news" warranty related letters discussed in Chapter 8, the goal is to refute the complaint without alienating the customer.

1. State the subject of your letter ("I am responding to your letter . . .").

2. Express understanding and concern for the customer's issues.

3. State the refutation, giving a detailed explanation. Do not address subjective issues such as taste or judgment. Keep "personalities" out of it. Focus only on the product or service issue at hand.

4. Offer whatever alternatives are possible: "We cannot make a refund in this case, but we can offer you a 15 percent discount on a replacement part. . . ."

5. No apology is called for here. Nothing is more annoying than declaring, in effect, "I'm sorry, but I'm right and you're wrong." However, do express your regret that the customer experienced a problem or is dissatisfied.

6. Express your hope that the alternative you offer will be of use or assistance.

— Product Defective: Mechanical —

Dear *(Name)*:

I am very sorry to learn that the *(product)* you purchased failed to perform to your satisfaction. There are two ways I can work with you to resolve the problem and get you up and running as quickly as possible:

1. I can send you a replacement *(part name)*, with complete directions on replacing the defective part. We believe this will resolve the problem most quickly.

2. If you prefer, you may return the entire unit to us, and we will replace the defective part, thoroughly test the unit, and return it to you, together with reimbursement for your shipping costs.

If you choose the second option, please take care to pack the unit in its original carton with all of the original shipping material. The carton and the shipping material are specially designed to prevent damage.

Please give me a call at *(phone number)* to advise me as to how you would like to proceed.

In the meantime, I apologize for the frustration and inconvenience you have been subjected to, and I thank you for your patience and understanding.

Sincerely,

———————

Dear *(Name)*:

I have received your letter of *(date)* in which you describe problems you have been experiencing with your *(product)*. Based on the information in your letter, I can only conclude that your unit is defective. Please do one of the following:

> Take it to the nearest authorized dealer and describe the problem to her. Please present her with this letter and ask for in-warranty repair/replacement. A list of dealers in your area is enclosed.

> Pack the unit in its original carton, with all original shipping material, and return it to *(address)*, marked to my attention: *(Name)*. I will ensure that it is given prompt and appropriate attention.

I am very sorry that you have had difficulty with the *(product)*.

Sincerely,

———————

Dear *(Name)*:

I am sorry you are experiencing problems with your *(product)*. I have discussed your description of events with our technical staff. Unfortunately, we can only conclude that your unit is somehow defective.

I have notified our technical service manager and have ordered a replacement unit. Production is planning to complete your new unit on *(date)*. Our technical service manager will contact you and schedule a time for our technicians to visit you and replace your old *(product)*.

I am very sorry these difficulties have occurred.

Sincerely,

— **Product Defective: Cosmetic** —

Dear *(Name)*:

I am sorry to learn that your *(product)* arrived with scratches and abrasions. Although these do not affect its performance, they certainly do have a negative impact on the pleasure you take in the product.

I am shipping a new body shell for the unit, along with instructions for replacing it. You should receive the replacement body shell in *(time period)*. You may discard the damaged body shell; there is no need to return it.

We appreciate your patience and understanding.

Sincerely,

———————

Dear *(Name)*:

I was sorry to learn your *(product)* arrived with cosmetic damage. I assure you that, although our technician proceeded with the installation and has the system running for you, we have every intention of replacing the damaged surface panels.

Our technician alerted the service center immediately upon noticing the damaged panels, and new replacement panels were ordered. We proceeded with the installation using the damaged panels to get your system running for you as quickly as possible. Just as soon as the new panels arrive, we will schedule another service call.

Thank you for your consideration, and I am sorry about the inconvenience.

Sincerely,

———————

Dear *(Name)*:

Thank you for your letter of *(date)* in which you summarize your dispute with *(Name of dealer)* over return and replacement of *(product)* because of surface scratches.

Disagreements over the extent and nature of cosmetic damage are often troublesome to resolve because of the high degree of subjectivity involved in assessing these issues.

I have two suggestions to make. The first is that you bring the unit to another authorized dealer. Perhaps his assessment of the condition of *(product)* will agree with yours more closely. The second would be to meet me at *(Name of dealer)* on *(date)*, when I will be in the area. Bring the unit with you, and I will examine it as objectively as I possibly can. If you are interested in the second suggestion, please call me at *(phone number)* to arrange an exact time.

I hope you find these alternatives helpful.

Sincerely,

— Product Failed to Perform as Promised —

Dear *(Name)*:

Thank you for your letter of *(date)*.

I have shown your letter to our technical staff here, and we are in agreement that the *(product)* is not performing up to specifications. We want to work with you to ensure that the *(product)* meets our specifications and your needs; therefore, we can pursue one of two courses. If you are confident that there is no problem with your installation, you may return the unit to the Service Department at *(address)* with a copy of this letter, and we will run a full series of diagnostic tests on it to determine whether or not it is operating up to specifications. If it is defective, we will repair or replace it. Alternatively, we suggest that you run the following checks on your installation, then retry the unit:

(list)

If you have any questions about these checks, please give our Technical Service Department a call at *(phone number)*. They will be happy to assist you.

Sincerely yours,

Dear *(Name)*:

I am very sorry to hear that our *(product 1)* has not performed to your expectations. I reviewed test results for your unit with *(Name)*, one of our Technical Representatives, and we both conclude that the *(product)* is performing up to specifications. The problem may simply be that *(product 1)* is not powerful enough for your application. I would be happy to review, by telephone, your use of *(product 1)*. With a fuller picture of your particular circumstances and needs, perhaps I can recommend an upgrade to *(product 2)*. We would be willing to give you full exchange value for *(product 1)*, should you want an upgrade.

I hope this offer proves helpful.

Sincerely,

— Product Unsuited to Application —

Dear *(Name)*:

Thank you for your letter, dated *(date)*, detailing your problems with *(product)*.

I have shared your letter with a number of people on our technical staff, and from the information you provide, we have concluded that the *(product)* is unsuited to the requirements of your application. We believe that what you need is *(alternative product)*, which is designed to meet the following requirements: *(list)*

If this sounds like what you need, we would be happy to exchange the *(product)* for *(alternate product)* plus the *($ amount)* difference in price. If you would like to speak to a member of our technical staff before making your decision, please call *(phone number)*.

Sincerely yours,

————————

Dear *(Name)*:

I have received your letter concerning your dissatisfaction with *(product 1)*.

I agree: you should be dissatisfied.

But it is not *(product 1)* that is at fault. We are.

We should have guided you more thoroughly in selecting the unit best suited to your application. *(Product 1)* is working as it should, but you need *(product 2)* instead. It provides *(percent amount)* greater power, and for what you want to do, it will better meet your needs.

We would be pleased to give you full exchange value for your *(product 1)* toward an upgrade to *(product 2)*. If you would like to take advantage of this, please call me at *(phone number)*, and I will arrange the details.

Sincerely,

— **Product Not Durable** —

Dear *(Name)*:

Your letter of *(date)* concerning the durability of our *(product)* was referred to me for response.

During development, the *(product)* was subjected to a standard series of durability tests and was found to be an exceptionally durable product *of its class.*

Those last three words are important. *(Product)* is not intended for heavy-duty *(type)* work, especially in the kind of environment you describe. More appropriate to your needs is our *(alternate product)*, which is made specifically for heavy-duty applications.

Unfortunately, because the *(product)* was used inappropriately, I cannot agree to a warranty repair or exchange. In fact, if you intend to continue using it under the same conditions, I would not recommend repairing it, since it will soon break down again. What I do recommend is upgrading to the *(alternate product)*, and I would be pleased to accept in trade your *(product)*, as is, for *($ amount)* off the price of *(alternate product)*. If you would like to proceed in this way, please give me a call at *(phone number)*.

I hope you find this helpful.

Sincerely yours,

Dear *(Name)*:

I am very sorry that you have found *(product 1)* "flimsy." I cannot say that this is the word I would use to describe it. Quite the contrary, for its size and weight, *(product 1)* is quite durable. However, size and weight are the critical issues here; *(product 1)* was designed to be very small and very light. It was designed for occasional users rather than frequent users with heavy-duty needs.

My suggestion is that you think about upgrading to *(product 2)*. What it gains in weight and size, it also gains in durability. Unfortunately, since *(product 1)* has been damaged, I am not in a position to offer you full exchange value for it. However, if you would bring the unit to any one of our authorized dealers (list enclosed), you will be given the best trade-in price possible.

Sincerely yours,

— Product Difficult to Use —

Dear *(Name)*:

Your recent communication with our Technical Support representative was shared with me. A number of our customers have found some difficulty with *(action)* when using the *(product)*. I know that the Technical Support representative to whom you spoke reviewed some procedures with you to make the *(product)* easier to use, but I thought you might find it useful to have the steps summarized here:

(list steps)

We are working on an add-on device to alleviate the kind of difficulty you have experienced, and I have added your name to a list of customers who will be informed just as soon as this add-on becomes available. We anticipate that the add-on will be merchandised as an upgrade available at very modest cost.

I hope you find this letter helpful. If you continue to experience difficulty, please don't hesitate to call Technical Support at *(phone number)*.

Sincerely yours,

Dear *(Name)*:

At *(Name of company)*, we believe we make the easiest-to-use *(product)* on the market. But the technology is complex, and we are far from perfect. We are constantly working on making *(product)* richer in features yet easier to use, and we anticipate making a major upgrade available by *(date)*. That upgrade will be offered at a greatly reduced price to our currently registered customers.

In the meantime, please feel free to use our Consumer Technical Line to help you get over the hurdles. The CTL is available from *(time)* to *(time)* *(number)* days a week and can be reached at *(phone number)*.

Sincerely,

— Product Failed Prematurely —

Dear *(Name)*:

Thank you for your letter of *(date)*. I am sorry to hear that your *(product)* malfunctioned after *(hours)* of use.

I agree that this is far short of the average life expectancy of the *(product)*, but it does fall beyond the expiration date of your warranty.

You are a valued customer, and while we cannot honor an expired warranty, we are willing to extend to you a substantial *(percent amount)* discount on a new *(product)*. If you would like to take advantage of this offer, please use the enclosed reply card to place your order.

Sincerely,

Dear *(Name)*:

As you know, your *(product)* is covered by a *(time period)* warranty, which expired on *(date)*. However, failure of *(product)* after only *(number)* months of use is very rare, and, expired warranty or not, we don't want you feeling short-changed. From the condition you describe, it is clear that the failure of your unit was due to a failure of *(part)*. Bring the unit into any authorized dealer (see list enclosed), show this letter, and the *(part)* will be replaced free of charge.

Thanks for your patience and understanding.

Sincerely,

— Product Performed Poorly/Not Up to Expectations —

Dear *(Name)*:

I was very sorry to read your letter of *(date)*.

We believe the *(product)* is a fine product, and we have received overwhelmingly positive performance comments on it. However, we want all our customers to be thoroughly pleased with what we make, and I would like to solicit your suggestions for improving the *(product)*. It would help us greatly if you would use the reverse side of this letter to list the improvements you'd like to see. In return, I offer the enclosed coupon which is good for a *(percent amount)* courtesy discount on any of our products.

Please mail your suggestions to *(address)*.

Sincerely yours,

— Advertising Misrepresented Product —

Dear *(Name)*:

I was very distressed by your recent letter regarding our advertising. Let me assure you that we do not want to mislead any of our customers. That's not a good way to do business, and it certainly is not the way *we* do business.

Based on the comments in your letter, I believe you misread our advertisement—which suggests to me that we may want to revise our advertising copy to prevent such misunderstandings in the future.

For now, the best I have to offer is our apologies and, if you would like, a full and prompt cash refund. Just repack the *(product)* in its original carton, including all accessories, and send it via *(carrier)* to the following address: *(address)*. Your refund will include reimbursement for your shipping costs.

Sincerely yours,

Dear *(Name)*:

At *(Name of company)*, we take great pains to make our advertising not only honest, but clear and straightforward. For that reason, I was particularly distressed to learn that you feel our advertising for *(product)* misled you.

Of course, you may return *(product)* to the place of purchase for a complete cash refund. Alternatively, you might want to consider the following products, which may be more suitable to your needs:

(list)

You may exchange your *(product)* at full value for any of these.

Sincerely,

— New Model Inferior to Old —

Dear *(Name)*:

Thank you for your comments on our new model *(product)*. I am sorry that you disliked the new features, but we are all grateful for your description of the pluses and minuses. I have passed your comments to our marketing and development staff for use in future modifications.

Since you own the older model, which, of course, will not become obsolete, you do have the option of returning the new model for a full refund. However, might I suggest that you continue to use the two side by side a bit longer? Customer response to the changes we have made has been overwhelmingly positive. Perhaps the new model will grow on you.

Sincerely yours,

———————

Dear *(Name)*:

Thank you for your comments comparing *(new model)* to *(old model)*. We have tried to incorporate into *(new model)* all the features our *(old model)* customers requested, while also improving favorite features of the earlier version. So far, customer response has been very positive, but it is critical comments like yours that are even more useful.

Please be assured that we will study your remarks and will incorporate your suggestions into our thinking for future versions of *(product)*.

Sincerely,

— Refund Demand —

Dear *(Name)*:

Your letter of *(date)* requesting a refund of the purchase price of *(product)* was referred to me for action.

You purchased the *(product)* on terms that specify no cash refund. This is not simply a matter of stubborn "company policy," it is part of the reason that we were able to offer the *(product)* to you at such a low cost. It is, in short, part and parcel of the bargain you made with us when you purchased the *(product)*.

Please note that you do not have to exchange the *(product)* immediately. You can return it for full store credit good toward any purchase now or in the future. This option should provide you with sufficient flexibility to allow you to make a more favorable product selection.

Sincerely yours,

_____

Dear *(Name)*:

We have received the *(product)* you returned, and a check in the amount of *($ amount)* is enclosed.

Might I suggest that you don't cash it?

At least, let me suggest that you consider an alternative to the cash refund you requested. If you decide to exchange *(product)* for any other item in our catalogue, we will give you a *(percent amount)* discount. If you decide to accept a catalog credit in lieu of a cash refund, we will credit your account *(greater $ amount)* instead of the *($ amount)* you paid for *(product)* originally.

It's your choice.

If you decide on one of the alternatives to a cash refund, just return the check to *(address)*, directing it to my attention.

Sincerely,

— Replacement Demand —

Dear *(Name)*:

We have received your letter of *(date)* requesting replacement rather than repair of the *(product)* you returned to our Service Department.

The *(product)* is an advanced modular system. Rarely is it necessary or desirable to replace the entire unit. In the case of your *(product)*, only one component, the *(component)*, was found to be defective. It makes no sense, therefore, to replace the entire unit.

Why not?

1. There is nothing wrong with the rest of the unit. We are certain of that because we have tested it thoroughly.

2. It is more economical to replace a single module than an entire *(product)*. This not only means that we save money, it means that we can keep our costs competitive—which means more reasonable prices for consumers like you.

3. Replacing the module resets your warranty. You get the same warranty period that you would have gotten with a brand-new—or replacement—unit.

Mr. *(Name)*, we are in business to ensure that you are pleased with the operation of your *(product)*. For that reason, we would not repair an item that should be replaced. Please be assured that there is no reason to replace your *(product)*.

You will receive your repaired *(product)* within *(time period)*. If you have any questions about it, please call *(phone number)*.

Sincerely,

— Will Never Buy Another Product from the Company —

Dear *(Name)*:

I don't blame you for being angry. There is no question that our *(product)* failed you and, worse, failed you repeatedly. I know that it doesn't help much to tell you that such failure, let alone repeated failure, is very rare. Rare or not, the point is that it happened to you.

Of course, if you would like, we will refund the full purchase price of your *(product)*, and, if you also would like, we will do so without further discussion. Just telephone me at *(phone number)*. We have the unit you returned, and I will authorize an immediate refund.

The alternative to this step is for you to try one more replacement *(product)*. If you would like, we will send a Service Representative to your site, free of charge, to supervise installation of the *(product)* in order to ensure that it is operating in an optimal environment. It doesn't make you feel any better to be told that you've been the victim of a very rare phenomenon. But it is true nevertheless. If you would like to proceed with this final replacement, please call me at the same number, *(phone number)*.

Thank you for your consideration.

Sincerely yours,

Dear *(Name)*:

I was very distressed to receive your letter dated *(date)* and I am sorry we have displeased you. Yet, unhappy as you letter made me, I am grateful for your candor. I have shared your letter with others, including the director of sales and the shipping manager. Together, we are discussing ways to prevent the kind of situation that unfortunately occurred.

Your remarks will certainly help us alter our procedures. Please consider giving us another try in *(time frame)*.

Sincerely,

— Will Advise Others Not to Purchase Company's Products —

Dear *(Name)*:

I can well understand your anger and frustration over the disappointing performance of the *(product)*. Certainly, advising others not to do business with us may give you some degree of satisfaction, after an understandably frustrating experience. But, before you do that, wouldn't it be better to allow us to work with you to resolve the problem?

I am convinced we have not exhausted all the options available to us. I would like to send a technical representative and a replacement *(product)* to you. Let him set the unit up—at no cost to you—and let him talk to your staff about its operation, including what you can and cannot expect from the *(product)*.

Then after you are up and running, you will be in a more advantageous position to decide on your next step.

Please call me at *(phone number)* if you would like me to arrange for our representative to call on you.

Sincerely,

Chapter
10

Service Complaints

How to Do It

Responding to service complaints can be an even more demanding and delicate task than responding to product complaints. Avoid taking sides. Instead, focus on the issues your customer raises, and try to resolve them. Orient your responses to the tasks or servicing at hand, not to personalities involved.

1. Acknowledge the complaint.
2. Express your empathy, understanding, and concern.
3. If there is a quick and ready fix for the problem, propose it.
4. If the situation requires investigation, explain how you propose to go about that.
5. If appropriate, apologize. Do not dwell on your company's culpability, but instead, emphasize your gratitude for the customer's patience and understanding.
6. Even if you find that the customer's complaint is not justified, express regret for bad feelings and any inconvenience the customer may have suffered.

Focus on the positive. Where there is no ready solution to a problem, provide the customer with the best alternative.

In all cases, follow up on service complaints with your staff. Explain to your staff that even if the customer is completely wrong, they still have the responsibility of creating satisfaction and lifelong relationships with customers. Use feedback from customers to enhance training programs and in coaching as well as counseling sessions. Even the most difficult customer situations can and should be resolved. Studies on this subject are quite clear: Customers recognize and tolerate imperfect products far more easily than they tolerate imperfect personalities. Further, even when products fail, positive service can in most cases save the relationship with the customer.

— Personnel Impolite or Unwilling to Help —

Dear *(Name)*:

Your letter regarding your recent unsatisfactory experience with my performance was referred to me by my supervisor. She discussed the entire matter with me.

We pride ourselves on the high quality of our technical support staff, and we take any negative reports very seriously. When I took your call, our load was very heavy, and I did not give you all the attention your problem deserved. Of course, my workload is no excuse, and I would like to convey my sincere apologies.

I understand that the problem with your *(product)* was indeed resolved to your satisfaction after another call to Tech Support. I am pleased by that, at least, and on behalf of *(myself)* and the total Customer Service/Technical Support Department, I once again offer our apologies.

Please call me at *(telephone number)*, or my supervisor at *(phone)* if you feel there is anything further we should do.

Sincerely yours,

cc: *(Supervisor)*

Dear *(Name)*:

Your recent unpleasant exchange with one of our Customer Service representatives was brought to my attention. I have discussed the incident with *(Name)*, the representative involved, and he acknowledges that, at the end of a very rough day, he lost his temper. He believes that he acted inappropriately and has asked me to extend an apology on his behalf.

We take pride in our professionalism, and we all apologize for this unfortunate breach of professional behavior. Thank you for your patience and understanding.

Sincerely,

— Exchange/Replacement Delayed —

Dear *(Name)*:

I wanted to follow up on this morning's phone call, in which I informed you that the replacement part you ordered, *(part)*, will not be available until *(date)*.

I apologize for any inconvenience the delay may cause you, and I will do everything I can to ensure that, when the part becomes available, delivery to you will be expedited. There is a possibility that I may be able to secure the part before *(date)*, and please be assured that I will continue to work on that possibility.

Again, I am sorry for the delay, and I greatly appreciate your patience and understanding.

Sincerely,

Dear *(Name)*:

As you were advised by phone, replacement of your defective *(product)* will be delayed by *(number)* days. This delay is due to an understocked supplier, but we can promise delivery of the replacement no later than *(date)*.

We greatly regret any inconvenience, and we are grateful for your understanding in this matter.

Sincerely,

— Exchange/Replacement Error —

Dear *(Name)*:

I was very sorry to learn about the error we made in sending you a replacement for *(part)* on your *(product)*.

I can appreciate how frustrating it is to receive a defective part to begin with and then be sent the wrong part to replace it. Ms. *(Name)*, our Customer Service Representative who handled your call remarked to me how patient and understanding you were. I wanted to write to express our appreciation for that—especially since you had every right to be annoyed.

I trust that by the time this letter reaches you, you will have received the correct part. If you have any questions or I can be of further assistance in any way, please don't hesitate to call me at *(phone number)*.

Sincerely,

Letter with correct part/product

Dear *(Name)*:

Here—at last!—is the part you ordered: *(part)*. I am very sorry that we made a mistake with the first shipment, and I greatly appreciate your understanding in this matter.

Sincerely,

— Unresponsive Repair Service —

Dear *(Name)*:

Your letter concerning your difficulty with our Repair Service was referred to me for action and response.

I reviewed the technician's logbook, and I agree that you were not given the prompt attention you deserve. I have seen to it that your repair is being expedited, and I am assured that the repair will be completed no later than *(date)*. I will personally call you just as soon as the work is completed.

I am sorry for the delay, but there *is* good news. The repair work is covered 100 percent by your warranty, so there will be no charge to you of any kind.

Please call me at *(phone number)* if you have any questions.

Sincerely,

———————

Dear *(Name)*:

Your letter concerning the delay you experienced in reaching a Technical Service Representative was referred to me for action.

Let me begin by apologizing for the delay. We try to be as responsive as possible, but sometimes, the volume of calls to our department prevents us from moving as quickly as we would like.

You can help us. Please have your Customer Number ready when you call. It is the quickest way we have for accessing all of your records—and that means that we can help you faster. Further, our least busy times are *(times)*. Calling during these times will result in faster service.

Sincerely,

— Repair Delayed —

Dear *(Name)*:

Pursuant to our telephone conversation this morning concerning the delay in servicing your *(product)*, this will confirm the revised scheduled delivery date of *(date)*.

I very much regret the delay, which as I mentioned, is due to a shortage of parts supplied by our manufacturer, who has just consolidated operations and in so doing, has made an unannounced cut in production.

I apologize for the inconvenience, and I have every confidence that we will meet—or *better*—the revised delivery date. In the meantime, if you have any questions, please call me at *(phone number)*.

Sincerely yours,

Dear *(Name)*:

We have completed the "tear down" of your *(product)* and have determined that it needs a new *(part)*. Unfortunately, we will be unable to obtain *(part)* before *(date)*, which means a *(time period)* delay in completing the repair.

Please be assured that we will do everything to expedite the repair work and return your *(product)* to you as soon as possible.

We apologize for any inconvenience the delay may have caused, and we appreciate your understanding.

Sincerely,

— Repair Unsatisfactory —

Dear *(Name)*:

I have completed a review of the service performed on your *(product)*, and I must report that I find that all the work has been done properly and the unit tests to specifications.

It is remotely possible that the problem you report is an intermittent one that does not show up in test results. I can offer two alternatives. Either we return the *(product)* to you in every expectation that it will perform—and continue to perform—as specified, or you can leave it with us, where we will run a continuous "burn-in" test over a *(number)-(hour, day, etc.)* period, in which time any hidden flaw should become apparent.

Please phone me at *(phone number)* so that we can further discuss this issue.

Sincerely yours,

———————

Dear *(Name)*:

I am sorry to hear that you are not pleased with the repair work done on your *(product)*. If you bring it back to our service facility, I will see to it that the work is inspected and retested, and we will make whatever adjustments are necessary.

Sincerely,

— Repaired Product Failed —

Dear *(Name)*:

I was sorry to hear that your *(product)* failed even after we repaired it. This is a rare occurrence, and it was our best judgment to repair rather than replace the *(product)*. We were wrong, and I want to apologize for any inconvenience.

By the time you receive this note, you should be up and running with a new unit. If you have any questions about its operation, please give our Technical Service Department a call at *(phone number)*.

Many thanks for your patience and understanding.

Sincerely yours,

Insert with repaired item

Dear *(Name)*:

The only thing more frustrating than the failure of a *(product)* is the failure of a recently repaired *(product)*. So I well understand your irritation with us over the recent repair work on your *(product)*.

I am confident that you will now find your *(product)* repaired to your satisfaction. If you have any questions, please call *(phone number)*.

I apologize for any inconvenience we may have caused you.

Sincerely,

— Repaired Product Returned in Worse Condition —

Dear *(Name)*:

Your telephone conversation with Ms. *(Name)*, one of our Customer Service representatives, was brought to my attention for action.

I am very sorry to hear that you are dissatisfied with the repair work on your *(product)*. In order to assess the quality of the work and to act on your claim that the item was returned in worse condition than when you sent it to us, I must ask that you ship the *(product)* to the Customer Service Department at *(address)*. Please mark it to my attention: *(Name)*.

I will see to it that the *(product)* and the repair work are evaluated quickly and thoroughly, and will advise you as to what *(Name of company)* believes to be the next appropriate step.

Please pack the *(product)* carefully in its original container, using the original shipping materials. Regardless of the outcome of our examination, you will be reimbursed for all shipping costs.

Sincerely,

Chapter
II

Product Recalls
and Safety Issues

How to Do It

Product recalls are either safety-related and, therefore, mandated by moral and legal obligation, or quality related and, therefore, voluntary. Any recall is an admission of a problem or potential problem. It is important to

1. Define and describe the problem clearly
2. Accept responsibility for the problem
3. Provide a crystal-clear and practical course of action for the customer
4. Create a message that will position your action and your company in their best light.

This last point bears some further explanation. Recall communications should tell the truth, the whole truth, and nothing but the truth, and they should tell it clearly. No fact should be distorted or obscured in order to make your firm look better. However, by emphasizing the positive, aggressive steps that your firm is taking to correct the problem—whether it is a matter of safety or quality—and by demonstrating your firm's commitment to the customer and its willingness to stand firmly behind its product, you may turn a potentially damaging situation into one that builds and strengthens your company's relationship with the customer. No letter can—or should—absolve your firm of the responsibility and, yes, the expense of a necessary recall program. But good communication can increase the effectiveness of the recall, can contribute to customer safety, and can actually build company image by demonstrating courage, honesty, and integrity.

In carrying out all aspects of a recall campaign, whether issues of safety or quality are involved, it is critically important that you understand all applicable laws and legally mandated procedures. Professional legal and liability advice should be secured. Furthermore, you must be aware that Section 15 of the Consumer Product Safety Act—a federal law—requires manufacturers, importers, distributors, and retailers to report any product defects that have the potential for creating a hazard. This is not a voluntary matter, but a federally required action. The U. S. Consumer Product Safety Commission publishes a *Recall Handbook,* which contains guidelines for reporting potentially hazardous product defects and for preparing for, initiating, and implementing product safety recalls. This important document is available from the U. S. Consumer Product Safety Commission, Office of Compliance and Enforcement, Division of Corrective Actions, 4330 East West Highway, Room 612, Washington, DC 20207 (301–504–0608). Nothing I have written in this chapter or anywhere else in this book is intended as a substitute for the information provided in the *Recall Handbook.*

SAFETY ISSUES

The U.S. Consumer Product Safety Commission (CPSC) recognizes three classes of hazard priority:

A **Class A Hazard** exists when a risk of death or grievous injury or illness is likely or very likely, or serious injury or illness is very likely.

A **Class B Hazard** exists when a risk of death or grievous injury or illness is not likely to occur, but is possible, when serious injury or illness is likely, or moderate injury or illness is very likely.

A **Class C Hazard** exists when a risk of serious injury or illness is not likely, but possible, or when moderate injury or illness is not likely, but is possible.

These classifications are issued by the CPSC in response to a firm's report of a potential hazard. Depending on the classification, a range of means of notifying consumers of the hazard must be employed. The letters, memos, and press releases in this chapter and elsewhere in this book *do not* cover the entire range of notices the CPSC requires or may require for Class A, B, or C hazards. Consult the CPSC *Recall Handbook* for a discussion of potential means for giving "maximum direct notice to the product distribution network" and to "consumers or groups who have or use the product."

All of this said, safety recall notices issued to consumers, distributors, and retailers should contain the following elements:

1. They should be specific and concise.

2. The words "Important Safety Notice" or a heading such as "Recall Notice" should appear in the lower lefthand corner of the envelope and at the beginning of each letter.

3. The letter or communiqué should state that the recall is for safety reasons.

4. The nature of the product defect or hazard, as well as the recommended action for the consumer, distributor, or retailer, should be contained in the letter.

While all of these elements are common to letters, memos, and notices sent to consumers, distributors, and retailers, the letters you send out should be appropriately individualized for your target audience. The letter to the consumer should be specifically addressed to the consumer, and it should advise the consumer on the course(s) of action she may (or should) take; the letter to the distributor should contain directives specifically intended for the distributor; and so on.

QUALITY ISSUES

As with the safety-related recall, a quality-related recall can be viewed as a liability—an admission that your firm goofed and failed to get it right the first time. Or such a recall can be regarded as an opportunity to demonstrate your company's commitment to ensuring the highest quality. The tone of the quality-related recall letter should convey that your firm is initiating the recall not because the product involved is *no good,* but because it is not *good enough* to meet your firm's high standards. The message is not, *We have failed,* but *We can—and will—do even better.*

Begin by stating the reason for the recall. Be sure to emphasize that the recall is voluntary. Provide full instructions on how the customer can obtain the repair or retrofitting. End the letter by making two points:

1. Reiterate your firm's commitment to the highest quality.

2. Express thanks to the customer for taking the time and effort to comply with the recall. Suggest that your firm and your customer are partners in excellence.

SAFETY-RELATED RECALL

— Important Safety Notice —

Dear *(Name)*:

We have learned that if the user of our Caffeinator Coffee Maker does not properly insert the filter holder, the filter holder could become dislodged under pressure, resulting in the potential release of steam, spillage of coffee grounds, and, under some circumstances, breakage of the glass carafe.

This situation can occur only when the filter holder has been inserted incorrectly.

To avoid such misuse and potential problems, we have taken two steps:

1. We have enclosed with this letter a special Product Instruction Label, which shows the correct way of inserting the filter and warns against the potential hazard of inserting it incorrectly.

2. We have manufactured a new-style filter holder, which can be inserted only one way: correctly. Just take this letter to *any* store that stocks the Caffeinator Coffee Maker, and you will be given the new filter holder free of charge.

Caffeinator, Inc., very strongly recommends that you apply the label to your coffee maker *now* and that you obtain the free replacement-model filter holder as soon as possible.

Please direct any questions concerning this Important Safety Notice to 1–800–555–2602.

Sincerely,

— Important Safety Notice: Product Recall —

Dear *(Name)*:

Our records indicate that you purchased a *(product)*, model *(model name)*, model number *(model number)* sometime between *(date)* and *(date)*.

Routine tests conducted as part of our ongoing quality control program indicate that failure of *(component name)* is possible under certain conditions of severe use. Failure could result in personal injury.

(Name of company) has reported this situation to the appropriate government agencies and has initiated a recall program to enable us to replace the *(component name)* with a new design that is not subject to failure.

In order to prevent personal injury due to possible failure of *(component name)*, you must bring your *(product)* to any authorized dealer in your area. This does *not* have to be the dealer who originally sold the unit to you, and a complete list of dealers in your area accompanies this letter. In most cases, the dealer can replace the *(component name)* while you wait. There is no cost to you for this part and procedure.

For your safety, it is extremely important that you have this replacement performed without delay. *(Name of company)* urges you to STOP USING *(product)* until *(component name)* is replaced.

If you have any questions concerning this Important Safety Notice and Product Recall, please telephone *(1–800–555–5555)*.

Sincerely,

— Quality-Related Recall —

Dear *(Product)* Owner:

As a *(product)* owner, you care about quality intensely. So do we. That's why we're asking you to bring your *(product)* to your nearest authorized dealer for FREE replacement of *(component name)*.

Why are we asking you to do this?

Tests in our ongoing quality-assurance program have indicated that the *(component name)* in a significant percentage of *(products)* does not perform up to our exacting specifications. Your enjoyment of *(product)* and our reputation as the finest producer of *(products)* in the world depend on each and every component performing precisely as it should. Therefore, we ask you to take a few moments to bring your unit in and allow us to improve performance.

Please note that the replacement of *(component name)* will be made at no cost to you. In most cases, the work can be performed while you wait, but we suggest that you confirm this with your dealer before bringing the unit in.

If you have any questions about this quality-related recall, please call Customer Service at *(phone number)* during regular business hours.

Sincerely,

Dear *(Name)*:

Your new *(product)* isn't good enough. Better bring it back.

That's right. Oh, sure, most companies would be happy with a *(part)* that tests to *(percent amount)* specified tolerances. After all, that isn't bad.

But it isn't good enough.

And that's why *(Name of company)* is asking you to bring your *(product)* to any authorized service facility (see enclosed list) for a free replacement *(part)*.

Get the most out of your *(product)*. Bring it to a service facility today.

Sincerely,

— Safety Advisory —
Please heed this important warning!

Dear *(Name)*:

Recently, various so-called "speed-enhancement" products intended for use with your *(product)* have become available from several third-party manufacturers. *(Name of company)* has tested the following products and have found them UNSAFE to use with *(product)*:

> *(list)*

All these products force your *(product)* to operate far in excess of specified tolerances. At minimum, this will reduce the useful life of the *(product)*. At worst, excessive speed could cause sudden failure, which could result in a safety hazard.

Use of the products listed above will result in the voiding of your warranty and *may* ultimately result in personal injury. We cannot be responsible for the product's performance if there is any alteration to our tested and proven designs.

Sincerely,

— Response to Customer Safety Question —

Dear *(Name)*:

Thank you for your letter concerning the safety of the paints used on our *(product)*. Since *(year)*, *(Name of company)* has used *(type of paint)* exclusively on all *(products)*. The manufacturer of this paint guarantees it to be environmentally safe, containing no lead or other heavy metals. The manufacturer guarantees the paint is wholly nontoxic once it has been baked on. It cannot be absorbed through the skin, and is flake and chip resistant.

If you have any further questions concerning this or any other safety-related issue, please call me at *(phone number)*.

Sincerely,

— Responses to Complaint of Safety Problem —

Dear *(Name)*:

Thank you for your letter of *(date)* advising us of a potential safety hazard with our *(product)*.

Please note that the *User's Manual* specifically addresses the issue you raise and warns against the procedure you describe. The hazard you point out is a real one, but it is only a hazard if our safety interlocks are bypassed mechanically.

Our *User's Manual* is crystal clear in this area. Please help us help you and be certain that no maintenance technicians bypass any of the interlock systems. They are absolutely critical to ensure personal safety.

Thank you for taking the time to comment.

Sincerely yours,

———————

Dear *(Name)*:

Thank you for your letter of *(date)* commenting on a possible safety hazard when using *(product)*.

Please note that operations you described are not within the intended use guidelines of the *(product)*. Using *(product)* for the purpose you describe is extremely hazardous and may cause injury or fatality.

Please protect your employees. Note page *(number)* of our operations manual. All safe intended uses of the product are described. Further, on page *(number)* is a specific list of restrictions on use of *(product)*. As noted in the manuals, permission is granted to copy and post these important instructions and restrictions.

Please conduct training programs to insure that *(product)* is only used for its intended purpose as recommended on page *(number)*. All the information you need to conduct such a program can be found on pages *(numbers)* of our manual.

We further ask that you contact your safety department and human resources department for assistance. We recommend that, in addition to training and reinforcement of correct procedures, disciplinary action should be defined to ensure that employees comply with all intended usage provisions.

Thank you for writing. Please call if I can be of further assistance. I will be glad to talk to your safety director and human resources director.

Sincerely,

Chapter
12

Service *as* Sales: Recommending Accessories *and* Additional Products

How to Do It

Gone are the days when a company could look on the Customer Service Department as either a necessary evil or a nice frill. Not only is customer service perceived in the marketplace as an essential product feature offering significant value, it is both too expensive and too valuable an asset to be regarded as either a grim necessity or a mere extra. Each customer service interaction with a customer presents an opportunity for generating revenue—for making a sale and cultivating continuing relationships. Sure, the Sales Department should be promoting accessories, upgrades, and other products, but often, customer service and customer support personnel are in an even more advantageous position to promote these items. Ideally, customers regard the customer support professional as an ally and "counselor," and are receptive to sales advice from her. Moreover, the customer support professional occupies a knowledgeable position from which to recommend (in detail) the most appropriate accessories, upgrades, and related products.

The Letter

All the letters in this chapter are sales letters, which is exactly what they should be. Customer service is a marketing function, and these letters have the potential of being very effective sales letters, which will not be automatically discarded as junk mail. To begin with, they are directed at a carefully targeted group: the owners of a certain product. Also, the letter arrives with a certain added credibility because it is targeted to users.

To preserve credibility, avoid "hard sell" tactics—once-in-a-lifetime offers and such. The tone should be informational and educational, but the structure of the letter should follow that of the basic sales letter.

1. Define the value of accessories, upgrades, or related products. Often, the basis of this additional value is to enhance or protect the initial investment in the original product, usually by expanding its capabilities or improving its operation.

2. Develop interest in the items offered.

3. Assume there are no objections by stressing cost effectiveness and value added.

4. Move the customer to act. Close the sale by telling your customer how to place an order or how to obtain additional information.

— Recommending Additional Products and Spare Parts —

Dear *(Name)*:

As a user of *(product)* you'll want to know about the following new products now available from *(Name of company)*:

(Product 1) is a great add-on enhancement to your *(product)*. It allows you to *(describe)* and to make more efficient and cost-effective use of your *(product)*. It's a great way to get more value from a wise investment.

(Product 2) is for users who *(describe)*. With this, you can customize the output from your *(product)* in the following ways:

   (list)

(Product 3) is for those who want the added flexibility of operating on house current, rechargeable batteries, or automobile battery. This inexpensive option greatly expands the utility of your *(product)*. We stock a full line of rechargeable batteries.

A current price list for all three of these fine products is enclosed. To place an order and secure expedited service, please call our Accessory Hotline at *(phone number)*.

Sincerely,

———————

Dear *(Name)*:

(Name of company) encourages self-maintenance as a cost-effective measure for our customers. You only make profits when your *(product)* is running. Accordingly, we stock a full line of spare parts, and each spare part comes with full installation instructions.

For *(product)*, we recommend that you keep the following spare parts on hand:

> *(list)*

These are all wearable parts, and having them readily available will reduce downtime to an absolute minimum. No special training is required for you to successfully install these wear items.

To place an order for these or other spare parts, refer to the Specifications section of your *User's Manual,* page number *(number)*, and call *(phone number)* to order by part number. Orders are filled within *(number)* days.

Thank you for contacting us.

Sincerely,

———————

Dear *(Name)*:

(Name of company) encourages rigorous preventive maintenance for all its *(products)*. Our experience indicates that customers who practice regular maintenance get far greater—and far more profitable—"up-time" performance from the *(product)*, something we both want.

You don't even need to keep replacement and consumable parts in stock. Join our Partnership Sharing Program, and let us carry the burden for you. Members of our Partnership Sharing Program have access to these parts:

(list)

Give us a call at *(phone number)*, and join the program today. Any of these parts can be available to you under four major plans:

> Regular ground carrier of your choice
>
> Two-day service
>
> Twenty-four-hour service

The fourth and best Partnership option is when we jointly schedule maintenance in advance with you. It is simple. We advise you *(number)* days before maintenance is needed. We ship parts using lowest-cost methods and ensure the parts are there for the scheduled maintenance.

Give a call today, and let us work out the best program for you.

Sincerely,

Dear *(Name)*:

Are you concerned about emergency breakdowns?

Do you worry about lost production if you do not have a needed part in stock?

Worry no more. Call *(phone number)* and join our Emergency Support Program. And what does the Emergency Support Program mean? Twenty-four hours per day, members of the program have access to the following parts:

> *(list)*

It's guaranteed! That's right, join today and you automatically have all the backup parts you need with no additional cost in your inventory budget. Who other than us, the original manufacturer, knows best what parts to keep on hand?

And we can insure minimum downtime. Parts, of course, can always be ordered in advance for regular maintenance. Additionally, we can ship on an emergency basis three different ways:

> Downtime is not serious at this moment? We will ship regular ground carrier or second-day air.

Is downtime moderately important right now? Let us know by 6:00 P.M. and the parts will be to you by 11:00 A.M. the following day.

Got a real emergency? We can ship counter-to-counter, next available flight.

The Emergency Support Program offers real value. Give us a call and join today.

Sincerely,

— Invitations to Order Accessories Catalog —

Dear *(Name)*:

I'd like to extend to you a very special invitation to accept a free copy of our extensive catalog of the most popular—as well as the hardest to get—accessories for your *(product)*.

We are your best source of accessories and supplies for your *(product)* because

> We are a one-stop source for all your *(product's accessories)*. We stock everything, even the hard-to-get items.
>
> We stock a vast inventory and have the most knowledgeable staff in the industry.
>
> We offer the lowest prices because of our vast buying volume.

Why not order your catalog today? It's absolutely free.

Sincerely yours,

————

Dear *(Name)*:

Are you getting full value from your *(product)*? Sure it's great for:

> *(list applications)*

But did you know that with the addition of a few value-added accessories, your *(product)* can also:

> *(list application)*?
>
> *(list application)*?

(list application)?

If you're not aware of our full line of terrific accessories, you don't know the full capabilities of your *(product)*! Why not get more value? Write or call for our free *Accessories Catalog* today.

(address)
(phone number)

Sincerely,

— Advisory of Availability of Accessories/Spare Parts —

Dear *(Name)*:

Our records indicate that on *(date)* you phoned our Customer Service Department to inquire about *(accessory)*. As of *(date)*, manufacture of that product will be discontinued, and it will no longer be available after present stock is exhausted. I thought you would like to know this.

If you are still interested in purchasing *(accessory)*, just call Customer Service at *(phone number)* and specify part number *(number)*. The cost of the accessory is *($ amount)*.

For your information *(accessory)* is being replaced by *(accessory 2)*, which includes the following features:

(list)

None of these features are currently in *(accessory)*. The price for *(accessory 2)* is *($ amount)*. If you would like to order it, please call Customer Service and specify item number *(number)*. *(Accessory 2)* will be shipped after *(date)*.

Sincerely,

Dear *(Name)*:

On *(date)*, you inquired about *(part)*. It is now in stock and available. If you would like to order the part, please call our Parts Order Line at *(phone number)*.

Sincerely,

— Recommending Specific Accessories/Spare Parts —

Dear *(Name)*:

Thank you for recent letter inquiring about accessories for your *(product)*.

We have two attachments available that will convert your *(product)* into a highly efficient *(type of device)*. The first, *(product 1)*, will allow you to perform the following additional operations:

(list)

The second, *(product 2)*, performs the functions listed above, plus the following:

(list)

(Product 1) is priced at *($ amount)*, whereas *(product 2)* is priced at *($ amount)*. If the additional functionality is important to you, *(product 2)* represents a particularly good value.

To place an order, please call *(phone number)*, and we will expedite delivery.

Sincerely yours,

———

Dear *(Name)*:

Thanks for your inquiry concerning the use of your *(product)* for *(application)*. Although *(product)* is not designed primarily for that application, we do have an accessory that allows you to adapt it for that purpose.

The *(accessory)* converts your *(product)* into a full-featured *(type of product)* excellently suited to *(application)*. At *($ amount)*, it costs far less than a dedicated *(type of product)*, and it maximizes the value of your investment in *(product)*.

To order—or if you have any further questions—just call me at *(phone number)*.

Sincerely,

— Recommending Related Products —

Dear *(Product)* User:

We're sure that you are enjoying and benefitting from your new *(product 1)*. That's why we want to tell you about *(product 2)*, which greatly extends the functionality and convenience of *(product 1)* at a modest cost.

Here's what *(product 2)* does:

(list)

While *(product 2)* is specially designed to work perfectly with *(product 1)*, it also functions as a stand-alone unit, in effect giving you the benefit of two great products in one.

To order—or to get answers to any questions you may have—call *(phone number)*.

Sincerely,

———————

Dear *(Name)*:

Thank you for recently purchasing a *(product 1)*. It has been our experience that customers who use *(product 1)* are serious about *(type of application)*. For that reason, please let me take a moment to tell you about *(product 2)*, which, used in conjunction with *(product 1)*, will take care of all your *(type of application)* needs.

Just look at what *(product 2)* allows you to do:

(list)

(Product 2) is available to owners of *(product 1)* at a very special price: *($ amount)* instead of the regular price of *($ amount)*. You may order by phone at *(phone number)* or by returning the enclosed card.

Sincerely,

— **Recommending Extended Service Contracts** —

Dear *(Product)* Owner:

Let's face it. It's tough for the manufacturer of the finest, most durable *(product)* to turn around and try to sell you an extended service contract to fix it when it breaks.

But let's face facts.

Even the best *(products)* require regular maintenance, and, even with proper maintenance, the high profits *(products)* create for you does wear them down.

Now, your warranty covers defects for the first *(time period)*, but it doesn't pay for

1. Regular maintenance
2. Anything that goes wrong after *(time period)*

With private contractors charging *($ amount)* for major maintenance, and repairs averaging *($ amount)* per call, it doesn't take a rocket scientist to figure out that the *($ amount)* per *(time period)* you pay for our *(time period)* extended service contract is money well spent.

Here's the protection you're buying:

   (list coverage)

In addition, with our extended service contract, you're automatically on the "A" list. Nobody on the other end of a phone is going to tell you that they'll "squeeze you in" a week from next Tuesday. We're there within *(time period)* each and every time you need us.

And there's one more thing. Our extended service contract entitles you to very special discount prices on equipment loaners—for those rare times when we can't fix your problem on site.

Please take note that to maintain continuous coverage, you must order the extended service contract by *(date)*. To order, call *(phone number)*. It's a painless way to protect your investment.

Sincerely,

Dear *(Name)*:

Understandably, most makers of *(product)* don't like to talk about what you do if it breaks down. And, the fact is, most new owners of *(product)* don't like to think about it, either. But, while your *(product)* is a great machine, it *is* a machine, and it will inevitably require service.

Now, the *(term)* warranty that is supplied with the *(product)* is generous. But our engineering is so advanced that, odds are, you'll own your *(product)* long after the warranty has expired.

Then you're on your own.

Unless, of course, you take advantage of our economical Extended Service Contract offer.

Here's what the extended warranty covers:

> *(list)*

And here's how long you're covered:

> *(list)*

Now here's what this valuable coverage will cost:

> *($ amount)*

Most importantly, here's what it might cost you if you *don't* choose coverage:

> *(repair item)*   *($ amount)*
> *(repair item)*   *($ amount)*
> *(repair item)*   *($ amount)*
> *(repair item)*   *($ amount)*

To order your Extended Warranty, just call *(phone number)*, and we'll do the rest.

Sincerely,

— Special Offers: Accessories/Spare Parts —

Dear *(Name)*:

As a user of *(product)*, you'll want to know about our new limited-availability special offers on some of the most popular accessories that will greatly enhance your enjoyment of *(product)*. Please look over the brochure I've enclosed, which tells you all you need to know about these accessories, available now at very special prices.

You'll want to look very closely at *(accessory 1)* and *(accessory 2)*, the price of which we've slashed *(percent amount)*.

As I'm sure you'll see from the brochure, now is a great time to order those accessories you've probably been "thinking about" for some time.

Sincerely yours,

Dear *(Product)* Owner:

We're delighted to send you the enclosed special catalog of highly discounted accessories for your *(product)*. Sit back, take a look through the catalog, and give me a call if you have any questions. I'm at *(phone number)*, and I'd love to discuss them with you.

Sincerely,

— Special Offers: Related Products —

Insert with product

Dear Customer:

Welcome to the family of *(product)* users.

As a member of this family, you are entitled to very special prices on products we know *(product)* users want and enjoy. These include:

> *(list)*

Why not take a look through the free catalog packed with your *(product)* documentation? To place an order—or if you have any questions—please call us at *(phone number)*.

Sincerely,

———————

Dear *(Name)*:

I thought that you, as a *(product)* owner, would be interested in hearing about our new line of related products, including:

> *(list)*

All these—and more—are available to *(product)* owners at significantly discounted prices *if* you order by *(date)*.

Why not take this opportunity to look through the enclosed brochure. To place an order—or if you have any questions—just call *(phone number)*.

Sincerely,

— Recommending Product Upgrades —

Dear *(Name)*:

Talk about a tough assignment!

Take the number-one *(product)*, which has been praised by industry insiders and professional consultants since it was first introduced in *(year)*, and make it better.

It wasn't easy, but that's exactly what we did.

We've made *(product)* easier to use, more powerful, and more flexible with the following features:

> *(list)*

And because you've already made a commitment to the *(product)* idea, we are offering you *(upgrade product)* at the special upgrade price of only *($ amount)*, *(percent amount)* of the price of the full product.

You may place your order with us by calling *(phone number)*, or you may visit any authorized *(Name of company)* dealer. Just mention this special upgrade number—*(number)*—to secure the upgrade price of *($ amount)*.

Sincerely yours,

———————

Dear *(Name)*:

As good as *(product)* is, *(upgrade product)* is even better.

Why?

Because we've taken everything we've learned in creating *(product)*, put it all together with everything you've taught us about using *(product)*, and added a fresh new dash of our own innovation to produce *(upgrade product)*.

Here's what's new:

> *(list new features)*

That's over *(number)* new product benefits and improvements.

Why not call *(phone number)* today for more information on our exciting new upgrade?

Sincerely,

— Special Offers: Product Upgrades —

Dear *(Product)* User:

When you purchased your *(product)*, you also purchased our pledge to keep you up to date with the very latest in *(type)* technology. At *(Name of company)*, we are always working to advance the state of the art in *(product type)*, and the new version of *(product)* is just such an advance.

(Product) incorporates the features that users like you have told us were most important, together with a few exciting new wrinkles of our own, including:

> *(list new features)*

Keeping up to date does, naturally, have a price. But for you, that price is very special. We are offering the *(product)* upgrade for only *($ amount)* until *(date)*, when it will be available only at the full price of *($ amount)*.

Why not reserve your upgrade today by calling *(phone number)*? As always, we will give your order priority attention.

Sincerely,

Dear *(Name)*:

When you purchased your *(product)*, we made a pledge to protect your investment. One important way in which we keep that pledge is to make certain that you are always on the leading edge of technology, and that means giving you the opportunity to purchase product upgrades and improvements as we develop them at very special prices.

Our new *(upgrade product)* is one of the most exciting upgrades we have ever developed. It includes a wealth of new features, producing benefits such as:

> *(list)*

Best of all, it is available to owners of *(product)* for only *($ amount)* during our initial upgrade program. That's a savings of *($ amount)* from the regular retail price.

To take advantage of this special offer, please call *(phone number)* no later than *(date)*, which is the expiration date for this program.

Sincerely,

Chapter 13

SERVICE *as* SALES: SECURING CUSTOMER REFERRALS, RECOMMENDATIONS, *and* TESTIMONIALS

HOW TO DO IT

Many people find it difficult or unpleasant to ask for such favors as referrals, recommendations, and testimonials. If you think of the request narrowly—asking somebody to give you something for nothing—asking such favors is, indeed, onerous. However, you need not think of the request this way. It is not that you are asking for something in return for nothing, but that you are offering an opportunity as well. The fact is that most people enjoy helping others and are certainly flattered by being asked to lend their name, judgment, and approval to a product or service. To be asked for a recommendation is to be honored.

Make It Easy

Unless your correspondent dislikes your product or service, the only typical resistance to your request may be an unwillingness by the referrer to take the time to think of something to say. Make your request easy on your correspondent by suggesting the kind of praise you would like to hear. You can come out forthrightly and declare: "I know that you are extremely busy, so I've taken the liberty of jotting down a few good words about our product. Perhaps these will help you frame your own remarks."

When requesting a written referral, it is a good idea to ask the correspondent to send his testimonial back to you. This allows you the opportunity to develop a collection of letters to send to others. Furthermore, no one is certain about any relationship. Having the letter sent to you allows the opportunity for examination and the avoidance of embarrassment.

Structure

There are various ways to structure this kind of request. If you are on familiar terms with your correspondent, a simple, friendly letter is appropriate. If you require something more businesslike, consider this outline:

1. Establish your relationship with the correspondent: "We have been doing business together now for eight years . . ."

2. Because of our relationship, I am asking for a referral, recommendation, or testimonial.

3. This will be of great value to my business because you are so highly respected . . .

4. I realize how busy you are; therefore, I have taken the liberty of jotting down a few good words about our product or service.

5. Please send the letter of recommendation to . . .

6. Any questions? Call me at . . .

7. Thank you. I am confident that this will mean a great deal to the success of . . .

— Requests for Referrals: New Customer —

Dear *(Name)*:

Congratulations! You've made the team.

Okay. Maybe it wasn't that hard. All you had to do was make one right decision—to purchase *(product)* from *(Name of company)*. But believe it or not, there are plenty of people out there who haven't made that decision yet.

You can help them, and here's how.

Just tell them about us. Tell them about the features that convinced you to join our team. For example,

(list features)

And we're sure you can think of more.

Don't forget to say something about our Super Service Plan, too. For instance,

(list points)

Now we don't expect a team recruiter to work for nothing. For every referral you make that pays off for us, you get three months of extended warranty coverage for free *(or other offer)*.

Valuable as that is, you'll get something even better: the eternal gratitude of a friend or colleague.

Sincerely,

— Requests for Referrals: Customer of Long Standing —

Dear *(Name)*:

You've been a client of *(Name of company)* for *(number)* years now, and I know that you agree: it's been a rewarding relationship.

How do I know?

Because over the years, a number of new clients have come to us, telling us that you've sent them or that you said such fine things about us, they just had to check us out for themselves.

Well, we think that that's just terrific, and we are very grateful for the kind words and new business. But isn't it time you got something out of it, too? We think so. That is why we would like to recognize your kind words by offering you a *(percent amount)* discount on your quarterly invoice for each referral you send our way.

It is, to coin a cliché, a win-win situation. You do a favor for a friend by turning her on to a firm you're pleased with. We get more business. And you get the satisfaction of a good deed done and at least one slightly shrunken account payable.

There's no formal arrangement here. Nothing to sign. Just make certain that you tell anyone you send our way to mention your referral. We'll do the rest.

Best regards,

———————

Dear *(Name)*:

As the cliché goes, you came to us for the prices, and you stayed for the service.

Well, how would you like to get the same great service at an even lower price?

At *(Name of company)*, we've discovered that our best salespeople are our customers. We thrive by word of mouth. What we'd like to do is encourage our customers to spread the word. Here's the deal:

For every new customer you send our way, we'll give you *($ amount)* off your current monthly service contract—up to a total of *($ amount)*.

Send us *(number)* customers, and your contract costs will be cut in half!

But there's more. In recommending *(Name of company)*, you're doing your friends and colleagues a big favor, for which they will thank you.

To enroll in our Customer Referral Program, just call *(phone number)*. We'll send you a special Word of Mouth Kit to make spreading the good word even easier.

Sincerely,

— Referral Forms —

Your name: _____

Your company: _____

Your account number: _____

Name of referral: _____

His/her company: _____

Telephone: _____

Fax: _____

Address:_____

_____

_____

Type of business:_____

_____

_____

Product(s) of interest to your referral:

_____

_____

_____

_____

_____

Okay for us to contact? ( )

OR

Wait for referral to contact us? ( )

Anything else we should know?

_____

_____

_____

Thanks!

— **Customer Referral Incentives** —

Dear *(Name)*:

Take a moment to answer a very stupid question.

Do you want to save money?

Now, here's another—and not so stupid.

Do you want to do someone a simple favor they'll thank you for again and again?

Put the questions together this way: *Do you want to save money by doing someone a simple favor they'll thank you for again and again?*

At *(Name of company)* we've learned that good as our sales representatives are, the best sales staff we've got is our small army of satisfied customers. If we did absolutely nothing to encourage it, our customers would talk us up and send new business our way.

But we don't believe in taking your good word for granted. That's why, for every new customer you send our way, we'll give you a *(percent amount)* discount on any *(Name of company)* purchase. All you have to do is ask your friend or colleague to mention your name when he or she contacts us. We'll do the rest. And if your referral places an order, we'll send you a special acknowledgment, together with a discount certificate.

It's our way of thanking you for your good words. Rest assured, your friend or colleague will thank you, too.

Sincerely,

— Requests for Permission to Use Customer's Name —

Dear *(Name)*:

We've had such an enjoyable and rewarding experience working together that I feel comfortable asking you for a favor.

Would you be kind enough to let me use your name as a reference in approaching *(Name)* of *(Name of company)*, for whom we are currently bidding on a contract to supply *(product/service)*? I know that, with you as a reference, we will be in a very competitive position for some very significant business.

I appreciate your consideration. Please give me a call at *(phone number)* with your permission or to discuss this request.

Sincerely yours,

Dear *(Name)*:

I have been approached by *(Name)*, who I understand is a friend and professional colleague of yours. *(Name)* has asked me to bid on *(project)*. It is a project I am especially excited about, and in order to give myself the best shot at it, I would very much like to use your name as a reference. I'm sure it would carry a lot of weight with *(Name)*.

I am scheduled to talk to *(Name)* on *(date)*, and I will give you a call shortly before that time to make certain that you are comfortable with my using your name.

Sincerely,

— Requests for Recommendation —

Dear *(Name)*:

Can you help me?

(Name of company) is currently considering us as a contractor for *(describe project)*, a project very similar to the one we worked on with you last year. Since that was such a rewarding experience for both of us, it seems natural that you would be the ideal reference for us, especially since I believe you are well acquainted with *(Name)* at *(Name of company)*.

I'd be very grateful if you could offer a reference letter about our performance. It would be particularly helpful if you could make the following points:

> *(list points)*

Just send the letter to me. We're very excited at the prospect of this contract, and I would appreciate any good words you can pass along. Thanks for your help.

All the best,

— Requests for Recommendation: Quid Pro Quo —

Dear *(Name)*:

I'm sure you'll understand that, in my business, a lot rides on a recommendation. I'm so sure you'll appreciate this fact because I know that your business operates exactly the same way. Our products are different, of course, but the one thing we both sell is confidence.

So, I have a suggestion to make.

Why don't we come to a mutual understanding whereby you can rely on me for referrals and recommendations and I can rely on you?

Sound good?

I think it will save a lot of time for both of us, and I know it will promote business—for both of us.

Can you join me for lunch sometime during the week of *(date)* so that we can discuss the arrangement and get it in gear? I'd appreciate a call.

Best regards,

— Requests for Testimonials —

Dear *(Name)*:

I've just come out of a meeting with some of our marketing people, who tell me that we need to redesign the packaging for our (product). What's this got to do with you?

I've heard you rave about *(product)* many times over lunch or a cocktail. I think one of the best things we could do to put some real punch in our packaging would be to put some of those raves into print—right on the package.

I'd like to quote you—something like this: "*(quote)*."

Coming from you, those words should move a lot of units for us, and it would get your company's name seen by a whole lot of our customers.

How about getting together for lunch during the week of the *(date)* to discuss this? We can eat at *(restaurant)*, and I'll let you let me buy.

All the best,

Dear *(Name)*:

I'm currently putting together a direct-mail letter to promote *(product)*. Now, I know you've been a loyal fan of *(product)* for years, and I'm writing to ask you to put some of your enthusiasm in writing. Can we quote you in the letter?

This is what I had in mind: *"(quote)"*

Of course, if you'd like to say something else, that's just fine. Call or fax me a quote by *(date)*, which is our firm deadline for getting this letter into shape.

I appreciate your consideration.

Sincerely,

— Requests for Testimonials: Quid Pro Quo —

Dear *(Name)*:

Let's swap our good names.

I mean it. You're the foremost supplier of *(product/service)* in the *(type of industry)* industry, and we're the best-known supplier of *(product/service)* in our field. What I'd like to do is capitalize on that happy coincidence by including a testimonial from you in our new direct-mail appeal and supply you with a testimonial for your next campaign.

It's a simple quid pro quo, and it's about time that we did it.

If this sounds as good to you as it does to me, why not give me a call at *(phone number)* to set this up?

I look forward to hearing from you.

Sincerely,

— Request for Recommendation in Person —

Dear *(Name)*:

Hello! I'm inviting you to lunch at *(restaurant)*.

A free lunch?

You bet.

Except, of course, for the string attached.

We'll be dining with *(Name)* of *(Name of company)*, a firm currently considering us for a contract to do *(project)*. What I'm convinced will put us over the top with *(Name of company)* is your personal recommendation. And, some time between the onion soup and the chocolate mousse, that's what I'm asking you to put in: a few *very* kind words about what it's like working with us.

Can you pencil in lunch on *(date)* at *(time)* or on *(date)* at *(time)*? Please let me know by *(day)*. And thanks. This will mean a lot to me.

Best regards,

— Recommendations in Response to Special Service —

Dear *(Name)*:

John Jones, our service technician, told me about the kind words you shared with him when he stayed late to finish repairing the *(product)*. This type of positive behavior is stressed in all our training programs. John perceived your emergency situation and performed exactly as we wanted him to perform.

(Name), it is always difficult for us to explain to new customers our flexible performance capability and the value it brings to the relationship. It is also difficult to teach these concepts in our training programs.

Would you be willing to help?

Would you mind writing a sentence or two describing how John's flexibility helped you save money? A few words in a memo addressed to me at the above address would be greatly appreciated. It would help us with our prospective customers as well as in training our employees.

Thanks in advance for the memo, and I look forward to our continuing positive relationship.

Sincerely,

Dear *(Name)*:

I appreciate the kind words you shared with Judy Jackson about her performance in handling your *(situation)*. Developing personal relationships is a very important part of our overall "customer-first" training program.

(Name), would you mind sharing your positive comments in a brief note?

Having a note available helps us demonstrate to new customers just what developing personal relationships means to us.

Thanks for your help.

Best regards,

Dear *(Name)*:

We're glad Susan Manning managed to get the *(product)* back on line so quickly for you.

No, she is not a magician; the fact is that at *(name of company)*, service technicians like Susan actually do have the real power to rattle the corporate cage and make things happen. Susan was well within her "influence sphere" when she pulled in advanced engineering support on an emergency basis. She recognized the seriousness of your situation and took appropriate action.

Fortunately, we do not have to do this very often. But we do recognize that the real world is an imperfect place, and that is why Susan, like other technicians, has the power she needs to take necessary action.

Would you mind helping us with other prospective customers? Would you mind expressing your satisfaction in a brief written note?

As I mentioned, these situations do not occur very often; however, when they do, it is important for our customers to know that we can take action. Your comments attesting to that fact would help us convey the total value we offer.

Thanks for your support.

Sincerely,

Dear *(Name)*:

I was happy to hear that Charles Gooden managed to keep you "limping" along through that urgent production run last week. That sort of creative response demonstrated by Charles is stressed in all our training programs and is an important part of the service we offer.

As you know, Charles had no choice. There were no available flights to get the parts shipped counter-to-counter any sooner.

Would you help us get the word out to others? Would you mind jotting down just a note or two discussing Charles's positive performance that we might be able to use in our communications with our prospective customers?

Of course, we always hope that nothing ever goes wrong. However, when something does go wrong, we are certainly happy that we can minimize the problem.

Thanks in advance for your help.

Sincerely,

Dear *(Name)*:

We were glad to help you develop certification charts on our *(product)*. I am happy things worked out for your customer with his *(special inquiry)*.

And, of course, we are very happy to help you keep a satisfied customer.

These special situations, while infrequent, give us the opportunity to clearly demonstrate how we individualize our customer support efforts.

If you could take the time—and without violating any special confidences of course—would you please write a brief note describing how we helped your customer save money? We would greatly appreciate the effort and the note would help us explain our flexible service approach to others.

If I am being presumptuous for asking, please allow me to apologize in advance. Either way, we were happy to help and would be happy to do the same in the future.

Sincerely,

Dear *(Name)*:

Great. Just great! Judy Perone told me that she took the opportunity to demonstrate what our *(product)* could do when you were escorting a prospect around your shop.

I hope her timely demonstration gets the sale for you, and I appreciate your compliments to her.

Would you mind jotting a note to her, which I can use in our company-wide customer service newsletter? Judy was there for a scheduled preventive maintenance. However, we always stress flexibility with all of our technicians. Like you, we are always trying to imbue the entire organization with this type of positive behavior. A note from you would certainly help our efforts.

Thanks.

Sincerely,

Part Two

Reaching Prospective Customers

Chapter
14

Selling *the* Service Advantage

How to Do It

Traditionally, the Customer Service Department has served active customers, while the great pool of potential customers was strictly the province of Sales. These days, state-of-the-art customer service is proactive, reaching out to potential customers in order to promote the "service advantage" as a key product feature.

This chapter presents a brief series of sales letters promoting customer service. The objective of these letters is to get prospective customers to think beyond the particular piece of hardware they are purchasing and consider the dimension of service. The task, therefore, is one of persuasion: getting the potential customer to think about customer service in a new way. Emphasize:

1. Service

2. Collaboration and partnership

3. Accountability

— **Introducing Customer Service** —

Dear *(Name)*:

A lot of companies think "Customer Service" is a synonym for "Complaint Department," and they'd just as soon you never called. That's not the way we do things at *(Name of company)*.

Sure, we're here for you if you have a problem with any of our products. But we're here for you when things are going just fine, too. Our job is not just to fix things, it's to make things work the best they can *for you* and *all the time.*

To do this job we offer the following services:

> *Customer Answer Line*—for all your questions about our products
>
> *Accessory Express*—for all your accessory needs
>
> *Self-Maintainer Service*—spare parts and instructions so that you don't have to do-it-yourself all by yourself
>
> *Development Line*—a place you can call to share your ideas about how we can serve you better and how we might improve the *(product)*

In addition to these services, we are troubleshooters when you need us to be. Just call the Service Hotline number: *(phone number)*.

When you buy a *(Name of company)* product you don't just buy a fine piece of hardware, you buy a commitment to total service. All of the time.

Sincerely yours,

Dear *(Name)*:

By now I'm sure you've admired your new *(product)* and examined it closely. But I bet you've overlooked one very important feature.

In fact, it is invisible—until you need it.

It's customer service and technical support. We put as much thought into both as our designers put into the physical hardware of *(product)*. We offer a full program of technical support, including an automated Answer Line to get you authoritative answers to your questions fast and a full complement of technical representatives to talk you through any installation, configuration, or operational issue. In addition, our customer service representatives are waiting to help you with answers to your questions about related products, upgrades, extended warranties, service contracts, and training seminars.

To try out your *(product's)* "invisible feature," give our developmental line a call at *(phone number)*.

Sincerely,

— Explaining the Benefits of Customer Service —

Dear *(Name)*:

Thank you for your inquiry about our customer support policy. Not everyone in the market for a *(product)* has the savvy to ask about service. Too many don't think about it or understand its value—until they need it.

But that's just the point.

At *(Name of company)*, Customer Service is not just the department you call when something stops working. We believe that "service" means more than just fixing things. We believe that "service" is about helping you get the most out of your *(product) all* the time; helping you learn how to use it most effectively and creatively in a wide variety of situations. We also believe that "service" is about keeping you informed of all the latest developments in *(product)* technology, so that the technology can serve you better.

And, yes, we *are* here when something stops working. We offer a twenty-four-hour Customer Hotline for emergencies and a quick-response fax for less pressing problems. We can dispatch a technician to your site within *(number)* hours. Whenever you've got a problem, we make it our problem, and we won't pass it back to you. We'll solve it.

Thank you for asking about us. After all, Customer Service is one of the main benefits of *(product)*.

Sincerely,

— The Personal Service Advantage —

Dear *(Name)*:

As a user of *(product type)*, you are undoubtedly accustomed to getting a lot of sales literature (maybe you call it junk mail) from sales departments and professional copywriters.

We could have sent you more of the same.

But we realized that the enclosed catalog tells you all you really need to know about our *(products)*—except for one very important feature they all share: The Personal Service Advantage. And then we asked ourselves: Who better to tell you about The Personal Service Advantage than the department directly responsible for it? Here then, is the word from *(company name)* Customer Service:

> At *(company name)*, the Personal Service Advantage Program is as simple as it is vital. We **guarantee** that when you call *(company name)* Customer Service any weekday between *(time)* and *(time)*, you will talk to a technical specialist within *(number)* minutes. If you do not want to hold for the next available technician, we **guarantee** that we will call *you* back within *(time period)*. We **guarantee** that the technician you speak to will have a complete and up-to-date copy of your *(product's)* service record.

In short, we **guarantee** that when you need us, we will be there for you. Absolutely and without fail.

So there it is: No sales letter, no professional advertising text. Just honest, friendly, prompt, personal service—when you need it.

Sincerely yours,

— Selling Customer Support —

Dear *(Name)*:

The last time we took count, there were *(number)* manufacturers turning out *(products)*. We assume that most of these products work pretty well. Oh, there are technological differences and cosmetic variations, but let's face it, what you buy from X, Inc. will probably work just about as well as what you get from Y or Z Corp.

Now I'm going to tell you that *(Name of company)* is different.

But the difference is not in metal, plastic, or technology. The difference is in the organization.

When you buy a *(Name of company)* product, you buy more than great hardware. You buy great service. Our Customer Support staff is the best in the business. It should be. We recruit our members from the ranks of the foremost consultants in the industry, and we devote an unprecedented *(percent amount)* of our total resources to ensuring that Customer Support offers excellence at all levels.

Customer Support not only rides to the rescue when you have a problem, we'll help you avoid problems in the first place with our Installation Service Line. We'll help you maximize your range of applications with our Imagination Line. We'll advise you on accessories and related products, ours as well as those from other manufacturers, through our Equipment Line.

With each *(Name of company)* product you buy, you buy a top-flight staff of consultants. Here to serve *you,* and they are backed by our total organization.

Why not look through the accompanying catalog? And when it comes time to place an order, just remember how much total added value you're getting for your money.

Sincerely,

Dear *(Name)*:

When you buy a *(product)*, don't just settle for features such as:

    (list)

These are terrific features—and our new *(product)* has them all. But they're not enough.

When you buy a *(product)*, you should also get great customer support, with:

    Customer Answer Line available 24 hours a day

    Hi-Tech support

    VIP purchasing power with Express Order Service

Maximizer training videos and seminars

400 Technical Service Representatives throughout the country

57 regional offices

300 authorized dealers

Our *(product)* comes with all these, too.

So when you're in the market for a *(product)*, look beyond the hardware. Look for the people behind the technology. Look for the *(Name of company)* label.

Sincerely,

Chapter 15

The Warranty *as* Product Feature

How to Do It

Like customer service, the product warranty is one of those vitally important things that companies (and customers) have traditionally taken for granted. Warranties are expensive to support, and for that reason alone they are a product benefit that a company should promote actively.

The task of the letters in this chapter is to show the warranty in a fresh light—as a product benefit significant as any other. Nobody likes to plow through the fine print of a standard warranty. So, use the letter to highlight in narrative and in list fashion, the features that make the warranty an exceptional value and benefit.

— Introducing the Warranty —

Dear *(Name)*:

Ask the folks in our R & D department, and they'll tell you its our cutting-edge technology that makes *(product)* a best buy. Ask the people in Marketing, and they'll mention our fantastic dealer network. Ask Production, they'll talk about how high volume gives you low prices.

Well, of course, they're all right.

Now ask those of us in Customer Service, and we'll roll out the *(Name of company) (number)*-year warranty.

No other manufacturer offers so much protection, which covers you 100 percent for *(number)* years on the following:

> *(list)*

And we make getting warranty service easy. Just call our Warranty Hotline, available *(hours)* a day, *(number)* days a week, and we'll take immediate action. Most of the time, we can diagnose it right over the phone. Often, we can even resolve it right over the phone. If necessary, we'll send replacement parts, and we'll do it via overnight courier. A fully qualified technician can be at your site within *(number)* hours of your call. And, if you have to return your unit for warranty servicing, we'll send you a loaner to tide you over.

We like to call our warranty policy *aggressive*. But, unlike a lot of other companies, it's the problem we attack, not you, or your patience.

So, when you tally up your list of the many benefits that make *(product)* great and make up total value, don't forget the warranty. It's our guarantee that we will never forget you. When considering a competitive *(product)* be sure to ask them to put their warranty in writing, as we have.

Sincerely,

Dear *(Name)*:

(Name) in our Sales Department tells me that you are considering the purchase of a *(product)*. Might I offer you just one word of advice? When you weigh your choices, look beyond the hardware and take a very close look at the warranty. Many warranties are remarkable for what they *fail to* cover. For example, most *(product)* warranties exclude the following:

> *(list)*

The trouble is, a lot can go wrong with the items on this list. We know it. That's why we cover them. Everything listed above is covered *plus* the usual list, including:

(list)

Remember, when you buy a *(product)*, you are also buying a warranty.

Sincerely,

— Extended Warranties Available —

Dear *(Name)*:

Thank you for your recent inquiry about the availability of extended warranty service for *(product)*.

Everyone has a few favorite features of our *(product)*, and one of the most highly praised is the original warranty that comes with it. In fact, people like it so much, they wish it could go on forever.

Well, we can't cover you quite that long, but we can extend full warranty service for up to *(number)* years. Here's how it works:

Original Warranty	*(coverage period)*	Free
Extended Plan 1	*(coverage period)*	*($ amount)*
Extended Plan 2	*(coverage period)*	*($ amount)*
Extended Plan 3	*(coverage period)*	*($ amount)*

You don't have to buy all this coverage at once, but you can purchase it at intervals of *(number)* months. And of course, the extended warranty is transferable. If you sell your *(product)*, the warranty goes with it. Quite a plus for helping you maintain resale value.

If you have any other questions concerning warranty and extended warranty coverage, please give us a call at *(phone number)*.

Sincerely,

Chapter 16

SELLING COMPANY PRIDE, PERFORMANCE, *and* CHARACTER

HOW TO DO IT

There are two reasoning tools customers use to judge service. One is simply performance. Did the package arrive on time and as promised? The other is more subjective. Did I receive *personal* service? Was I dealing with human beings who treated me like a person, or was I dealing with a company that treated me like a number? Did I enjoy the transaction? Did the company demonstrate how important I am to their future?

The Customer Service Department is a component critical of a firm's personality. As far as customers are concerned, it represents the company's sincerity and ability to keep its promises. This role should animate all transactions for which Customer Service is responsible. It can also be embodied more deliberately in correspondence designed to sell a company's pride, performance, and character.

There is no one set of formulas that work for these letters. The idea is to inject into them a sense of pride and personality, with an emphasis on accountability. These are statements of identity, a declaration of Who We Are.

The strongest type of letter in this category is also the least pretentious. It is the personal guarantee of service: In essence, a letter introducing yourself as a customer service professional, promising that you will be responsible personally for rendering great service.

There is little downside risk in using letters like these, provided, of course, that the company is willing to live up to what the letters promise.

— The Capsule History and Statement of Principles —

Dear *(Name)*:

It gives me great pride to introduce *(Name of company)*.

We were founded in *(year)* by *(Name)*, a young college professor who realized that cultural organizations often lack the funds to maintain a full staff of exhibition and publishing experts. *(Name)* established *(Name of company)* as a research, writing, and interpretive planning firm that offers cultural organizations an effective blend of technical expertise, interpretive skills, museum experience, and creative talent.

In *(year)*, our company helped plan and launch the *(Name)* Museum in *(Place name)*. The following year, we designed the popular *(Name)* exhibit at the *(Name)* Institution, and created the highly successful catalog that accompanied the exhibition. Since then, we have assisted such cultural institutions as:

(list)

(Name of company) can place at your institution's disposal experts in:

Management

Writing

Editing

Production

Packaging

Marketing

Audience survey

Feasibility studies

Market testing and analysis

Grant proposals

Graphic design

Video concepts

Whatever your institution's needs, *(Name of company)* gives you systematic, formula-free, personalized help. Our editors, writers, designers, meeting and program planners, curatorial specialists, and exhibit experts work alongside you every step of the way to bring your special projects to successful completion.

For more information, please call *(Name)* at *(phone number)*.

Sincerely,

— Performance Sales Letters —

Dear *(Name)*:

When fire tore through their sales offices, *(Name of company)* lost hard copy of just about every transaction record and lead file it had. It knew insurance would pay for the building and the furniture, but how would the company recover from losing what was its stock in trade?

The paperwork was gone, but there were the computers. Of course, the fire did quite a number on them. Damage was severe. But *(Name)*, chief operating officer of *(Name of company)*, collected every machine, every tape, and every soggy and charred diskette he could find, and then he gave them all to us.

"See what you can do," he said. And there wasn't much optimism in his voice.

Drives and tapes were warped, even melted partially. But we went at them and were able to recover 85 percent of the data—virtually every transaction record and better than 90 percent of *(Name of company's)* vital lead files.

And we did it all in less than a week.

That is performance. And we can do the same for you.

(Name of company) is technology driven and service-oriented. The combination cannot be beat, and where your data recovery needs are concerned, we just don't give up.

We also specialize in data protection and archiving—to prevent losses before they occur. Why not call *(phone number)* for a free assessment of your data protection and recovery needs?

We deliver performance when you really need it.

Sincerely,

— Letters from Customer Service Manager/Director —

Dear *(Name)*:

I'm writing to congratulate you on your recent purchase of a *(product)* from *(Name of company)* and to introduce myself. I'm *(Name)*, director of Customer Service, and I'm committed to protecting your investment in *(product)* and helping you to get the most out of it.

In many companies, Customer Service is the same thing as the Complaint Department or Repair Shop. Well, we will act on any complaints you may have, and we'll also deliver speedy warranty repair or replacement. But most of all, we're here to help you in your day-to-day use of *(product)* to ensure you receive maximum value from your investment.

If you have any questions—or problems—just give us a call at *(phone number)*. I promise you won't get a busy signal.

Sincerely yours,

———————

Dear *(Name)*:

We're not one of those organizations where the left hand never knows what the right is doing. At *(Name of company)*, we talk to each other, and that's why I'm writing to you. *(Name)*, one of our sales representatives, tells me that you are considering the purchase of *(product)*.

I'm not going to tell you how great *(product)* is. I'm sure *(Name)* has already done that. But I do want to let you know that our *(product)* comes with a value you'll find nowhere else: *us*.

The *(Name of company)* Customer Service Department is committed to helping you get the most out of your investment—*(number)* hours a day, *(number)* days a week. How do I know? I'm director of the department, and I've been helping our customers for *(number)* years now. Become a *(Name of company)* customer, and you will be assigned your own customer service representative—but you will also have a direct line to me. Always. Many of our competitors will likely say they can do the same. But, ask them if they have been assigning personal customer service representatives for *(number of years)*.

So please think about our commitment to customer support as you con-template acquiring a new *(product)*. And if you have any questions now, please give me a call at *(phone number)*.

Sincerely,

— Personal Guarantee of Great Service —

Dear *(Name)*:

I'm writing to you directly because I know you want me here when you need me. My name is *(Name)*, and I am your Customer Service Representative. When you call *(phone number)*, you won't be getting the "Customer Service Department," you'll be getting me, and I am 100 percent committed to answering any questions you may have or resolving any dif-ficulties you may be experiencing. I personally guarantee great service. It's my job, my responsibility, and my pleasure.

Sincerely,

Dear *(Name)*:

You don't know me. But you will, if you purchase a *(product)* from *(Name of company)*.

I'm *(Name)*, customer service representative, specializing in *(product)*. I can:

> Help you through installation
>
> Help you get up and running
>
> Help you get the most out of your *(product)*
>
> Help you find the accessories and other products you need

In all modesty, I can tell you that nobody knows the *(product)* better than I do.

I personally guarantee that, with *(product)*, you will get the best, fastest, and most thoroughly committed customer support in the industry.

Sincerely,

Part Three

INTRADEPARTMENTAL and DEALER COMMUNICATIONS

Chapter 17

EXPLAINING *and* IMPLEMENTING PROCEDURES *and* POLICIES

HOW TO DO IT

Old-style managers frequently wrote memos ranging from the prescriptive to the dictatorial. The ideal was to make each memo an expression of something called "Company Policy"—an inflexible standard according to which all actions were conducted and by which all employees were judged. This approach no longer reflects the state of the art, especially in service-oriented operations. Managers no longer look upon personnel as "their people" to be controlled, but rather as assets to be developed. The notion of a management hierarchy has given way to the concept of a departmental team. The goal of most memos nowadays is to cultivate and foster the team.

The memo should convey the necessary information and guidance, but it should do so in an inclusive way that invites the active collaboration of all personnel. In this way, the state-of-the-art memo is not so much a directive as it is an effort to motivate and define common purpose.

— Cover Memos: To Accompany *Customer Service Handbook* —

Date:

To: All Customer Service Representatives
From: *(Name)*, Director of Customer Service
Subject: *Customer Service Handbook*

The handbook that accompanies this memo is the work of a lot of people with a lot of experience. It is the work of you, of me, of all of us in the Customer Service Department.

It is a valuable book that deserves your careful attention.

But it is *not* the Bible of Customer Service. Use it, learn from it, and add to it. But never delude yourselves into thinking what's printed here is "Company Policy" meant to be followed unquestioningly. Each customer is an individual, and each customer situation is unique—at least as far as the customer is concerned. No handbook can take the place of common sense, sympathetic understanding, patience, and creative imagination. It can only be a guideline.

Finally, please remember that the *Customer Service Handbook* is a "living" document. It changes frequently because we—you and I—continually add to it and delete from it. I invite you to make the ongoing composition of our handbook part of your daily job. Make notes. Identify new issues and concepts. When necessary, we will produce a revised edition.

Date:

To: All Customer Service Representatives
From: *(Name)*, Director of Customer Service
Subject: *Customer Service Handbook*

Please take a quick look at the Table of Contents of the *Customer Service Handbook* that accompanies this memo. It is divided into two broad sections: "Procedures" and "Strategies." The "Procedures" section covers policies that, for legal, safety, financial, or technical reasons, *must* be followed. However, even when following these policies, do not use the words "policy" or "procedure" with the customer. Explain *why* you must act in a certain way. Don't just say, "our policy is . . ." The "Strategies" section contains a wealth of ideas that you *might* use in dealing with a number of issues.

In order to assist customers effectively, please familiarize yourself with both sections.

— Announcing New Policy/Procedure —

Date:

To: All Customer Service Representatives
From: *(Name)*, Director of Customer Service
Subject: New Procedure for Evaluating Warranty Coverage

For some time, most of us have felt that asking customers who make warranty claims whether their *(product)* had been subjected to abuse was not only a rather silly question, but an offensive and alienating one.

I believe we are all in agreement that Customer Service should not be in the business of alienating customers. Therefore, let's not ask the question anymore, and indeed, let's not prejudge any warranty situations. If the customer's warranty is in force and you cannot resolve her issue over the phone, proceed on the assumption that the unit has failed and should be returned for warranty repair or replacement.

Please consider this standard operating procedure from now on.

———————

Date:

To: All Customer Service Representatives
From: *(Name)*, Director of Customer Service
Subject: New Procedure for Processing Refund Requests

As a Customer Service Representative, your primary responsibility is to ensure that customers are aware of their range of options in any given situation. This includes those occasions when a customer "demands" a cash refund.

Dissatisfied customers usually assume that a cash refund is their best, indeed, their only desirable option. In the past, it has been our policy simply to comply without comment to requests for refunds (provided, of course, that all warranty and return conditions were met). In operating this way, the customer believed we were doing our jobs and we believed we were doing our jobs.

But we weren't.

We need to make our customers aware of the desirability of exchange or credit in lieu of a full cash refund. When a customer "demands" a cash refund, after you confirm the validity of the claim, please reply to the customer this way:

> Of course, I'll process that refund immediately. You might want to consider an exchange or credit, however, since you receive a *(percent amount)* allowance greater than the actual cash value.

Please proceed this way from now on.

— Emergency Revision of Policy/Procedure —

Date:

To: All Customer Service Representatives
From: *(Name)*, Director of Customer Service
Subject: Evaluating Safety-Related Issues

Effective immediately, this department is revising guidelines for telephone evaluation of safety-related issues. From this date on, if a customer presents an issue that may be related to any of the unit's power supply components, please advise the customer to stop using the unit immediately and return it for warranty evaluation and repair or replacement.

Do NOT advise running self-diagnostic procedures in cases where issues may be related to the power supply.

———

Date:

To: All Customer Service Representatives
From: *(Name)*, Director of Customer Service
Subject: Warranty repair to be handled by dealers, not independent
          repair facilities

Effective immediately: Advise all customers to bring any units requiring *warranty* repair to their local dealer and *not* to an independent repair facility. Assist the customer in determining the most conveniently located dealer.

Reason for this policy change: We have received many complaints from customers concerning poor or inadequate warranty repair service from various independent shops. Until Quality Assurance and this department complete the establishment of a formal network of factory-authorized repair facilities to supplement our dealer network, it is important that customers bring their warranty repair work only to the dealers, who are directly responsible to the company.

— Inviting Comments and Suggestions Regarding Policies/Procedures —

Date:

To: All Customer Service Representatives
From: *(Name)*, Director of Customer Service
Subject: Your Ideas

A lot of companies have boxes for staff suggestions. Here, we need more than your suggestions. We need your ideas, your day-to-day guidance. We've got a *Customer Service Manual* because, through the years, *you* and others in your position wrote it.

The manual is not finished. Please keep writing.

I hope that you will continue even more vigorously to share your ideas at our weekly staff meetings.

———

Date:

To: All Customer Service Representatives
From: *(Name)*, Director of Customer Service
Subject: Suggestions

We have few rules in our Customer Service Department, but many suggestions—and the more suggestions we have, the more effectively we can serve our customers.

Please contribute your ideas as often as possible, either at our biweekly meetings or through the E-mail network.

Date:

To: All Customer Service Representatives
From: *(Name)*, Director of Customer Service
Subject: Ideas

Notice a special problem? Or, did you discover a creative new solution? Jot a note and place it on our public bulletin board. Remember, we compile all these notes several times a year and add them to our procedure book.

Chapter 18

SCHEDULES and WORK ASSIGNMENTS

HOW TO DO IT

These memos are often the written distillations of meetings. Use tabular form to make schedules clear. In cases where special assignments or overtime assignments are being made, be certain to acknowledge additional or special effort.

— Schedule/Assignment Memos —

Date:

To: All Customer Service Representatives
From: *(Name)*, Director of Customer Service
Subject: Work assignments

As we agreed in our meeting this morning, *(Name 1)* will take responsibility for *(assignment 1)*, *(Name 2)* will handle *(assignment 2)* and *(assignment 3)*, and *(Name 3)* will take *(assignment 4)* in addition to covering the phones during the regular lunch hour. *(Name 1)* will be responsible for collecting and reporting customer response data, and will meet with me briefly every other *(day)* to discuss trends.

Date:

To: All Customer Service Representatives
From: *(Name)*, Director of Customer Service
Subject: Schedule for *(date)* to *(date)*

From *(date)* to *(date)*:

> *(Name 1)*, *(Name 2)*, and *(Name 3)* will handle the Customer Support Line during regular hours
>
> *(Name 4)* will handle the CSL during off-hours and weekends
>
> *(Name 1)* will compile Trouble Reports for the period
>
> *(Name 2)* will compile the Customer Profile for the period

All of us will meet at *(time)* on *(dates)*.

— Special Assignments —

Date:

To: *(Name)*
From: *(Name)*, Director of Customer Service
Subject: Customer response survey

Thanks very much for volunteering to take on this important special assignment.

As we discussed at yesterday morning's meeting, you will be responsible for collecting data from all customer service representatives on a biweekly basis. You will input the data and using the *(Name of computer program)*, tabulate the results. Every other *(day)*, we will meet for a review of trends. You will also prepare quarterly analyses, which will be due on *(date)*, *(date)*, *(date)*, and *(date)*.

———————

Date:

To: *(Name)*
From: *(Name)*, Director of Customer Service
Subject: Customer Service tutor assignment

I am very pleased that you have agreed to serve as a tutor to our Customer Service Representatives. As you know, this is a new program for which we all have high hopes. I am confident that you will devote the same high degree of energy and imagination to this special role as you do in serving your customers from day to day.

Again, thanks for taking on this very important assignment.

— Overtime Assignments —

Date:

To: All Customer Service Representatives
From: *(Name)*, Director of Customer Service
Subject: Saturday phone coverage

As we reviewed during yesterday's meeting, hourly employees of this department are expected to cover the phones on Saturday in rotation, according to the following schedule:

(Name)   *(Dates)*
(Name)   *(Dates)*
(Name)   *(Dates)*
(Name)   *(Dates)*
(Name)   *(Dates)*

Compensation will be at the rate of time-and-a-half.

Any variations in this schedule must be cleared with me at least two days prior to the Saturday in question. Remember, our goal is to provide coverage even when other companies do not.

————

Date:

To: All Customer Service Representatives
From: *(Name)*, Director of Customer Service
Subject: Overtime assignments

In our continuing effort to provide a customer service edge, we will be adding to our support staff. Until we can bring staff up to a sufficient level, however, I am assigning the following overtime schedule. Compensation for all overtime will be at time-and-a-half.

(Name) *(days)* *(hours)*

(Name) *(days)* *(hours)*

(Name) *(days)* *(hours)*

(Name) *(days)* *(hours)*

(Name) *(days)* *(hours)*

(Name) *(days)* *(hours)*

If any of these assignments present irreconcilable conflicts for you, please report to me no later than *(time)* on *(date)*.

Thank you for your effort and cooperation during this transitional period.

— "Work Team" Memos —

Date:

To: All Customer Service Representatives
From: *(Name)*
Subject: Team involvement

As reviewed during our meeting, the best way for us to maintain maximum responsiveness to our customers as well as maximum departmental flexibility is for all of us to become more involved in scheduling and assignment of responsibility.

Therefore, the new schedule board, now prominently located at the front of the office, will serve as the overall guiding—and evolving—plan for the department. Special projects as well as routine work responsibilities will be listed. All assignments and work loads over the upcoming *(period)* can be observed at a glance. All of us can see and become involved in changes. Of course, anyone needing to change the schedule must get their colleagues involved in the discussions.

It will be a great system, allowing everyone to have maximum flexibility. We will, however, all have to compromise and cooperate.

Date:

To: All Customer Service Representatives
From: *(Name)*
Subject: Approval of schedule changes

The new scheduling system has now been in place for *(time period)* and seems to be working well. Be advised that I do not need to be involved with, nor personally approve, every schedule change. If you and your team members agree on changes, and the changes you need still enable us to meet our stated goals, then go ahead and implement your ideas without me. I will continue to focus attention on the overall goals and direction of the department.

There may be occasions, unfortunately, when our goals and objectives on customer coverage and responsiveness must be compromised. While we hope these incidents will be rare, when they do occur, please ask me to join your discussions.

Thanks.

Date:

To: All Customer Service Representatives
From: *(Name)*
Subject: Schedule changes

The new scheduling system has now been in place for *(time period)* and generally seems to be working quite well. I do, however, seem to be drawn too frequently into conflict-resolution meetings. These discussions are consuming a good deal of our total available person-hours.

Remember, when we first established our self-directed work teams the subjects of cooperation and compromise were discussed extensively. Further, we all attended a one-day workshop reviewing techniques for conflict resolution.

I would ask you all to redouble your efforts at compromise and cooperation. The primary reason for team involvement in the schedule in the first place was to allow each person to have a voice, while still meeting our customer service goals and responsibilities. If we cannot handle team conflicts, we will have no choice but to revert back to a central planning and coordination system. Personally, I think a centrally planned system would be a step backward. However, we must maintain our overall standards and goals.

Thanks.

Chapter 19

UPDATES *and* ADVISORIES:
NEW PRODUCTS

HOW TO DO IT

These memos and letters are intended to keep customer support staff and dealers informed of the status of new products. They can also serve to generate or maintain a high level of enthusiasm over the product. Everyone knows that a company must sell its new products to the outside world of potential customers, but it must first sell these products internally. The enthusiasm of customer service staff and the dealer network cannot be taken for granted. Use these memos and letters to:

1. Announce new products

2. Advise staff and dealers of the design, production, and delivery status of new products

3. Advise staff and dealers of any delay in product release or other problems

4. Highlight special benefits of new products

   Provide complete information, giving reasons for any release delays. Always advise personnel and dealers as to what they should communicate to customers.

— New Product Memos —

Date:

To: All Customer Service Representatives
From: *(Name)*, Director of Customer Service
Subject: New Products

As you know, we will be introducing our new line of *(products)* during *(season)*. All should be available by *(date)*. Within the next *(time period)*, you will be receiving spec sheets, sell sheets, and catalog copy on each of these items. I expect you to do your customary thorough job in making yourselves familiar with the special benefits of the new products and communicating your enthusiasm for the new line to our customers.

On *(date)*, I'd like us all to get together in the conference room at *(time)* for a meeting to review the new benefits and to get your ideas on selling points to emphasize. Let's budget *(amount of time)*, since I expect we're going to have a lot of exciting ideas to share.

———————

Date:

To: All Customer Service Representatives
From: *(Name)*, Director of Customer Service
Subject: *(Product)*

Our new *(product)* will be available by *(date)*. As of *(date)* the earlier model *(earlier model)*, will be available only for clearance. You should begin promoting the new *(product)* at that time.

Sell sheets will be distributed by *(date)*.

— Cover Letter: To Accompany New Product Sell/Spec Sheets —

Dear *(Dealer Name)*:

We are proud to enclose the spec sheets for the new *(products)* in our *(name)* series.

The *(products)* will be available to you no later than *(date)*.

Be sure to highlight the following specific new values for your customers:

(list)

You should also be certain to point out the following improvements in design, many of which were made expressly in response to the customer comments *you* reported to us:

(list)

If you have any questions, please don't hesitate to call me at *(telephone number)*. I'm excited about the new line, eager to see it perform sensationally for you, and ready to answer your questions.

Sincerely,

———————

Dear *(Dealer Name)*:

Here are the specification sheets for our new line of *(products)*. We're particularly excited about the following features:

(list)

We hope that you will direct your customers' attention to the extremely tight tolerances we have achieved in these areas:

(list)

We believe these much tighter tolerances will significantly increase durability. Please make the specification sheets freely available to prospective customers. We are confident that you will find them to be valuable sales tools, and you should encourage customers to take the specs and do a little comparison shopping on their own.

Sincerely,

— Product Release Status/Date —

Date:

To: All Customer Service Representatives
From: *(Name)*, Director of Customer Service
Subject: Status of *(Product)* Release

I know we've got a lot of customers out there eager to order *(product)*. The bad news is that while we were hoping to make the product available by *(date)*, well *ahead of* schedule, it will not be available before *(date)*. The good news is that this at worst puts it *on* schedule.

Put customers on a callback list, which of course you should maintain faithfully, including tickler file.

Date:

To: All Customer Service Representatives
From: *(Name)*, Director of Customer Service
Subject: *(Product)* release date

(Product) will be shipped to the regional distribution centers by *(date)*. You can promise your customers delivery beginning *(date)*.

You should point out to your customers that anticipated demand will be very high and that they should place their orders as early as possible.

— Product Release Early —

Date:

To: All Customer Service Representatives
From: *(Name)*, Director of Customer Service
Subject: *(Product)* to be available early!

(Product) had been scheduled for *(date)* release. In large part because of the customer interest all of you reported, production was accelerated, and *(product)* will now be released on *(new date)*.

Now is the time to go back to your callback lists and let your interested customers know about the early availability. You should take back orders as well.

And incidentally, this is ample evidence that our input does make a big difference in marketing and production schedules. Let's keep up the great work!

Date:

To: All Customer Service Representatives
From: *(Name)*, Director of Customer Service
Subject: *(Product)* available *(date)*!

In response to your reports of customer demand, the production schedule for *(product)* has been fast-tracked. The new release date is *(date)*.

Please call your backorder and callback customers now!

— Product Release Delayed —

Date:

To: All Customer Service Representatives
From: *(Name)*, Director of Customer Service
Subject: Release of *(product)* delayed

Given the level of enthusiasm you have reported from our customers, this is not news you want to hear. The release of *(product)* has been pushed back *(number)* months to *(date)*.

Please proceed as follows:

1. Inform any callback or backorder customers to whom you specified a release date. This may result in some cancellations, but I'd rather risk a few of those than lose our credibility on a larger scale.

2. Inform your customers that the delay is due to a shortage of *(materials)* from a major supplier. Make no "excuses" beyond this.

3. Let your customers know that you are sharing this scheduling information in order to be of greatest help to them.

4. Assure your customers that the new date is firm.

Date:

To: All Customer Service Representatives
From: *(Name)*, Director of Customer Service
Subject: *(Product)* release date pushed back to *(date)*

Due to quality assurance issues, the decision has been made to delay the release of *(product)* until *(date)*. As you are well aware, *(product)* is an important product for us, and we want to take the time to make sure we handle it right.

Since the rescheduling is relatively minor, you need not call your backorder customers. However, should any of them call to inquire about the release date, do inform them of the rescheduling. Chalk it up to tweaking and fine-tuning—which is what the extra time does amount to.

— Product Release Rescheduled —

Date:

To: All Customer Service Representatives
From: *(Name)*, Director of Customer Service
Subject: Release of *(product)* rescheduled

The release of *(product)*, planned for *(date)* originally, has been rescheduled to *(date)*.

Since this news is coming early in the design process, I don't expect it will cause us any problems. However, if you have discussed the product with any of your customers and have specified a release date, you may want to advise them of the change in schedule.

Dear *(Dealer Name)*:

As you know, *(product)* was scheduled for release by *(date)*. Unfortunately, supplier shortages have forced us to reschedule that release to *(date)*. The company will make additional promotional materials available, and we will extend our media ad campaigns into the new release period.

Please inform all your interested customers, and be sure to use the new promotional materials.

Sincerely,

— Product Development/Release Problems —

Date:

To: All Customer Service Representatives
From: *(Name)*, Director of Customer Service
Subject: Problems with *(product)* release

Development work on *(product)* has encountered some unanticipated snags and is consuming a good deal more time than anticipated. At this point, we unfortunately have no word on a new release date.

If you have customers to whom you have mentioned the original anticipated release date, I suggest you call them and advise them that that release date was "overly optimistic." Further advise them that you will call back when you have a firm release date. You can inform your customers that we are incorporating additional product improvements and have, therefore, chosen to push back the release date.

———

Dear *(Dealer Name)*:

Recent technical developments in the industry have prompted *(Name of company)* to reevaluate the design of *(new product)*. This reevaluation process will take approximately *(number)* months, making it necessary to reschedule the release date of this product. At this point, we estimate release in *(month and year)*.

In the meantime, *(current product)* remains the most advanced *(device)* available today, and you should continue to promote it as such.

Sincerely,

— Availability Advisories —

Date:

To: All Customer Service Representatives
From: *(Name)*, Director of Customer Service
Subject: Availability of *(product)*

Please advise your callback and backorder customers that due to exceptionally heavy demand, *(product)* will be available no later than *(date)*. Promise availability by this date, but tell them that earlier availability is possible; you have assigned the customer's order top priority; you will do your best to expedite delivery.

Dear *(Dealer Name)*:

(Product) has entered the final stages of production and will be shipped to you no later than *(date)*. This is a firm date, and you can inform your customers accordingly.

Sincerely,

— Memo to Limit Quantities —

Date:

To: All Customer Service Representatives
From: *(Name)*, Director of Customer Service
Subject: Limit quantities on *(product)*

Because of exceptionally heavy demand, we must limit per-customer quantities to *(number)*. Reorders will be taken after *(date)*.

Please stress that this action is our earnest effort to be fair to all of our customers. Emphasize that the reorder date is not far off, and promise to call back just before that date.

— Backorder Policy Memo —

Date:

To: All Customer Service Representatives
From: *(Name)*, Director of Customer Service
Subject: Back Orders

You are encouraged to take back orders on all items not available immediately. But please, when the item becomes available, follow through by E-mailing a tickler memo to Shipping to confirm delivery of the back order. Once that is confirmed, call your back order customer to advise her of the shipment.

— Product Cancelled —

Date:

To: All Customer Service Representatives
From: *(Name)*, Director of Customer Service
Subject: *(Product)* cancelled

As of *(date)*, production of *(product)* is being cancelled and that product should now be sold as a clearance item priced at *($ amount)*. Quantities on hand are limited.

Please make the necessary correction in your current Price Book. Revised Price Books will be issued on *(date)*.

Dear *(Dealer Name)*:

As of *(date)*, production of *(product)* will end—it will be discontinued. *(Name of company)* will stock spare and replacement parts for *(product)* through *(date)*.

As of *(date)*, limited quantities of *(product)* will be available to you as a clearance item.

Sincerely,

Chapter 20

UPDATES *and* ADVISORIES: PRODUCT MODIFICATIONS *and* WARRANTY CHANGES

HOW TO DO IT

It is very important that the customer service staff and the dealer network are informed fully of any modifications in product specifications or changes in warranty terms. It is not sufficient to send a pro forma memo with this information. The memo should underscore and highlight the significance of the modifications or changes and should include a rationale for them. Explanation of reasons and development of the context in which an action is taken give relevance to that action, and makes it meaningful to the frontline personnel who deal with products and customers. Further, when reasons are documented properly, front line personnel are less likely to rely on highly offensive positions such as: "Management has advised . . .," "Our new policy position is . . .," "I must follow the procedure . . .," and so on.

— Modification Memos —

Date:

To: All Customer Service Representatives
From: *(Name)*, Director of Customer Service
Subject: Modification of *(type of feature)* of *(product)*

In response to consumer comment, the *(type of feature)* included in *(product)* now offers a bypass mode. The benefit of this modification is significantly enhanced flexibility and economy of operation in situations where the full range of functions is not necessary.

Please advise your customers who have purchased the earlier model that their unit may be retrofitted with the new feature at a cost of *($ amount)*. The retrofit may be performed at any authorized dealer.

———————

Date:

To: All Customer Service Representatives
From: *(Name)*, Director of Customer Service
Subject: Modification of *(product)* specifications

As of *(date)*, the specifications for *(product)* will be modified as follows:

   (list modifications)

The reason for these modifications is to achieve improved throughput.

You will receive updated spec sheets by *(date)*.

— Cover Letters: To Accompany Modification Spec Sheet —

Dear *(Dealer Name)*:

Enclosed are the new Spec Sheets for the *(Name of company)* *(product)* line. They reflect changes made to upgrade the *(feature[s])* of these products. Your customers will like the changes we've made—*if* you point them out. Here are the highlights to hit:

(list highlight features)

If you have any questions about any of the modifications, please call me at *(phone number)*, and I'll give you the answers you need.

Sincerely,

_____

Dear *(Dealer Name)*:

In response to customer request, we are introducing modifications in the following *(product)* features:

(list modifications)

A complete spec sheet is enclosed.

In discussing these modifications with your customers, please emphasize the gain in performance and the fact that the modifications were made in response to customer feedback.

Sincerely,

— Modification Status/Date —

Date:

To: All Customer Service Representatives
From: *(Name)*, Director of Customer Service
Subject: Modifications of *(product)*

Quality Assurance has completed its recommendations for modifications to be made to *(product)*. The modifications will be incorporated into production models beginning *(date)*. We will prepare Upgrade Notices for your current customers by *(date)*. If you have occasion to speak to any of them before then, let them know that an Upgrade Notice is on the way and that the voluntary upgrade will be performed free of charge at any authorized dealer. Don't go into the details. Just advise them that a full explanation is about to be sent to them.

Dear *(Dealer Name)*:

(Product) models manufactured after *(date)* will incorporate the following slight modifications:

   (list modifications)

We believe these modifications will enhance performance and durability of the *(product)* significantly.

Sincerely,

— Modification Early —

Date:

To: All Customer Service Representatives
From: *(Name)*, Director of Customer Service
Subject: Modification of *(product)* ahead of schedule

As you were advised, *(product)* is being modified to include the following features:

   (list)

These modifications were scheduled to be introduced beginning on *(date)*. The date of introduction has been pulled up to *(date)*. All units manufactured after this date will incorporate the modifications.

Since no upgrade program is available, current models may be sold at a clearance price of *($ amount)*, beginning *(date)* until supplies are exhausted. Please explain the benefits of the modifications to your customers.

———

Dear *(Dealer Name)*:

As you were advised in our letter of *(date)*, the specifications for *(product)* are being upgraded significantly. (Please see enclosed spec sheet.) The modifications were announced for *(date)*.

We feel so strongly about the value of these upgraded performance specs however, that we have accelerated the modification program so that units manufactured after *(date)* will incorporate the new specifications.

A dealer-installable upgrade kit will be made available by *(date)* for owners of the current and earlier models of *(product)*. The price of the kit is yet to be determined.

Sincerely,

— Modification Delayed —

Date:

To: All Customer Service Representatives
From: *(Name)*, Director of Customer Service
Subject: Modification to *(product)* delayed

The modifications that were scheduled to be introduced into our *(product)* line by *(date)* have been pushed back to *(date)*.

Please advise your customers of this change in schedule and offer them the option of receiving shipment now on models with the current specifications or placing back orders for the modified models.

Please refer to my memo of *(date)* for a summary of the nature and benefits of the modifications.

Dear *(Dealer Name)*:

Please be advised that the modifications to *(product)* announced on *(date)* will be delayed. The new shipment date for the modified *(product)* is *(date)*.

(Name of company) apologizes for this delay, especially after we whetted your appetite with the *(date)* announcement. Please convey to your cus-

tomers that we are devoting extra time to testing the design revisions to ensure optimum performance. As you appreciate your customers' patience and understanding, we are grateful for yours.

Be assured that the additional time spent will result in a product even better and more reliable than anticipated.

Sincerely,

— Modification Rescheduled —

Date:

To: All Customer Service Representatives
From: *(Name)*, Director of Customer Service
Subject: *(Product)* modification rescheduled

We had planned originally to introduce minor modifications into the *(product)* line by *(date)*. This work has been assigned a low priority, and the modifications will not be introduced until *(date)*. The proposed changes are of a minor cosmetic nature. Neither I nor Marketing believes it necessary to discuss the modifications with customers at this time.

———

Dear *(Dealer Name)*:

The minor modification announced for *(product)* has been rescheduled from *(date)* to *(date)*. Please continue to sell the current version of *(model)*. The modification will be made available as a low-cost upgrade along with the release of the new version.

Sincerely,

— Announced Modification Changed —

Date:

To: All Customer Service Representatives
From: *(Name)*, Director of Customer Service
Subject: Change in proposed modification to *(product)*

My memo of *(date)* advised you of a modification proposed to *(product)* and asked you to solicit customer response. Your work elicited a vigorous response from our customers, and as a result, the proposed modifications have been changed as follows:

    (list)

It is anticipated that the new specifications will be introduced into production models after *(date)*.

Dear *(Dealer Name)*:

On *(date)* we sent you notification of an anticipated modification to *(product)* designed to *(describe function)*. R&D reevaluated the proposed modification and has made significant improvements, including:

    (list)

A revised specification sheet is enclosed. The date set for the release of the modified *(products)* remains the same as before, *(date)*.

If you have any questions, please call me at *(phone number)*.

Sincerely,

— Modification Cancelled —

Date:

To: All Customer Service Representatives
From: *(Name)*, Director of Customer Service
Subject: Proposed modification to *(product)* cancelled

The modifications proposed for *(product)* (see my memo of *[date]*) have been cancelled. With an entirely new model scheduled to appear by *(date)*, it was felt that modifications to the current product would not be cost-effective.

If you have mentioned the proposed modifications to customers, advise them of the cancellation and the introduction of a new model scheduled for *(date)*. The new model will incorporate the functionality of the proposed modifications, together with many other improvements. You will be given detailed sell sheets on the new models by *(date)*.

――――――

Dear *(Dealer Name)*:

After careful study, our marketing and R & D departments have concluded that the following modifications we had planned to introduce into *(product)* do not represent an improvement significant enough to make them cost-effective:

> *(list proposed modifications)*

In view of this, these modifications will not be made at this time. Please direct any questions to me at *(phone number)*.

Sincerely,

— Warranty Changes: New Terms —

Date:

To: All Customer Service Representatives
From: *(Name)*, Director of Customer Service
Subject: New warranty terms for all product lines

As of *(date)* the warranties provided with all our products will specify a *(time period)* unconditional refund/replacement period and an additional *(time period)* replacement/repair period.

We want to ensure that no competition ever offers a better warranty.

――――――

Dear *(Dealer Name)*:

(Name of company) is pleased to announce the following new terms for warranties on products released to you after *(date)*:

> *(list terms)*

We are confident that these new terms will allow you to offer a warranty that is highly competitive. Please create opportunities to discuss these superior new terms with your customers.

A copy of the full warranty is enclosed.

Sincerely,

— Warranty Changes: Coverage Expanded —

Date:

To: All Customer Service Representatives
From: *(Name)*, Director of Customer Service
Subject: Expanded warranty coverage for *(product)*

Good news! Effective as of the date of this memo, warranty coverage for *(product)* is extended to include *all* impact damage, whether incurred during shipping or at any time during the warranty period.

Letters informing customers of this change are being prepared and will be mailed by *(date)*.

———————

Dear *(Dealer Name)*:

Our company has decided to expand warranty coverage on all new *(product)* warranties as well as those currently in force. Here are the details of the expanded coverage:

(list)

We urge you to ensure that your new customers are fully aware of the benefits of our expanded warranty coverage. We also suggest that you take advantage of an opportunity to create goodwill among your current customers by sending each of them a letter announcing the coverage.

This is a significant sales opportunity.

Sincerely,

— Warranty Changes: Coverage Reduced —

Date:

To: All Customer Service Representatives
From: *(Name)*, Director of Customer Service
Subject: Reductions in warranty coverage on *(product)*

As of *(date)*, warranty coverage on *(product)* will no longer include the following:

> *(list)*

These items are now considered consumable. Current warranties will, of course, remain in force as per their original terms.

Please note that even with the reduced coverage, our warranties remain among the best in the industry and are still to be promoted as a positive selling point.

———————

Dear *(Dealer Name)*:

Please be advised that, beginning with *(products)* made available to you after *(date)*, our standard warranty will no longer cover the following:

> *(list)*

These items will be covered by the Extended Warranty, which is available for *($ amount)*.

As you know, even with the reduced coverage, our warranties remain among the most generous in the industry and continue to be a powerful selling point.

Sincerely,

— Warranty Changes: Availability/Cost of Extensions —

Date:

To: All Customer Service Representatives
From: *(Name)*, Director of Customer Service
Subject: New prices for Extended Warranties

As of *(date)*, the cost of extended warranties will be increased as follows:

(product)	*(extended warranty term)*	*(cost)*
(product)	*(extended warranty term)*	*(cost)*
(product)	*(extended warranty term)*	*(cost)*
(product)	*(extended warranty term)*	*(cost)*
(product)	*(extended warranty term)*	*(cost)*

This is a good opportunity to sell extended warranties. Urge your customers to order extended coverage now, before the price increases.

———————

Dear *(Dealer Name)*:

Please be advised that, as of *(date)*, the retail cost of the Extended Warranty for *(product)* will increase to *($ amount)*.

The increase is necessary to meet our own rising costs for providing the fullest possible service. Even at the new price, we are confident that your customers will be impressed by the benefits of the Extended Warranty, and the new price ensures that *(Name of company)* will be able to continue to provide the same efficient high level of service your customers have come to expect.

Sincerely,

Chapter 21

UPDATES *and* ADVISORIES: SHIPPING, BILLING, *and* DELIVERY CHANGES

HOW TO DO IT

These memos and dealer communications must include the relevant information in succinct form:

1. What will happen

2. When it will happen

3. Why it will happen

4. What action to take because it is happening

— Shipping Procedure Change —

Date:

To: All Customer Service Representatives
From: *(Name)*, Director of Customer Service
Subject: Shipping procedure change

Beginning on *(date)*, all customer service representatives will be authorized to enter shipping orders directly rather than transmitting them to the Shipping Department. The only occasions on which customer service representatives will have to go through the shipping clerk is if the items ordered for shipment are listed as "Currently Unavailable."

———————

Date:

To: All Customer Service Representatives
From: *(Name)*, Director of Customer Service
Subject: New Shipping Procedures

Beginning *(date)*, Management Information Systems is putting into operation new software that will reduce order turnaround time from *(number)* days to *(number)* days. Please estimate delivery times based on this number and advise your customers accordingly. You may take the opportunity to point out to your customers that our quicker delivery allows them to hold smaller inventory levels.

— Billing Procedure Change —

Date:

To: All Customer Service Representatives
From: *(Name)*, Director of Customer Service
Subject: Billing Procedure Change

Beginning on *(date)*, we will be using the new billing software, which will allow us to track marketing and distribution data more accurately. If you are not yet up to speed on the new system, please read the manual distributed to you last week. *(Name)*, our software consultant, will be available from *(time)* to *(time)* on *(days)* to answer any of your questions concerning the new system.

———————

Date:

To: All Customer Service Representatives
From: *(Name)*, Director of Customer Service
Subject: Billing to customer number

Beginning *(date)*, all customers will be assigned a customer number when they place orders. All billing will be linked to this number. Please advise your customers that use of their customer number will significantly reduce order processing time.

— Carrier Change —

Date:

To: All Customer Service Representatives
From: *(Name)*, Director of Customer Service
Subject: Change in carrier for standard delivery

Beginning on *(date)*, all our standard ground shipments will be handled by *(carrier 1)*. As before, expedited air shipments will be handled by *(carrier 2)*.

We have changed carriers to improve efficiency and reliability. We are confident your customers will be happy with the change.

Date:

To: All Customer Service Representatives
From: *(Name)*, Director of Customer Service
Subject: *(Name of carrier)* to become our standard carrier

I am pleased to inform you that, beginning on *(date)*, *(Name of carrier)* will be our standard contract carrier. *(Name of carrier)* is a fine company with a reputation for a high level of service. We are looking forward to a profitable relationship that will greatly benefit our customers.

Date:

To: All Customer Service Representatives
From: *(Name)*, Director of Customer Service
Subject: Carriers

We use *(carrier A)*. However, customers may request any other carrier. If another carrier is selected, the customer must absorb shipping charges over *(carrier A)* rate.

Chapter 22

UPDATES *and* ADVISORIES: HANDLING SPECIAL PROBLEMS

HOW TO DO IT

These are vital bulletins concerning problem reports and corrections to errors. Problem reports are especially important to customer service personnel. Such memos should include:

1. The nature of the problem.

2. What is being done about it.

3. When a fix is expected.

4. What to advise customers, including temporary solutions.

    Error correction should include:

1. Announcement of the error.

2. The correction.

3. What is being done to inform customers and others.

4. What to advise customers.

In these straightforward informational memos, it is usually not necessary to apologize for errors, make excuses, or to explain why they happened.

— Reports of Product Problem —

To: All Customer Service Representatives
From: *(Name)*, Director of Customer Service
Subject: *(Part)* in *(product)* malfunctions under *(set of conditions)*

Between *(date)* and *(date)*, we have received *(number)* customer reports of the *(part)* in our *(product)* malfunctioning under the following conditions:

    (list)

The Engineering Department has been informed of these reports and is attempting to recreate the failures in the lab. In the meantime, please record carefully any customer reports of such failures, noting in particular the following:

    (list)

We will send a monthly report to the Engineering Department, showing the impact of this problem on customer satisfaction.

Tell your customer that we are aware of the problem and are working on a fix. For now, advise the customer to avoid using *(product)* under the conditions noted above. Be certain to get the customer's name and number. We are planning to keep customers advised of our progress on this issue.

———————

Date:

To: All Customer Service Representatives
From: *(Name)*, Director of Customer Service
Subject: Report of paper jamming with Model 15 copier

Since *(date)*, many of you have reported a significant number of customer complaints about paper jamming with the Model 15 copier. These reports have been turned over to Engineering for action. Please advise your customers that we are aware of the problem and are working on a free upgrade modification to correct it. In the meantime, advise your customers to load no more than 100 sheets of paper in the tray at a time. Be certain to identify all customers calling on this issue and load the *(flag)* against their name. We will be supplying progress reports to these customers.

— **Error in *Owner's Manual*** —

To: All Customer Service Representatives
From: *(Name)*, Director of Customer Service
Subject: Error in *(Product) Owner's Manual*

Please note that the *(Product) Owner's Manual* contains an error on page *(number)*. The text reads:

> *(quote)*

It SHOULD read:

> *(corrected quote)*

Notice of the error, together with the correction, is being sent to all customers. In the meantime, please advise any customers who call concerning *(product)* of the error. Read and fax them the correction. Tell them that a hard copy of the corrected text is being mailed to them.

———————

Date:

To: All Customer Service Representatives
From: *(Name)*, Director of Customer Service
Subject: Error in *Owner's Manual* for *(product)*

Page *(number)* of the *Owner's Manual* for *(product)* provides inaccurate instructions for operating *(feature)*. The correct way to activate *(feature)* is:

> *(list steps)*

When customers call complaining of the following problems—

> *(list problems)*

please point out the error in the manual and go over the correct procedure with them. Fax a copy of the corrected procedure to them, and follow up with hard copy.

All customers are receiving a copy of the corrected procedure.

— Error in Advertising —

To: All Customer Service Representatives
From: *(Name)*, Director of Customer Service
Subject: Error in advertising for *(product)*

Our ad for *(product)*, which appeared in *(magazine, etc.)* on *(date)*, listed inadvertently the specifications for *(another product)*.

Please be prepared to advise customers who inquire about *(product)* or *(another product)* accordingly. The correct specifications are attached. Send a copy by fax or mail to any customer who inquires.

Dear *(Dealer Name)*:

An advertisement that appeared in *(list magazines, newspapers, etc.)* on *(date[s])* described the *(product)* incorrectly as fully automatic. As you are well aware, *(product)* has automatic and manual modes.

Please take extra care to ensure that your customers and potential customers are well aware of this important feature.

(Name of company) greatly regrets the error.

Sincerely,

— Error in Announced Specifications —

To: All Customer Service Representatives
From: *(Name)*, Director of Customer Service
Subject: Error in announced specifications for *(product)*

Our *(season)* catalog misprints one of the specifications for *(product)*. The catalog shows *(number)* r.p.m. The *correct* specification is *(number)* r.p.m.

Please advise any customers interested in this product, or a related product of the error. The corrected version is attached. Send any interested customers a copy of the corrected version.

Dear *(Dealer Name)*:

The specified duty cycle for *(product)* listed in the sell sheets distributed to you on *(date)* is incorrect. The *correct* duty cycle for *(product)* is as follows:

> *(list)*

Corrected sell sheets are enclosed. Please take a moment—now—to replace the incorrect documents.

We regret and apologize for the error, and we appreciate your understanding.

Sincerely,

Chapter
23

UPDATES *and* ADVISORIES: NOTIFICATION *of* RECALL

HOW TO DO IT

In any recall situation, especially recalls related to safety issues, it is imperative to recognize your responsibilities as noted in Chapter 11.

It is, of course, vitally important to inform all customer support personnel and the dealer network of any recalls. Such notifications are not intended to substitute for letters written to customers. Where possible (or mandated), communication with the customer service staff and dealers should be coordinated with communications to the customer. *Do not* leave customer service staff or dealers to learn about the recall from the customer! The recall notification should:

1. Announce the recall.

2. Explain why the product is being recalled.

3. Explain precisely which product is being recalled. As relevant, provide manufacturing dates, lot numbers, and so on.

4. Explain the procedures that have been instituted.

5. Explain how customer service personnel and dealers should advise customers. If the recall is safety related, it is best to stop all product use until repair or retrofit is completed.

— Departmental Safety-Related Recall Memo —

To: All Customer Service Representatives
From: *(Name)*, Director of Customer Service
Subject: Recall of *(product)*

Following reports of a failure-prone *(part)* in *(product)*, *(Name of company)* has initiated a safety-related recall.

The CPSC was duly notified on *(date)*, and letters were mailed to customers beginning on *(date)*. The mailing will be completed by *(date)*. Please be prepared to answer customers' questions relating to the recall, which has been classified as a Class C hazard by the CPSC. A risk of injury, while not likely, is possible.

Reason for recall: Failure of *(part)* is possible after prolonged stop-and-go use.

Safety issues: Failure of *(part)* could cause a structural failure that could result in personal injury.

Action customer should take: Take the unit to any authorized dealer for replacement of *(part)* with a reinforced *(part)*. There is no charge for this service. *Advise customer to stop using unit until the replacement has been made.*

Action we will take: Authorized dealers will replace *(part)* with a reinforced *(part)* at no charge.

Time required for replacement: Most dealers should be able to perform the replacement on a same-day basis, but advise customer to call the dealer in advance.

Be prepared to supply customer with name(s) of authorized dealers in his/her area.

— Safety-Related Dealer Recall Advisories —

Dear *(Name)*:

On *(date)*, due to customer reports of failure of *(part)* in *(product)*, *(Name of company)* is initiating a recall program. The problem was duly reported to the CPSC on *(date)* and has been classified as a Class C hazard.

We are shipping on a rush basis reinforced replacement *(parts)* to all dealers in our network. You will receive these parts no later than *(date)*.

Customers are being instructed to return the unit to the nearest authorized dealer for replacement of *(part)*. Please see customer recall letter enclosed.

Sudden failure of *(part)* could cause structural failure of the unit and result in personal injury. Please advise any customers who call you directly about the product that:

1. The recall has been initiated.

2. The recall is important for their personal safety and the operation of the unit.

3. The replacement of the part will be made at no charge.

4. The unit MUST NOT BE USED until the replacement is made.

Please perform the replacement in accordance with our Standing Agreement on Recall Issues. We ask that you do all in your power to expedite service to make the replacement a same-day operation.

Sincerely,

— Departmental Quality-Related Recall Memo —

To: All Customer Service Representatives
From: *(Name)*, Director of Customer Service
Subject: Recall of *(product)* for quality-control problems

From *(date)* to *(date)*, we received *(number)* complaints concerning the failure of *(part)* on *(product)*. In consultation with Quality Control, we have determined that this is an unacceptably high failure rate and warrants recall of units manufactured between *(date)* and *(date)* for replacement of *(part)*. We feel strongly that the *(product)* should supply better service.

Letters were sent out to customers beginning on *(date)*. All letters will have been mailed by *(date)*.

Customers are instructed to bring their *(product)* to an authorized dealer after *(date)* and before *(date)* for free replacement of *(part)*. The reason for the recall is given as: "*(part)* is subject to possible premature failure."

There is no safety hazard to the customer if the product is used as is.

— Quality-Related Dealer Recall Advisories —

Dear *(Name)*:

Between *(date)* and *(date)*, the Customer Service Department received *(number)* complaints concerning the failure of *(part)* in *(product)*. *(Name of company)* has determined that this represents an unacceptable failure rate and has, therefore, decided to recall units manufactured between *(date)* and *(date)*. Please understand, however, that there is no safety-related danger if the product is used as is.

Customers are being sent letters (mailing will start on *[date]* and will be complete by *[date]*) advising them to bring the *(product)* to an authorized dealer after *(date)*.

All dealers will be rushed sufficient quantities of replacement *(parts)*. Dealers are instructed to perform the replacement in accordance with our Standing Agreement on Recall Issues. We further ask, that you make every effort to perform the replacement on a same-day basis as a goodwill gesture to your customers.

Please note for yourselves and your nonrecall customers that the recall applies only to units manufactured between *(date)* and *(date)*. The problem with *(part)* has been reported in no other units.

A copy of the customer advisory letter is enclosed.

Sincerely,

Chapter 24

Reporting Recurring Problem

How to Do It

One of the most valuable functions of a Customer Service Department is to collate, evaluate, and report problems and other issues raised by customers. The intradepartmental memos in this chapter motivate personnel to report problems regularly and advise them as to reporting procedures. Such memos may be treated simply as straightforward statements of procedure, but it is even more useful to think of them as opportunities to motivate staff to take an active role in quality control and continuous improvement of products and services. It is important that the memo demonstrates that the problem reports are taken seriously and acted upon. Problem reporting should be portrayed as one of the most creative and constructive aspects of the customer service professional's role.

Far too often, customer service is seen as the complaint department. Dealing with the company's problems creates stress. Too often, rewards are few and opportunity for positive recognition infrequent. Burnout rate is high. Allowing the customer service representative to handle special projects related to problem study and analysis is a positive step. Use this opportunity to help representatives bond to the team and to the company. Allow them to participate fully and make vital contributions to the success of the business.

— Problem Reports: Intradepartmental Memos —

To: All Customer Service Representatives
From: *(Name)*, Director of Customer Service
Subject: Problems with *(product)*

Since *(date)*, many of you have been reporting frequent customer complaints about difficulty operating the *(feature)* of *(product)*.

I have shared these reports with Design, which is considering modifications for future models of *(product)*. In the meantime, with the current product, you should advise customers who call to report this problem that they should try operating the *(feature)* in the following sequence:

1. *(step 1)*

2. *(step 2)*

3. *(step 3)*

This should avoid any engagement difficulty.

———

To: All Customer Service Representatives
From: *(Name)*, Director of Customer Service
Subject: Problems with *(product)*

If you have been hearing customers complain about *(problem)*, you're not alone. Since *(date)*, we've logged *(number)* of complaints about this—enough to warrant an alert to Design.

If you receive a call concerning this problem, advise the customer that:

1. It is a known problem.

2. We are working hard on a solution. Assure the customer that he will be notified of a fix just as soon as one becomes available. Flag the account so that we can provide the customer with a status report.

3. In the meantime, a replacement for *(part)* if it fails will be available at no charge.

— Explaining Importance of Reporting Problems —

To: All Customer Service Representatives
From: *(Name)*, Director of Customer Service
Subject: *Please* report problems

I know how difficult it is juggling a dozen phone calls from a dozen anxious customers. The temptation is to put off all "paperwork," including reports of customer-reported problems. *I* understand, but I also ask that *you* understand how vitally important the customer problem reports are.

1. They help us do our jobs better by keeping us all informed.

2. They help other departments improve our products.

3. They help us to deal with customers' product issues more effectively.

Please make the extra effort to keep problem reports up to date, and file them in a timely manner.

To: All Customer Service Representatives
From: *(Name)*, Director of Customer Service
Subject: Problems with *(product)*

You are the vital first link in product redesign and improvement. Please report all customer complaints and comments in detail bearing on durability, performance, and cosmetic appeal. *Tell* your customers that you are making a full report of their complaint or comments. *Thank* them for taking the time to comment, or even to complain. We value their input.

— Procedure for Reporting Problems: How To —

To: All Customer Service Representatives
From: *(Name)*, Director of Customer Service
Subject: Reporting Problems

As a Customer Service Representative, you *live* with problems. Everybody tells you their problems.

Why keep all these problems to yourself?

Share them with us!

Not only will it make you feel better, it's an important part of your job.

Begin by keeping your Customer Problem Log up to date. Every other week, prepare a Customer Problem Summary Report. This should be sent to me no later than *(day)* of the following week.

If you run across any extraordinary problem or a repeated problem, please make a Problem Report immediately. You may send it to me through E-mail.

— Reporting Problems: To Whom? —

To: All Customer Service Representatives
From: *(Name)*, Director of Customer Service
Subject: Reporting problems: Who wants to hear?

Generally, we hear customers report problems in five areas:

1. Shipping.

2. Billing.

3. Product quality.

4. Premature product failure.

5. Product design/performance deficiency.

Report any significant problems in these areas directly to the appropriate department:

1. Shipping problems to Fulfillment.

2. Billing problems to Billing.

3. Product quality to Quality Assurance.

4. Premature product failure to Quality Assurance and Production.

5. Product design/performance deficiency to Design.

— Reporting Problems: Accountability —

Date:

To: All Customer Service Representatives
From: *(Name)*
Subject: Problems

This memo is to confirm agreements reached during our meeting on *(date)*. During the general discussion period, we concluded that the department had been investing considerable resources into resolving the following issues:

   (list of key issues)

We need to generate current costs the company is incurring while these issues remain unresolved, so that we can make appropriate recommendations to management.

Adjust your time sheets accordingly. Hours invested in resolving these particular issues should be noted. Of course, log hours invested in resolving other issues too. We will track our time investment into these issues over the next month or so and evaluate what these problems are truly costing the company. These studies will help us determine how much should be invested in solving the problems and how urgent each problem is.

———

Date:

To: All Customer Service Representatives
From: *(Name)*
Subject: Value added

On your ongoing time reports be sure to track time invested in positive public relations, constructive advertising, education of the customer, responding to sales-related questions, and *(other issues)*.

Your weekly time sheets form the database supporting our customer service reports to management. These reports, in addition to helping us determine departmental contributions, enable us to identify key customer concerns.

Knowing these concerns enables us to better target advertising, sales effort, direct mail campaigns and training efforts.

Thanks.

— Reporting New Solutions —

Date:

To: All Customer Service Representatives
From: *(Name)*
Subject: Continuous education

This is a reminder.

Don't forget about our *Problem Solution Manual,* an ongoing departmental project.

Every time you research a unique solution to a particular problem, be certain to write the solution up, assign it the proper issue identification code, and give a copy of your solution to each rep in the department.

We must continue this effort as it is the best way to build department-wide intelligence, increase our response time in getting answers to customers and keep us two steps ahead of the competition.

One last point. When using the *Problem Solution Manual,* you don't need to specifically mention it to customers. After all, we would not really want a customer to accidentally mention our system to a key competitor. Let the competition figure out how to do it on their own.

Thanks.

— Keep Alert —

To: All Customer Service Representatives
From: *(Name)*
Subject: Keeping alert

The *(name)* team did a super job in identifying and quantifying the *(type)* problem for us. Judy was first to notice that the volume of calls concerning *(problem)* seemed to be growing.

She perceived the trend and quickly alerted her total team to be especially observant. Everyone on the *(name)* team made special note of what was happening, and within three days we noticed a definite trend and immediately alerted engineering and production.

The *(problem)* was traced back into production, and quality control corrections were made. All customers impacted by the problem have been contacted, and corrective customer action was taken.

Overall, the quick identification and tracking of the *(problem)* enabled us to get a solution out in the field at a low cost in dollars as well as customer satisfaction. Keep alert. This is the kind of stuff that builds company-wide appreciation for what we do in customer service.

Chapter 25

DEPARTMENTAL EVALUATION

HOW TO DO IT

The memos in this chapter are not intended to serve as full-scale employee evaluations, but as more routine expressions of feedback concerning individual and collective employee performance. A fuller discussion of written communication with employees is found in *The New Handbook of Business Letters* by Jack Griffin (Prentice Hall, 1993). However, these memos are included here to underscore the importance of putting *all* evaluations in writing, even casual, day-to-day comments. Memories are short and unreliable, and in an era jammed with litigation and loaded with regulation, a reliable paper trail is essential. Beyond this, concise written evaluations are more powerful and effective than a word or two dropped into office conversation. This goes for praise as well as evaluations that suggest a need for improvement.

Improvement Needed

As a general rule, evaluation of performance should evaluate performance, *not* personality. In customer service of course, it is always tempting to stray into the area of personality, since working with customers naturally raises such issues. However, focus on specific performance issues wherever possible. If for example, customers have complained about calling

Customer Service only to be kept on hold for an excessive amount of time, don't write an evaluation suggesting that staff members are lazy or slow, but address the issue of reducing hold time. Issue guidelines for accomplishing this *and* solicit suggestions from the staff. The message should not be *You* need improvement, but *We* need improvement. Be careful when handling these productivity issues. For example, our obvious solution when "time on hold" exceeds the standard is to shorten the average length of the call. However, pushing the staff to shorten call length could very well cause even greater customer dissatisfaction.

Thanks for a Job Well Done

Behavioral psychologists long ago and repeatedly demonstrated that positive reinforcement is a more effective means of motivation than negative reinforcement. This does not mean you should avoid pointing out problems and areas that require improvement, but it does suggest that the customer service manager should also be generous with memos acknowledging special achievements, extra efforts, and jobs well done. The secret to effective praise is to be as specific as possible and relate the praise to specific behavior, not general "goodness." "You handled the adjustments on the Smith account masterfully, and that resulted in one very satisfied customer" is far better than "Thanks for another great job."

Soliciting Employee Evaluation and Suggestions

Invite—don't just ask for—employee evaluation and suggestions. Make it clear that these are important documents that are taken seriously and are acted upon. Old-style managers were content with an obedient army of functionaries. State-of-the-art managers work to forge a team, in which all members contribute actively. This means ensuring channels of communication that flow both ways: from manager to staff, and from staff to management. Make it clear to staff members that they are problem *solvers,* not mere problem handlers, and that it is vitally important for them to share information on problem solving.

— Memos: Improvement Needed —

To: All Customer Service Representatives
From: *(Name)*, Director of Customer Service
Subject: Need to decrease telephone customer hold time

Looking over our recent performance statistics, it is clear that we are doing an excellent job in achieving high levels of customer satisfaction. However, our longest-calls-on-hold number is consistently out of tolerance. Part of the problem, of course, is that there are just too few of us. Another part of the problem is the amount of time we devote to each customer call. Well, the time we spend with our customers is one reason they are so pleased with our service.

Put these two halves of the problem together, and you've got one tough challenge. We do need to cut down our hold time, but we need to do it without cutting short our conversations with other customers.

I'd like to meet with all of you at *(time)* on *(date)* in my office to brainstorm this area for improvement.

———————

To: *(Name of Customer Service Representative)*
From: *(Name)*, Director of Customer Service
Subject: Improving follow-up

I am very well aware of the volume of customer calls you handle, and I am pleased by the speed and efficiency with which you attend to our customers' issues. Yet this speed and efficiency comes at a cost in follow-up. I would be happy to see you sacrifice some volume in new calls in order to call again and follow up with customers to ensure that they are satisfied. It is this follow-up that adds a dimension of depth to our service.

Don't you agree that it's worth a try? Think about what it will take, and let's brainstorm this in our next staff meeting.

— Memos: Thanks for a Job Well Done —

To: All Customer Service Representatives
From: *(Name)*, Director of Customer Service
Subject: Rise in accessories sales

Sales of accessories to our *(product)* line have risen significantly this last quarter. Why? Because all of you have been counseling your customers effectively on the value of such items as *(list)*. In taking the extra time to promote these items, you are not only boosting our bottom line, but you are protecting and enhancing the value of our customers' original investment in our product.

Well done all around.

To: *(Name of Customer Service Representative)*
From: *(Name)*, Director of Customer Service
Subject: Improvement in customer follow-up

I want to thank you for taking to heart my suggestion about devoting more telephone time to following up on individual customer issues.

How do I know you've been acting on my remarks?

(Name), in Sales, told me that a customer couldn't say enough good things about our level of service, and she mentioned you in particular: that you had actually called back to make sure that all of her concerns had been addressed.

You didn't just make a customer happy, you forged a *relationship.*

Thanks for the great work.

— Memos: Soliciting Evaluation by Employees —

To: All Customer Service Representatives
From: *(Name)*, Director of Customer Service
Subject: Evaluation of *(name of project)*

(Name of project) is in its ____nth *(week, month, year, etc.)*. It's time that we assessed its utility and effectiveness, and the best way to do this is to

go to those who administer operation of the project each and every day. That's *you*.

I ask that you assess the utility and effectiveness of *(name of project)* briefly in the following areas:

> *(list)*

and using the following criteria:

> *(list)*

This is an opportunity for all of us to improve a program that affects our customers and our own jobs significantly.

— Memos: Soliciting Employee Suggestions —

To: All Customer Service Representatives
From: *(Name)*, Director of Customer Service
Subject: Suggestions, anyone?

This is our company and our department. Just as we listen to our customers and act on what they tell us, we also must listen to each other. We have very valuable information to share with each other.

The trouble is that the volume of feedback has been falling off lately. Now, maybe that means everything is perfect. If that's true, then silence is golden. However, if you feel as I do, that we can always do even better, please don't keep it to yourself. Let's generate some ideas for improvement.

Suggestions can be transmitted to me through E-mail. If you like, share them with others on the network. If you prefer to submit a suggestion on paper anonymously, please do so. The old suggestion box is still next to the watercooler. If you would like to talk with me privately, just give me a buzz.

The silence is eerie. Please speak up.

Chapter
26

THE INTRADEPARTMENTAL NEWSLETTER

HOW TO DO IT

Perhaps the real question is not *how* to do it, but *why* do it. Why an intradepartmental newsletter?

Just as the effective customer service representative possesses or develops a service personality—an eagerness to help, knowledge of the relevant products and services, and abundant imagination (which allows him to step into the caller's shoes)—so the effective customer service department must possess or develop a collective service personality. Call it team spirit. Call it a clear sense of mission. Above all, call it a sense of purpose beyond simply taking complaints: a mission to train, to educate, and to understand and resolve problems.

One way to develop, maintain, and reinforce this collective service personality is through sharing ideas and attitudes. This can be done through regular periodic meetings and conferences of course, but another very special way of sharing is through a newsletter.

Purposes of the Newsletter

The intradepartmental newsletter serves six major purposes:

1. It broadcasts information, often more effectively than E-mail or photocopied sheets of paper. (By the way, consider "publishing" your newsletter via E-mail. Who says it's got to be on a sheet of paper?)

234

2. It is a vehicle for sharing new ideas.

3. It is a vehicle for sharing feelings, positive and negative.

4. It is a vehicle for airing problems.

5. It is a vehicle for sharing excellence.

6. Finally, it is a means for forging a departmental identity and personality.

How is task number 5 accomplished?

Mainly through discussion of situations that illustrate the effective service personality. Also, through tips and reminders, the director of customer service (and others) reinforce desired behaviors and problem-solving responses.

Certainly, the intradepartmental newsletter need not be elaborate. If you have access to a laser printer and multiple font software, you can introduce various magazine- or newspaper-like typographical touches. Any degree of "slickness" beyond this might well be perceived as a waste of resources—not so much by your supervisors as by those you supervise.

— *At Your Service:* Two Sample Issues —

1
OUR NEW 300-DPI COLOR DYE SUBLIMATION PRINTER SHIPS!
By *Ralph Thaler*

After two years of development, the new Chromatic Color Dye Sublimation Printer is shipping at last. Sell sheets have been distributed, together with briefing sheets from Marketing and from Product Testing.

The new unit has everything our customers have been asking for:

Four-color, 32 MB full-frame buffer

Color adjustment through front-panel controls

Contrast and sharpness adjustments

Photographic-quality printing

Expect a small flood of installation questions, since there are so many variables. The printer team is ready for the influx, and overload will be handled by the peripherals team.

2

SHIRLEY JOHNSON NAMED SERVICE REP OF THE QUARTER
By *Harmon Jeffrey*

Shirley Johnson's specialty is high-volume graphic printers, and she has been troubleshooting these for customers since 19__. She is known for her command of the technology and for her friendly, calming telephone presence.

"No. You didn't break it. Just reset it, and it will start working again. Trust me." That's the way Shirley builds personalized relationships.

The Sales Department loves her almost as much as customers do. "Shirley generates leads nonstop," says Henry Sharp, director of sales. "Customers rely on her for sound advice on product purchases and upgrades."

Asked how she approaches customer service, Shirley responded: "A customer service rep needs two things above all: knowledge of the product, and imagination. Imagination lets you put yourself in the customer's shoes, feel what he's feeling. Once you do that, it's easy to give a high level of service."

Shirley makes her home in Springfield, with husband, Greg, a sales representative for Maniken Industries, and their two sons, Biff (age ten) and Scooter (age four). She devotes her free time to senior citizen volunteer work at the Springfield Senior Center, and to gardening. Her day lilies won first prize in last year's National Show.

And why did Shirley make Service Rep of the Quarter? Consider these specific situations:

(list)

Congratulations, Shirley!

TIP OF THE MONTH
from *Art Vandalay*

Never put the customer on hold without first getting permission. For example: "Could you hold for a moment?" means you have about ten seconds or less. "It will take me about three minutes to look that up" means you have about two minutes, and so on.

FROM THE DIRECTOR
Super Idea

Special thanks to *Carl,* who suggested that tracking hours invested in "positive P/R" would be a significant benefit for demonstrating the customer service contribution. We will start tracking P/R time and list it in our monthly report as a contribution to advertising.

—Fran Wilson

3

DYE SUBLIMATION ISSUES
By *Art Vandalay*

Those of you fielding calls from customers concerning the 300 dpi Color Dye Sublimation Printer already know it's a big hit. However, it does present some frustrating problems for certain customers. *At Your Service* urges you to read bulletins 1234 and 1235, which cover the most common issues, especially those concerning installation with an SCSI-2 interface.

The key here is patience, talking customers through the unfamiliar territory of super high-performance computer printing. However, everyone should also be aware that the direct mail campaign is having an effect. The educational call load is diminishing.

AVOIDABLE MISTAKES
by *Herbert Kistler*

Here are two mistakes and how to avoid them.

1. *The unexpected bill.* If a customer asks you how much a service or product costs, make sure you know the exact amount. If you do not have the correct figure, then quote a not-to-exceed estimate. Under no circumstances should you put the company in the position of billing for costs beyond our quote. When this occurs, customer satisfaction evaporates.

2. When you take an order, the best way to prevent errors is simply to repeat the information: "That's three number 54s in blue, green, and red. Correct?" Then follow up with a confirmation by fax or mail.

TIP OF THE MONTH
from *Fran Wilson*

One of the major challenges we face is that we can't *see* our customer. Talking on the phone, it is, of course, impossible to pick up on those elements of body language and facial expression that convey understanding and satisfaction. It is up to us to make up for this deficiency. Always follow up with a phrase such as, "Have I answered your question?" Never assume. Also, use good voice modulation. High and low tones help to clarify meaning. Back-up complex things with fax.

FROM THE DIRECTOR
When a *Product Fails*

When a product fails, we've got one solid resource left: our accountability. When a customer tells you that he is having a problem with a product, respond to the *problem,* not the customer.

"What exactly is wrong with the product?" Or: "Please tell me just how our product let you down."

This not only wins a measure of approval for taking responsibility, it serves as an education—for us and for our company. If you succeed in getting the customer to tell you how we've disappointed her, we have taken a big step toward avoiding doing the same to others in the future.

But don't leave it here. Offer direct help while simultaneously empowering our customer.

"What can I do to resolve this problem to your complete satisfaction?"

Maybe the customer will even come up with a solution to the problem that *you* have offered to share with *him*.

—Fran Wilson

Part Four

INTERDEPARTMENTAL COMMUNICATIONS

Chapter 27

COMMUNICATING *with* *the* SHIPPING DEPARTMENT

HOW TO DO IT

Are you running a customer service department or are you running the customer satisfaction philosophy for the company? More progressive companies—and customer service directors—recognize that customer service is far more than order entry, complaint handling or technical support. Customer service is becoming a clearing house tracking all customer-related issues. Progressive operations recognize service for what it really is: a vital resource capable of fully supporting the organization's continuous improvement efforts. The financial controller advises all departments on the financial health of their respective budgets as well as the financial health of the corporation. In progressive operations, customer service is advising all departments on their customer service health as well as tracking the corporate ability to produce customer satisfaction. For example, perhaps a warehouse stocking problem has occurred. Service can and should identify and track the cost of this recurring shipping problem. This can be done by tracking the total number of hours dedicated to this particular problem—a time study.

How customer service can help

Do not assume those outside your department are fully aware of what your operation does and the value of the contribution you offer. Customer service is still emerging as a function. Many still perceive it is a complaint department, and a simple one at that.

Start from where you are. Track where customer service time is being invested. Don't track just call volume or call length. Run a balance sheet. Track things like total time invested with issue A or issue B. Your goal is to report on how an important resource is utilized and what kind of payback the organization is receiving. Return on investment is an important business concept, and you will gain more corporate attention if you start communicating what customer service learns in a language the business understands. For example, perhaps engineering is aware of a problem with operation of a widget. Assume, however, that while engineering is aware of the problem, it does not have sufficient resources to fix the problem. Say $20,000 is required. However, if customer service reports to engineering—and management—that living with the problem in the field is costing $10,000 every month in customer service time, then the problem gets a completely different perspective. Not fixing the problem is far more costly than fixing it. Helping the organization to uncover these significant issues is what contemporary customer service is all about.

Communicating Customer concerns and comments

In developing reports and memos, always stress cooperation and coordination. Be a member of the corporate team. Customer service should not be complaining about problems and mistakes; customer service, as is true with all functions of the company, should be making a contribution to the future solution. It should be helping the total organization improve quality products and services.

Do not randomly report every problem or mistake. Be analytical, plot things. Get your customer service representatives involved in the mission. They will become more involved with the total job function and gain more satisfaction. Look for trends. Is the problem getting better or worse? Consider costs, the most important business consideration. How much does living with the problem cost? Does the fix cost more than living with the problem? And, of course, be absolutely certain to measure praise as well.

Customer service centers for some of my clients actually receive more praise about the company than complaints.

It is critically important to focus on the most significant issues, as not all problems are worth solving. The tone of these communications deserves careful attention. Do not scold, warn or reprimand other departments. It is a fair assumption that no one is deliberately trying to destroy the company. While it is perfectly appropriate—and helpful—to suggest solutions to problems that come to light, the principal purpose of these memos and reports is to provide enough information so that the concerned departments can recognize the nature, extent and cost of the problem and seek an appropriate solution. Always supply support information such as time study sheets reflecting how much dealing with the problem costs.

Suggesting new procedures or other changes

This is another potentially delicate matter. The spirit of the memo should be one of colleague speaking to colleagues. Avoid words like *must* or *should*. Use words such as *suggestion, idea, test out, try, might, could.*

Wherever there is the potential of encroaching on another department's turf, tread respectfully. Remember, however, the important role you play. If you truly want to play the role of leading the corporate customer service philosophy, then you should be involved in service-oriented issues, no matter where they originated. You should bring issues to the attention of the organization and lobby for resolutions.

Unfortunately, too many still view Customer Service as the corporate cudgel for use in subduing unruly customers. They may actually insist that customer service is at fault for not keeping customers "quiet." Our role is not to keep the customers quiet, our role is to listen and convert the customers' concerns into positive and constructive actions which ultimately are converted to improvements and profits.

— Memo: How Customer Service Can Help Your Department —

Date:

To: *(Name)*, Shipping
From: *(Name)*, Customer Service
Re: Shipping follow-up

We'd like to put shipping issues in our next customer-satisfaction survey, including issues related to timeliness, carrier, and packaging. This would be one part of a general customer satisfaction survey.

Can we get together and talk about appropriate questions—the questions that would be most useful to you? I'll call you next week for an appointment.

— Memos: What Customer Service Needs From You —

Date:

To: *(Name)*, Shipping
From: *(Name)*, Customer Service
Re: Shipping information Customer Service needs

The number of calls concerning changes in shipping schedules is increasing. See the attached chart covering the past three months. It would save money and improve customer satisfaction, if we proactively advised customers of changes.

Can we get together at *(time)* on *(date)* to set up a system?

———

Date:

To: *(Name)*, Shipping
From: *(Name)*, Customer Service
Re: Trouble reports

The key to good customer service can be found in treating each customer as an individual. However, many customer complaints are standard. It helps us do our job most efficiently, to assist you and our customer, if we are prepared in advance to deal with the most common of problems. Toward this end, I would like to discuss with you several shipping issues we do not fully understand. Armed with your answers, we should be able to deal with more shipping problems directly. After all, the last thing we want to do is transfer calls around the company.

— Memos Communicating Customer Concerns/Comments —

Date:

To: *(Name)*, Shipping
From: *(Name)*, Customer Service
Re: Foam peanuts

Based on customer calls—or, I should say, the absence of customer calls—you are all doing a great job. We hear very few complaints about shipping.

With a single exception.

Between *(date)* and *(date)*, we invested no fewer than *(number)* hours dealing with complaints about the use of foam peanuts as shock-absorbing material. The chief complaint is that the material is difficult and annoying to handle, and housekeeping staff complains that it clogs vacuum cleaners. A secondary complaint is that it is an unsound material ecologically.

I would like to share these comments and their costs with you in greater detail. I believe we should consider alternative shock-absorbing materials. Even if peanuts are cheaper, we are driving up customer-service burden costs and creating dissatisfaction.

I'll call you next week, and perhaps we can discuss alternatives and strategies.

Date:

To: *(Name)*, Shipping
From: *(Name)*, Customer Service
Re: Communication with customers

The good news is that Customer Service gets very, very few complaints about Shipping. Generally, an order is placed, we ship it, it arrives, and the customer is pleased.

Now, you would expect dissatisfaction when something goes wrong—say a shipment is delayed. But we have found that the greater source of dissatisfaction is not the fact that the shipment may be delayed, but that no one advised the customer, or the news came too late.

We need to develop a new strategy for advising customers on slippage. Let's meet to discuss.

———————

Date:

To: *(Name)*, Shipping
From: *(Name)*, Customer Service
Re: Thanks for rush delivery

Just a note to pass along this comment from one of our customers, *(Name)* at *(Name of company)*: "Your Shipping Department did a phenomenal job in expediting my shipment. I needed it. I needed it fast. And they got it to me."

Nice work.

cc: Newsletter and management

— Recurring Fulfillment Problems —

Date:

To: *(Name)*, Shipping
From: *(Name)*, Customer Service
Re: Frequent item errors

Between *(date)* and *(date)*, our department invested *($ amount)* in dealing with shipping problems. However, only *(number)* of these calls concerned late shipments; the balance were complaints about the wrong item or items having been shipped. Therefore, wrong items shipped is costing us *($ amount)*/month.

Certainly, *(number)* calls is no disaster, but we couldn't help noticing a pattern in the complaints. Almost always, the erroneously shipped item was one or two product i.d. numbers away from the correct item. This suggests some problem in picking.

Can we reduce this problem? Not only are we spending *($ amount)*/month to handle the calls, but all the wrong items must be returned for refund.

Date:

To: *(Name)*, Shipping
From: *(Name)*, Customer Service
Re: Damaged shipments

The attached chart shows the cost Customer Service incurred dealing with damaged-goods calls. Most of our callers feel that the damage was not so much the result of random accident as it was due to inadequate packaging. Increasing costs suggest that we should reconsider packing procedures, particularly for the following kinds of merchandise:

   (list)

— Suggesting New Procedures —

Date:

To: *(Name)*, Shipping
From: *(Name)*, Customer Service
Re: Bubble Pack vs. Foam Popcorn

Between *(date)* and *(date)*, *(number)* customers have mentioned to us that they find the Styrofoam "popcorn" we use to protect small-parts shipments annoying (at best) and (at worst) unsound environmentally. We have invested *($ amount)* discussing the issue with customers.

The number of complaints and comments on this issue seems to me significant enough to impact sales. Therefore, I suggest that you consider the feasibility of switching to bubble pack insulation. At least *(number)* of our customers have reported that they can—and do—reuse bubble pack, whereas styro popcorn is nothing more than a disposal nuisance.

Why not let our customers feel good about us from the very moment they unpack their shipments? Remember, even if bubble pack costs more, we must consider your costs as well as ours to understand *total* cost.

I'd appreciate your thoughts on adopting this new procedure as soon as possible.

— Mediating Customer Disputes —

Date:

To: (Name), Shipping
From: (Name), Customer Service
Re: Order number (number)

The problem comes down to this: (Name), the customer, claims that he specified and was promised delivery by (date). Your department has no record of this date—either from (Name) or from your personnel. (Name) has asked for a (percent amount) discount as compensation for our having missed the promised delivery date. However, he cannot furnish me with the name of the shipping staff member with whom he had communicated and from whom he secured his delivery date.

My suggestion is that we do not reduce this to an our-word-against-his situation. But I do not think there are sufficient grounds to justify our granting a discount. Instead, I suggest that we write (Name), expressing our regret that the order was not shipped at an optimum date for him and providing instructions to him so that he can ensure future shipments are made exactly where and when he wants them. If you agree, I'll draft a letter.

Chapter 28

COMMUNICATING *with* *the* BILLING DEPARTMENT

HOW TO DO IT

Communicating About Problems

Where money misunderstandings or errors are involved, customers are quick to feel victimized. Their thinking runs: "If I noticed a wrong invoice *this* time, what have I missed in the *past*"? It is therefore crucial that Customer Service work with Billing to correct errors and resolve conflicts quickly. It is also important the customer be made to feel that Customer Service is helping *her* to resolve the problem, that she is not being victimized or left to fend for herself. The memo should recommend a course of action consistent with this purpose.

— Memo: How Customer Service Can Help Your Department —

Date:

To: *(Name)*, Accounts Receivable
From: *(Name)*, Customer Service
Re: How we can help with slow accounts

As you know, Customer Service often serves as a "front door" to your department. Customers call us frequently with particular billing questions. Working with you, we are always capable of reaching a solution.

Customer Service is in a strategic position to reach out to customers as well as to receive calls from them. This is true particularly in chasing up slow payments. We can help accelerate your slower accounts by managing an incentive program and by ensuring customer satisfaction with the product and service.

I think that it would be productive for our departments to meet on this issue. I'll call you for a meeting, and perhaps we can develop some creative solutions.

— Memo: What Customer Service Needs From You —

Date:

To: *(Name)*, Billing
From: *(Name)*, Customer Service
Re: Request for information exchange

As you know, customers seeking billing information frequently call us rather than contact you directly. Our practice has been either to retrieve the necessary information from you and convey it to the customer, or simply to transfer the call to your department. We think it would make for greater efficiency all around and create greater satisfaction if we could handle simple billing inquiries directly. This way we would save time, you would save time, and most of all, the customer would save time—and would have to deal with a single person rather than get bounced from one to the other.

It should be an easy matter to get the necessary billing information on our terminals. If you like the idea, let's meet to discuss the technical stuff—say *(day)* at *(time)*? Please give me a call at ext. *(extension number)* to let me know.

— Memos: Communicating Customer Concerns/Comments —

Date:

To: *(Name)*, Accounts Receivable
From: *(Name)*, Customer Service
Re: Invoice format complaints

A significant number of our customers have been experiencing some difficulty understanding the breakdown of charges on invoices. In all honesty,

I can appreciate the problem. The present invoice format was tailored to our old accounting software and is anything but "user friendly." The fact that we've gotten customer comments on it suggests that it is time to rethink the format.

This may also help encourage prompt payment of balances due.

Date:

To: *(Name)*, Accounts Receivable
From: *(Name)*, Customer Service
Re: Customer comment on new statement format

I thought you would like to know that we have received *(number)* calls since *(date)* from people who are very grateful for the new, simpler Customer Statement Invoice. The customer response has all been positive, and I am confident that the new format will encourage a prompter settlement of accounts.

Congratulations!

Date:

To: *(Name)*, Billing Department
From: *(Name)*, Customer Service
Re: Incentives for prompt payment

Customers routinely ask us if we offer any incentives for prompt payment of balances due. At this point, of course, all we can do is point out our 30-day net terms and tell customers that there is no finance charge for accounts paid within 30 days. Judging from the steady volume of calls relating to this matter, perhaps it is time that we gave some thought to more positive incentives, perhaps a 1 or 2 percent discount for accounts paid within ten days or something similar.

If you would like to discuss this, please give me a call at ext. *(extension number)*.

— Recurring Billing Problems —

Date:

To: *(Name)*, Accounts Receivable
From: *(Name)*, Customer Service
Re: Invoices sent to shipping address

We have recently had a number of calls—about *(number)* since *(date)*—amounting to *($ amount)* in handling charges regarding invoices sent to shipping addresses instead of billing addresses. In some cases, this was merely a minor annoyance, but in other cases, the customer was embarrassed when *his* client received a bill he should never have seen, let alone have been asked to pay.

I wanted you to be aware of this serious problem. We should address this issue because our handling costs are high and, even more importantly, we are creating dissatisfaction. Let's discuss. How about *(date)* at *(time)*?

———————

Date:

To: *(Name)*, Accounts Receivable
From: *(Name)*, Customer Service
Re: Repeated billing error, account *(account number)*

Ms. *(Name)* called this afternoon—for the ____nth time in *(number)* weeks *(months)*. Repeatedly, we give her credit for a returned item (invoice number *[number]*), and repeatedly, that charge reappears on her next statement.

It happened again on the current invoice.

As usual, we've entered the credit up here, but please doublecheck the system to ensure that—this time—the credit sticks.

If there are any problems or questions, please call me at ext. *(extension number)*.

Date:

To: *(Name)*, Accounts Receivable
From: *(Name)*, Customer Service
Re: Confusion of product codes

Since the codes on the following products were changed on *(date)*, several customer invoices have contained errors because the codes were not updated properly:

   (list products and codes)

Please run a check on outgoing invoices to ensure that the new product codes have been entered correctly. Customers—understandably enough—find this particular kind of error quite baffling, and they seem to waste a lot of time trying to figure it out before they finally give up and call us.

— Problem Account: Suspend Credit —

Date:

To: *(Name)*, Accounts Receivable
From: *(Name)*, Customer Service
Re: Account # *(number)*

As you requested, I contacted *(Name)* regarding his account (number *[number]*) on *(date)*. He does not dispute the charges, but he does report serious cash-flow problems. He promises to contact me within *(time period)* with a payment proposal. I have advised him that, in the meantime, we had no choice other than to suspend his credit with us. However, we will continue shipping product on a cash-in-advance basis.

Accordingly, please put account number *(number)* on "hold" status until further notice.

Date:

To: *(Name)*, Accounts Receivable
From: *(Name)*, Customer Service
Re: Account number *(number)*

Following a lengthy conversation with this account, I must recommend that
we suspend credit until their outstanding balance is made current.

This firm has been a good customer, and we must do our best not to alien-
ate it. But it has clearly suffered a number of reversals, and we need to wait
until its situation stabilizes before extending additional credit. We have
informed *(account)* that it will now be served on a cash-in-advance basis.

— Problem Account: Refer to Collections —

Date:

To: *(Name)*, Accounts Receivable
From: *(Name)*, Customer Service
Re: Account number *(number)*

As per your request, I have attempted to contact *(Name)* repeatedly regarding his past-due account (number *[number]*). I have been unsuccessful in
reaching him.

Please refer this account to Collections for further action.

— Suggesting New Procedures —

Date:

To: *(Name)*, Billing
From: *(Name)*, Customer Service
Re: Introduction of quick-pay incentive

The results of our recent customer survey are in. Of special importance to
your department is an indication that *(percent amount)* customers would
pay their invoices within ten days of receipt if we offered a minimum of
(percent amount) discount on the total due.

I suggest you run the numbers on this and see how we would net out. I am reasonably confident that this incentive could save us real money in improved cash flow.

Please give me your thoughts on this.

Date:

To: *(Name)*, Accounts Receivable
From: *(Name)*, Customer Service
Re: Monthly billing option

We've been casually testing the waters with some of our customers to assess their response to a change from quarterly to monthly billing. *(Percent amount)* of the *(number)* we asked responded favorably to monthly billing.

Unless I'm mistaken, the cash-flow benefit monthly billing would give us outweighs the expense of issuing monthly statements, and not only do we *not* have customer resistance to monthly billing, we actually have some customer preference.

Let's discuss making the transition to this new procedure.

Date:

To: *(Name)*, Accounts Receivable
From: *(Name)*, Customer Service
Re: Cover note with invoices

Let's consider the benefits of including a personalized insert or cover note with invoices.

The note could be used to advise of important extra services, accessories, and so on, and it could also be used to highlight incentive programs, including our *(percent amount)* discount offer for balances paid before *(number)* days.

Finally, an insert or cover note personalizes the transaction and helps develop a stronger relationship with the customer.

Let's talk over some specific suggestions in greater detail.

— Mediating Customer Disputes —

Date:

To: *(Name)*, Accounts Receivable
From: *(Name)*, Customer Service
Re: Per hour dispute, account number *(number)*

At your request, I have spoken to *(Name)* regarding her dispute with the *(date)* bill for *(number)* hours. She received your breakdown of the service hours, but she still believes the figure is inflated. I suggested that she furnish us with a point-by-point statement of her counterclaim. Let's examine it and see if there is any realistic room for negotiation.

Chapter 29

COMMUNICATING *with* ENGINEERING, DESIGN, *and* PRODUCT TESTING DEPARTMENTS

HOW TO DO IT

The vital contribution customer service offers to engineering, design, and testing is far more apparent today than in the past. Customer service is a sounding board echoing the customer's attitude in real time. Market research can and does provide hard data reflecting what the customer might think about this or that issue. However service, responding to particular questions on a daily basis, quickly picks up the customer's live pulse.

Research evaluates customer attitudes concerning a particular range of preprogrammed questions. Service looks at current customer response on any issue or question and extrapolates what is happening now into the near-term future. Service can effectively discover early indicators of a problem thereby offering vital information before the trend—to say nothing of market damage—becomes significant.

Service also helps the organization flavor, temper, and judge the quality of data received, and tempering data is an important element in evaluating risk. Hard research converts customer perceptions and feelings into statistics; however, statistics are not always correct. (Remember the New Coke/Old Coke fiasco? It is now known as one of the classic marketing blunders. Yet the market research completed to confirm the decision suggested that customers *wanted* the New Coke formulation.) Customer service contact with customers yields fresh, frank information direct from the "trenches." Make sure that Engineering, Production, Assembly, and Test are aware of the potential and kind of information customer service can furnish. As always, be certain to pass along reports indicating positive customer comments as well as areas of concern.

Communicating concerns and problems

One of the weightier responsibilities of Customer Service is to communicate possible problems, flaws, and defects in products. As in any other situation where Customer Service communicates customer response to particular departments, care must be taken to filter the remarks in order to ensure that the data being conveyed reflects probable trends or significant anomalies. This degree of judgment requires intelligence, which must be gathered over time. Customer service must study what is happening. Time logs must be used to determine the amount of effort invested in resolving this or that issue, and time invested must be translated into dollars spent on issues. In short, Service must become another data source, helping the organization with its continuous improvement efforts.

Generally, these memos should reflect a preliminary trend or a likely outcome based upon a number of customer responses. In the usual case, resist the temptation to report every incident. Track things, keep records, and convert activity into cost. Remember, the organization responds most to dollars. (There are exceptions, of course. Obviously, if a single safety-related or other liability issue pops up, then immediate action is necessary.) Become part of the total company analysis process. Our purpose is not to ram numbers down the organization's multiple departmental throats, but we must ensure that the organization hears and responds to the voice of the customers.

Always pay close attention to the correct language engineering or production needs. I am familiar with a case in which customers had to suffer for six months with a faulty pump design for a hand lotion dispenser. Customer service knew perfectly well that a problem existed and that it was costing the company plenty. Unfortunately, what service did *not* know was the correct engineering terminology necessary to describe the particular pump parts. The internal confusion continued until Service learned the language, and then the problem was resolved within a week.

— Memos: How Customer Service Can Help Your Department —

Date:

To: *(Name)*, Design
From: *(Name)*, Customer Service
Re: Customer response reporting

As you know, Customer Service reports to your department whenever we get a significant response from our customers concerning some design feature of our products.

We are reworking our reporting formats, and I would like to incorporate any suggestions you may have. I suggest we get together to discuss a set of procedures before the new fall line hits the market in *(month)*.

————————

Date:

To: *(Name)*, Engineering
From: *(Name)*, Customer Service
Re: Tweak hotline

As you know, Customer Service has been providing technical feedback to customers for some time now. However, our continuing analysis suggests we are having difficulty with parameter adjustments. I would like to set up a series of special screens, which our Customer Service Representatives can access for particular applications. Essentially, this would make Customer Service a "front door" for Engineering, and I am confident it would enable us to serve our customers more effectively; reduce cost, and create new levels of satisfaction. Certainly, it would save your department time by relieving your staff of having to back us up so frequently.

If this appeals to you, let's get together to discuss implementing the service.

Date:

To: *(Name)*, Product Testing Department
From: *(Name)*, Customer Service
Re: How we can help you design tests

Please feel free to make use of Customer Service as a resource for defining customer concerns and interests. The kind of anecdotal and informal information we can supply is no substitute for formal product tests, but combined with information from the Marketing Department, I believe our data can be very valuable in helping you design the tests.

For example, with *(Name)* lotion, we learned that our product claim of "richer and thicker" was discounted because the customer did not *feel* the lotion *was* richer and thicker. Unfortunately, this was not learned until after the introduction, and expensive modifications had to be developed.

Let's discuss critical issues concerning the upcoming new *(product)* and how we might help.

It would be helpful if you would alert us to issues of particular interest.

— Memo: What Customer Service Needs From You —

Date:

To: *(Name)*, Design
From: *(Name)*, Customer Service
Re: Design questions

In order to conduct the telephone survey we discussed on *(date)*, we have created the following list of questions concerning the following issues:

     (list)

How do the questions look to you? Your suggestions and corrections will enable us to modify our questions in order to get the kind of information that will be most useful to you.

— Memos Communicating Customer Concerns/Comments —

Date:

To: *(Name)*, Design
From: *(Name)*, Customer Service
Re: *(Design feature)* on *(product)*

Since it was introduced last *(month)*, we have received some *(number)* comments concerning *(design feature)*. Unfortunately, none of these comments were positive, with most of the customers who spoke to us questioning why *(design feature)* had been changed.

Here is a summary of the comments:

   (list)

Resolving these issues has cost us *($ amount)* to date. Unfortunately, the current trend is that customer complaints regarding *(design feature)* are increasing. Based on current trends, within *(number)* months, our costs will be significant, and customer satisfaction will suffer. Let's discuss.

Date:

To: *(Name)*, Product Testing
From: *(Name)*, Customer Service
Re: Identifying focus and trial groups

Would you like us to recruit current customers for participation in focus and trial groups? A number of our customers have expressed interest in participating in product tests. They like the idea of being at the forefront of product development and having a voice in it.

If you are interested in our doing some recruiting, please let me know.

Date:

To: *(Name)*, Design Department
From: *(Name)*, Customer Service
Re: Add *(feature)* to *(product)*?

Recently, one of our customers dropped a casual suggestion that I think is worth consideration. Her idea was to add *(feature)* to *(product)*. Her reasons for this were *(list)*. I asked her if she would pay a premium to upgrade to a *(product)* that included this feature. She said that she would do so without hesitation.

Just thought I'd pass the information on.

— Recurring Product Problems —

Date:

To: *(Name)*, Design
From: *(Name)*, Customer Service
Re: *(Part)* jams with rapid use

One of the top five customer complaints we get concerning *(product)* is the tendency for *(part)* to jam with rapid use. Now this is a well-recognized problem, and the *Owner's Manual* cautions specifically against reengaging *(part)* before it has fully recycled. Clearly then, there is nothing faulty with the product, but there does seem to be an identifiable weakness in the overall design.

I believe *(product)* would be enhanced greatly if a solution to the jamming of *(part)* could be effectively designed.

The big question, of course, is: Do you have the resources to implement such a design change? Let us help you get the resources you need. Let me make some points.

As I mentioned, this is one of the top five issues my department handles. Over the past year, we have averaged *($ amount)* per month on this issue, representing a total investment of *($ amount)*. Unfortunately, during the past quarter, the trend in complaint calls has been increasing at the rate of *(percent amount)* compounded annually. At this growth rate, I must plan to spend *($ amount)* on this issue over the next year. This is serious and growing rapidly.

Even more importantly, we have not been able to accomplish: *(list)* because so much of our capability is being consumed on the jamming problem. And worst of all, customer satisfaction is certainly suffering. This is going to impact sales.

Let's put together a comprehensive report. The report should include not just the resources you need but also the costs I incur if we don't get this fixed.

How about a meeting on *(date)* at *(time)* to discuss further?

Date:

To: *(Name)*, Product Testing
From: *(Name)*, Customer Service
Re: Complaints about finish deterioration on *(product)*

Each month we get *(number)* complaints from customers who are frustrated by finish detoriation on *(product)*. While none of these complaints relates to product performance or reliability, they are still a significant concern. Surface finish is an important customer satisfaction issue. For example, our previous history suggests that for every complaint we get, there are ten to fifteen complaints we do *not* get.

Could we please set up a test on surface finish detoriation to determine what, if anything, can be done? I'm certain some of our customers will even help us by allowing us to evaluate their Real-world Applications.

Chapter
30

COMMUNICATING *with* the QUALITY CONTROL DEPARTMENT

HOW TO DO IT

The importance of quality is increasing. However, the presence of a quality control department, as a separate department responsible for checking quality, is declining. More and more, each individual in every job is expected to build quality into every operation. While the quality control department may play an ombudsman or lobbyist role throughout the organization, quality control is now being built into every job requirement.

As in other problem-reporting communications, a discriminating approach is called for. Watch for problem trends, identify them, assess the cost impact or customer satisfaction impact, and pass the information on. Observe your own culture carefully and blend the information you offer into the quality improvement mainstream. Build a constructive relationship with the quality control effort over time.

— Memos: How Customer Service Can Help Your Department —

Date:

To: *(Name)*, Quality Control
From: *(Name)*, Customer Service
Re: Regular reporting of problems

As you know, we report to you whenever we run across any unusual or significant pattern in customer calls. We are in the process of more formally tracking our activity so that we can better provide feedback to you and others. Over the past several months, we have tracked all calls and developed a logging system as noted on the attached form. Does information presented this way help you? Give me a call, and let's discuss further.

———————

Date:

To: *(Name)*, Quality Control
From: *(Name)*, Customer Service
Re: Check your batting average

You've called on us to ask customers specific quality-related questions in the past. You should also know that we routinely keep detailed "trouble and cost logs" and have the software to search them for specific issues and specific products. We're available to help you chart quality-related trends and can go as far back as *(year)*.

— Memos: What Customer Service Needs From You —

Date:

To: *(Name)*, Quality Control
From: *(Name)*, Customer Service
Re: Report on areas of concern

We don't like to make trouble in Customer Service, but we do a lot of looking for it. To help us increase our sensitivity to possible trouble areas with *(products)*, it would be helpful if you could furnish a list of areas of concern relating to the following items:

   (list products)

This will help us formulate how we track data from customers so that the information supports your efforts here in the plant.

Date:

To: *(Name)*, Quality Control
From: *(Name)*, Customer Service
Re: Information on sensitive areas

Please keep us posted on current quality-control issues and concerns so that we can put customer calls in context more effectively. If we have an idea of the problem areas, we will know better what to look for when we deal with customer servicing issues. We would like to receive special bulletins for any particularly hot issues.

— Memos Communicating Customer Concerns —

Date:

To: *(Name)*, Quality Control
From: *(Name)*, Customer Service
Re: Durability of *(product feature)*

Recently, we have received a number of calls (*[number]* since *[date]*) complaining that *(product feature)* on *(product)* seems insufficiently durable—"flimsy" is the word most of our callers have used. Our response is that the part is, and *must* be lightweight, and that it has passed rigorous tests.

Perhaps you can supply us with more information on testing and the quality-control process as they relate to this product. It would help us to have specific information to pass on to our customers.

Thanks.

———————

Date:

To: *(Name)*, Quality Control
From: *(Name)*, Customer Service
Re: Recycled materials concerns

Usually, customers are very pleased by our inclusion of high percentages of recycled materials in *(product)*. Lately, however, we have gotten some calls expressing concern over such materials—as if we were selling second-hand goods.

Can you furnish us with good, solid quality-control data concerning the durability of recycled materials? We would like something more than our own subjective impressions to pass on to our customers.

— Recurring Product Problems —

Date:

To: *(Name)*, Quality Control
From: *(Name)*, Customer Service
Re: Repeated failure of *(part)* on *(product)*

From *(date)* to *(date)*, customer service representatives have logged *(number)* calls complaining about the failure of *(part)* on our *(product)*. We have invested *($ amount)* in replacing *(part)*, and the trend is increasing.

Here is a typical complaint:

> *(quote complaint)*

I am sending this memo to your department as well as to Engineering and Product Testing. The failure rate is high and certainly warrants investigation. In addition to the costs mentioned above, we are having a negative impact on customer satisfaction.

––––––––––

Date:

To: *(Name)*, Manager, Quality Control
From: *(Name)*, Director of Customer Service
Re: Surface durability of *(product)* poor

I am directing this memo to you and to *(Name)* in Engineering, because I'm not sure whether we have a quality control issue here or something more basic. Between *(date)* and *(date)* we received no fewer than *(number)* of complaints about cosmetic damage to *(product)* resulting from normal use. Our cost of handling these complaints during the period in question is *($*

amount). In addition to processing costs, we have also had to replace *(number)* of units. This is a serious issue.

I have names and numbers for follow-up if we need more information on how these products were used.

Would you please review this issue and give me some feedback?

Date:

To: *(Name)*, Quality Control
From: *(Name)*, Customer Service
Re: Purchases of "stale" *(food product)*

Since *(date)*, Customer Service representatives have logged *(number)* complaints concerning "stale" *(food product)*. The purchases were made in stores generally throughout the Midwest. So far, the following lot numbers have been reported:

    (list)

Going by the expiration dates on these items, they should have been perfectly fresh.

I have all names, phone numbers, and corresponding lot numbers on file for your review.

In all cases, we are sending out coupons for free replacement product. Double-value coupons are being distributed. However, even though we are replacing product, we are still creating negative advertising. We need a quick assessment.

Chapter
31

COMMUNICATING *with* *the* MARKETING DEPARTMENT

HOW TO DO IT

As with Quality Control, the relationship between Customer Service and Marketing can be extraordinarily productive, providing Marketing with an opportunity to hear from customers directly and frankly. Ideally, the relationship between the two departments should be collaborative, with both sharing perceptions of customers' concerns, issues, wants, and requirements.

Take care in creating memos for Marketing that you do not usurp the role of that department. Your emphasis should be on reporting what you see and hear, and offering your perceptions. However, developing an overall strategic position is normally not a customer service function. When you report on numbers of calls received concerning a particular issue, be sure to provide a context in which the significance of the number can be interpreted: "Between April 1 and June 31, we received 1,123 calls concerning Brand X Software; 654 callers mentioned that they would like the program a lot more if it included feature Y."

— Memos: How Customer Service Can Help Your Department —

Date:

To: *(Name)*, Marketing
From: *(Name)*, Customer Service
Re: *(Product type)*: view from the front lines

As you would expect, most of the calls we get ask us for troubleshooting of one kind or another. But we also get a good deal of commentary· from customers on features they would like to see, particularly in a *(product type)*. Typically, dealing with this commentary consumes about *(percent amount)* of our normal resources. I would like to work with you to put together a questionnaire our representatives could use to probe a little more deeply concerning *(product type)*. I believe that, used in conjunction with your market surveys, this information "from the front lines" could help us hit the target—the first time.

If you agree, let's get together on it. Please give me a call at ext. *(extension number)*.

Date:

To: *(Name)*, Marketing
From: *(Name)*, Customer Service
Re: Complaints galore

Our approach to customer service is more than damage control. We try not only to deal effectively with customers' problems, but we keep careful analytical records of these problems. We also track costs the company incurs to handle problems. Costs include our time, free product or service we must give away, as well as "negative" advertising the company may incur. These records provide a vivid picture of what customers *don't* want, and, I believe, because of that, they provide a context for thinking about what it is they *do* want.

Consider the attached charts showing costs incurred to handle *(problem)*, which occurred with *(product)*. These charts (and many similar charts we have going back the last *[number]* years) are available for your inspection.

— Memos: What Customer Service Needs From You —

Date:

To: *(Name)*, Marketing
From: *(Name)*, Customer Service
Re: Helpful questions about targeted products

Customers are very frank with us. I suspect they tell customer service representatives things that don't get on marketing surveys. I'd like to take advantage of the special relationship that exists between our representatives and our customers by preparing our representatives with a set of questions that might help you fine tune your marketing efforts.

Please give us a list of target products—items you would like us to focus on—and a list of questions about them. Our staff will work them into customer calls as appropriate and report to you at regular intervals.

———

Date:

To: *(Name)*, Marketing
From: *(Name)*, Customer Service
Re: Marketing profiles for selected products

Believe it or not, the easiest problem for us to deal with is when the customer buys a product and it falls apart or just plain refuses to work. In these situations, the performance criteria are pretty much black and white.

More difficult for us are calls concerning products that fail to operate up to customer expectations. Sometimes we can address these calls in technical terms, but very often, the issues involved are far more subjective. In these cases, it would really help us to have target market segment profiles available, especially for certain products, including:

> *(list)*

These target markets will help us focus on our plan versus customer expectation, and we will be better able to assess precisely where the customer's perceptions varied from our own. We will be better able to determine if the customer's current usage is consistent with our intended usage.

— Memos Communicating Customer Concerns/Comments —

Date:

To: *(Name)*, Marketing
From: *(Name)*, Customer Service
Re: Market for a "no-frills" *(product)*

We get a good many calls asking for help with some of the more elaborate features of *(product)*. Many of these callers express a good deal of frustration and have let us know that, if a no-frills version of *(product)* were available, they would buy it. They find certain features of the present *(product)* downright annoying, especially:

> *(list)*

We get enough of this kind of comment to suggest that the feature-set of *(product)* warrants further study from Marketing.

Attached is a detailed caller log where it has been converted to dollars. This reflects our costs in dealing with this issue. Further, we have also estimated "negative" advertising the company receives as long as the problem persists. I realize that there are costs associated with changing the current feature-set. As you evaluate the need versus cost, however, please be certain to include our cost figures.

———

Date:

To: *(Name)*, Marketing
From: *(Name)*, Customer Service
Re: Disposable *(part)*

We get a lot of calls from customers asking us if there are better—more thorough and less tedious—ways of cleaning *(part)* after use. We have heard from *(number)* of customers over the past twelve months. This number of customers represents *(percent amount)* of our call volume.

Perhaps a market for disposable *(parts)* is worth investigating. This segment may be larger than we think. Usually, every customer call expressing a certain attitude represents *(number)* customers with the same attitude who are not calling.

Date:

To: *(Name)*, Marketing
From: *(Name)*, Customer Service
Re: Extending extended warranties

Let's look into the feasibility of offering extensions to our extended warranties. During the past *(number)* months *(number)* customers have asked for warranty extensions representing *(percent amount)* of our total call volume. Each call represents *(number)* customers with similar interests.

Of course, Engineering will need to calculate durability versus the cost of coverage, but I think we should be investigating the market for this service now.

— Transmitting/Summarizing Dealer Comments —

Date:

To: *(Name)*, Marketing
From: *(Name)*, Customer Service
Re: Dealer reaction to *(product)*

(Name), our dealer in *(place)*, just called to say that his customers are very excited about the new *(product)*. I asked him what they liked especially, and he gave me a short list:

    (list)

The first two items seem to be the most important to his customers.

I'll keep you updated on additional dealer response and full statistical analysis, but if *(Name's)* experience is any indication, it looks like we've got a winner and we should continue to hit the new features hard in our advertising program.

———

Date:

To: *(Name)*, Marketing
From: *(Name)*, Customer Service
Re: More colors for *(product)*

I don't know if any of the dealers have communicated with you on this issue directly, but they are certainly talking to us. Customer Service gets a substantial number of customer requests for a larger selection of colors in our *(product)* line. The most popular color requests seem to be (in no particular order):

> *(list)*

Judging from these comments, it seems high time to test the market for a variety of colors. *(Percent amount)* of our dealers have already asked for larger color selections, and this issue represented *(percent amount)* of our total call volume over *(number)* months.

Date:

To: *(Name)*, Marketing
From: *(Name)*, Customer Service
Re: Dealers want a more active role in marketing

I've been asked by *(percent amount)* of our dealers over the past *(number)* months to convey to you their desire to be included more closely in the marketing loop. Now from where I sit, it seems to me that Marketing maintains a reasonably high level of communication with the dealer network and is generally responsive to them. However, it seems that many of the dealers do not share this perception. This is an area of concern to me, as this type of call is consuming *(percent amount)* of my available resources.

My suggestion is that you set up a series of meetings with the dealers and let them air their concerns and suggestions.

Chapter
32

COMMUNICATING *with* *the* ADVERTISING DEPARTMENT

HOW TO DO IT

Anyone who deals with the customer is part of the overall advertising effort, and Customer Service is no exception. Typically, there is an advertising department, or agency, which handles both ad design and placement for formal campaigns. However, the advertising agency or department does not operate in a vacuum. It needs input from sales, customer service, product planning, market research, and other functions. It needs to know how well it is doing. It needs to know how well the target customer is responding to the campaign. It needs to know if the campaign is consistent with the corporate objectives. And, perhaps most important of all, it needs to know what is missing from the campaign.

Transmitting Customer Concerns and Response to Advertising

Customer Service is in the perfect position to help control the overall advertising message. For example, assume Customer Service notices an increase in the number of inquires focused on where the product can be purchased. This could be a clear signal that the ongoing advertising campaign should be focused more on the product's distribution network. Or, suppose customer service measures a heavy inquiry load related to product operation or preventive maintenance. Again, this information will be very valuable to the advertising effort, as the message can be tilted to focus on education related to these particular issues. Customer service is usually most sensitive to the information content of advertising, since such a big part of the Customer Service mission is education of customers. Feedback on this aspect of advertising is very valuable.

Customer Service as an Advocate for the Dealer Network

Dealers, like every other group, are, of course, free to communicate with the advertising department directly, but they probably won't. They more typically would express their concerns to the sales or customer service representatives. Often, Customer Service is cast in the role of advocate for the needs and desires of individual dealers or the dealer network. Dealer comments, like end-user customer comments, need to be catalogued, evaluated, and offered with an interpretation in order to be useful to the continuing advertising campaign.

Transmitting Critical Responses

Criticism of advertising should not be confused with criticism of the advertising department or agency. In the healthy organization, confusion will not occur. In all communications customer service should be focused on the needs, interests, and concerns of the customer. The personal concerns of the Customer Service department are not very relevant; the concerns of the customer as defined and interpreted by the Customer Service department are extremely relevant.

Criticism is not a matter of declaring one's likes and dislikes. Its goal is to assess the effectiveness of an ad or ad campaign, always providing data and explanation for any judgment expressed. Most importantly, do not provide cold statistics alone. Advertising is very expensive in all its many forms. Whenever possible, convert your data into dollars.

Use this type of thinking: "If we adjust the campaign to include A-type education, we can save dollars in customer service activity." Or, "We are spending dollars dealing with this false impression created. This money can be saved if the campaign is adjusted to offer clarification on issue B."

In supporting advertising, Customer Service must be politically astute as well. Many times a campaign is neither misleading nor inappropriate to the mass of the product's consumers or potential consumers. However, the campaign may be offensive to a small but highly organized group. Customer Service must be especially alert to this situation. If this occurs, then the problem must be identified and assessed quickly. Be very aware that a small organized group that is ignored can in many cases effectively rally support for its cause with the larger group. When this occurs, the product and company ultimately pay the price.

— Memos: How Customer Service Can Help Your Department —

Date:

To: *(Name)*, Advertising
From: *(Name)*, Customer Service
Re: Advertising effectiveness

One of our customer service representatives makes it her business to ask certain customers about our product ads. Basically, she puts it this way: "How did you find information that helped you make your decision to buy *(product)*?"

We've gotten some interesting responses, which I've enclosed.

If this kind of information is useful to you, more of us could be asking this question. Let me know at ext. *(extension number)*.

Date:

To: *(Name)*, Advertising Director
From: *(Name)*, Director of Customer Service
Re: Customer concerns

We, like you, are ultimately in customer education. For that reason, I would like to offer our findings on customer concerns during the past *(time period)*. The attached charts show how we have been investing our resources. Please note that *(percent amount)* of our resources representing a total of *($ amount)* has been invested in resolving customer concerns related to the following issues:

   (list)

Could we adjust the advertising so that these issues are addressed more directly? I'll call you so that we can set up a meeting.

— Memos: What Customer Service Needs From You —

Date:

To: *(Name)*, Advertising
From: *(Name)*, Customer Service
Re: Effective advertising

As you requested, we are working to monitor, collect, and collate customer response to the new ads. What would help you most? What kinds of responses do you want to monitor? A simple list would be very helpful for us.

Thanks.

Date:

To: *(Name)*, Advertising
From: *(Name)*, Customer Service
Re: Tear sheets

Please make certain that all current advertising tear sheets are distributed in quantity to Customer Service. Our representatives need to be completely up to date with our current advertising in order to respond to customer concerns most effectively. We do not want Customer Service Representatives saying, "What did the ad say?" to our customers.

Date:

To: *(Name)*, Advertising
From: *(Name)*, Customer Service
Re: Backup for performance data

Please attach full back up for any specifications or performance data contained in any ad to all tear sheets. We *do* get questions about our performance claims from time to time, and the right answer can help to close a sale or to keep customer expectations within the bounds of reality. Further, it is very important that we resolve customer concerns on the first contact.

— Memos: Communicating Customer Concerns/Comments —

Date:

To: *(Name)*, Advertising
From: *(Name)*, Customer Service
Re: Customer safety concerns

During the past *(time period)* we have tracked the following safety-related comments.

   (list issues)

What is significant is that these calls, as a total group, represent *(percent amount)* of our total call load. Clearly, these calls suggest that safety is a significant customer concern and, therefore, a potential selling point, for the following products:

   (list products)

Perhaps we should be hitting the safety issues or these products harder in our advertising.

Date:

To: *(Name)*, Advertising
From: *(Name)*, Customer Service
Re: Our customers are self-maintainers

Approximately *(percent amount)* of our call load is from customers who need help and guidance with various do-it-yourself maintenance and upgrade procedures. The volume of such calls strongly suggests that *our customers are self-maintainers*. I think we would be well served by tilting the self-maintenance and do-it-yourself upgradability of our products in our ads.

If you would like to look over our call logs, they're available.

Date:

To: *(Name)*, Advertising Director
From: *(Name)*, Director of Customer Service
Re: Advertising the "Service Advantage"

I really would like to see more of our ads highlight the Service Advantage. This company devotes a lot of resources to this department, and I think we should exploit this very significant asset more effectively. Based on our analysis over the past *(time period)*, *(percent amount)* of our customers were unaware of our significant service offerings.

There are a lot of companies making the kind of products we make, but there are very few companies who do what we do. As you know, we really stand behind our product, and we support it 100 percent. Let me specifically list how we differ from the competition:

> *(list)*

Please, let's talk about strategies for publicizing this aspect of *(Name of company)*.

— Transmitting/Summarizing Dealer Comments —

Date:

To: *(Name)*, Advertising
From: *(Name)*, Customer Service
Re: Dealers tell us that customers want flexibility

A number of our dealers have mentioned that a major sale-maker for our line of *(products)* is flexibility of application. Two of the dealers who spoke with us mentioned that our advertising does not stress the flexibility issue sufficiently, and that they would like to see this feature highlighted in future ads.

You might want to contact these two dealers directly to discuss the matter further:

> *(Names and phone numbers)*

Date:

To: *(Name)*, Advertising
From: *(Name)*, Customer Service
Re: Dealers featured in ads

A number of our dealers remark to us from time to time that they feel excluded from our ads.

I think they have a good point.

Our dealer network is a very positive product asset, providing:

1. Knowledgeable sales assistance.

2. Factory-authorized, factory-trained service.

3. Local convenience.

4. Company oversight and maintenance of company-mandated standards.

Can we play up some of these qualities in our ad campaigns?

Date:

To: *(Name)*, Advertising
From: *(Name)*, Customer Service
Re: Dealers tell us customers' warranty concerns

As might be expected, our dealers report that customers ask them a good many questions about our warranty policies. The concern expressed by some of our dealers, however, is the very basic nature of many questions— basics they think that should be covered in ad copy, but aren't.

As the dealers see it, then advertising should devote more space to the warranty as a desirable product benefit. Some copy highlighting comparatives would be particularly effective, since our warranty is just about the best, most comprehensive, and most generous in the business.

— Transmitting/Summarizing Customer Response to Advertising —

Date:

To: *(Name)*, Advertising
From: *(Name)*, Customer Service
Re: Customer response to new *(product)* ad

As you requested, from *(date)* to *(date)*, our customer service representatives asked all callers these three questions:

1. Did you see the ad for our new *(product)?* If so, where?

2. Are you interested in *(product)?*

3. Did you find the ad about *(product)* informative?

Of *(number)* responding to question 1, *(percent amount)* said they saw the ad. The media placement most effective is:

> *(list distribution covering where ad was seen)*

Of *(number)* responding to question 2, *(percent amount)* said they were definitely interested in *(product)*.

Of *(number)* responding to question 3, *(percent amount)* said the ad was very informative.

Detailed figures and selected notes from customer service representatives are enclosed. Based on this quick survey, however, it seems that the ad is successful in stimulating interest and in providing information.

Date:

To: *(Name)*, Advertising
From: *(Name)*, Customer Service
Re: Customers want product pictures

We've received a number of calls from customers asking us to send photographs of the following products:

> *(list)*

The reason? Our ads don't illustrate the merchandise.

Of course, it's up to you to judge the effectiveness of the recent print-media ads. That's a dollars-and-cents issue. But I do want to advise you that a significant number of customers like to *see* the product before they even consider buying it. To help you judge if the cost is worth it, we are sending *(number)* of photos per month responding to customer requests. Cost of photos plus processing cost is currently running at *($ amount)* per month.

Date:

To: *(Name)*, Advertising
From: *(Name)*, Customer Service
Re: Customer responses to latest *(product)* ad

We seem to have struck a nerve—at least among *(number)* callers since *(date)*, with our most recent *(product)* ad. These calls represented *(percent amount)* of our total volume! These callers, all women, have pointed out that the ad portrays women in a secretarial rather than an executive role. Two callers were upset enough to remark that the ads "turned them off" to our product.

Perhaps this response is sufficient to warrant rethinking the ad—or, at least, using a different photograph.

— Customer Complaints: Misleading Advertising —

Date:

To: *(Name)*, Advertising
From: *(Name)*, Customer Service
Re: Misleading new *(product)* ad

Since *(date)*, customer service representatives have handled *(number)* calls from customers disappointed that *(product)* lacks *(feature)*. Our new ad led them to believe that *(product)* included *(feature)*.

(Number) callers (representing *(percent amount)* of total volume) making the same point is more than casual coincidence, and I therefore recommend that your department review the text of the new ad in order to make it clear that *(product)* includes *(features)*, but not *(feature)*.

If you would like to examine our complaint log, just give me a call at ext. *(extension number)*, and I'll pull the relevant comments and cost calculations.

Date:

To: *(Name)*, Advertising
From: *(Name)*, Customer Service
Re: Photo in *(date)* ad making *(product)* look much bigger than
             actual size

Since *(date)*, two customers have called our representatives to remark that they were disappointed by *(product)*. Based on the ad, they expected something much bigger.

Now two calls isn't a lot, and after looking at the ad myself, I think the whole matter is very much a judgment call. However, you may want to give the photo some further thought.

Date:

To: *(Name)*, Advertising
From: *(Name)*, Customer Service
Re: Recent *(product)* ad leading customers to believe accessories
             are included

We have had *(number)* calls *([percent amount]* of total volume) since *(date)* from customers who thought that parts were missing from their *(product)* package. The reason? Our most recent television advertising led them to believe that the following accessories were included:

        (list)

Fortunately, our callers have taken this misperception in good humor, chalking it up to their own error. But I do think that we need some sort of disclaimer, making it clear that the accessories are available at additional cost.

— Customer Comments: Ad Supplies Insufficient Information —

Date:

To: *(Name)*, Advertising
From: *(Name)*, Customer Service
Re: Customer comments on *(product)* ad

Customers rarely make unsolicited comments to us about our ads, so when they do, they're probably worth listening to.

Since *(date)*, we've received about *(number)* calls—about *(percent amount)* of our total volume—from customers asking for information about *(product)*. Well, great. The ad piqued their interest. But the downside is that many of these customers complained that, while the ad was "cute" and "attractive," it really didn't say enough about the product.

You may want to consider adding some "hard" material to the ad. I think that could be done without altering the pitch radically.

If you want to discuss these customer comments in greater detail, just give me a call at ext. *(extension number)*.

———

Date:

To: *(Name)*, Advertising
From: *(Name)*, Customer Service
Re: Compatibility issues

Many of the calls we handle in Customer Service are pre-purchase questions about compatibility among systems. We have no problem dealing with such questions, but we have come to believe that many of the most basic compatibility issues would be more effectively dealt with in our advertising. Consider working the following kinds of information into ad copy:

  (list)

These are the issues prospective customers most frequently raise with us. Dealing with these basic issues is currently running *($ amount)* in customer service costs. Not only are the costs significant, but, remember, we only get one-tenth or less of the total concerned customers calling us.

Chapter 33

COMMUNICATING *with* SALES: TRANSMITTING LEADS *and* ADVISING *of* PROBLEMS

HOW TO DO IT

Antediluvian companies looked on customer service as a necessary evil. "Necessary" because customers expected it. "Evil" because it exposed problems while generating no revenue. New-paradigm corporate thinkers, however, have come to realize three things:

1. Customer service is a highly desirable product benefit.

2. Customer service representatives make sales and/or generate leads.

3. Customer service representatives help turn customers into salespeople.

Reporting Leads

A company's best customers are its current (satisfied) customers. They are the group most likely to purchase additional products, including accessories, upgrades, and products related to what they already own. They are more likely to promote growth by touting the product's value with word-of-mouth advertising. The customer service rep who is doing his job looks for opportunities to educate current customers about new products. In some companies, the CSR is empowered to make a sale directly. In other firms, he puts the customer in touch with a sales associate. This should not be done casually. It is always best to write the lead down, including:

Date

Name

Company

Product(s) lead is interested in

Product(s) lead already owns

Phone number

Best time to call

Relevant comments (if any; for example, "X is a customer of very long standing." or "X is the key decision maker.")

— Transmitting Leads: Essential Information —

Date:

To: *(Name)*, Sales
From: *(Name)*, Customer Service
Re: Lead on *(product 2)* sale

One of our customers, *(Name)*, who owns a *(product 1)*, mentioned that she was thinking about upgrading. Please give her a call about *(product 2)*. She's at *(phone number)*. Best to call between *(time)* and *(time)*. I told her she could expect a call by *(date)*. If you can't meet this, please advise before *(date)*, and I will reschedule to fit your needs.

———

Date:

To: *(Name)*, Sales
From: *(Name)*, Customer Service
Re: Lead on *(product)* sale

Mr. *(Name)*, of *(Name of company)* at *(phone number)*, called today seeking repair information for his *(number)*-year-old *(product)*. After giving him the information, I suggested that he consider upgrading to a new unit. He was receptive.

He is expecting a call from you. I estimated you would be in touch by *(date)*.

Date:

To: *(Name)*, Sales
From: *(Name)*, Customer Service
Re: Lead from current customer

(Name 1), who purchased a *(product)* from us in *(year)*, happened to mention that his associate, *(Name 2)*, is very interested in purchasing a *(product)*.

(Name 2's) number is *(phone number)*. His address is *(address)*. Our customer tells us that we should feel free to use his name in making this call.

Date:

To: *(Name)*, Sales
From: *(Name)*, Customer Service
Re: Sales lead

(Name) recently brought her ancient (*[number]* years old!) *(product)* in for nonwarranty repair. We have just phoned *(Name)* with a repair estimate. The cost of repair, as you might expect, is high, and I suggested to the customer that she consider purchasing a new unit.

She is expecting your call at *(phone number)*. I recommend you try to reach her by *(date)*.

— Memos: How Customer Service Can Help Your Department —

Date:

To: *(Name)*, Sales
From: *(Name)*, Customer Service
Re: Call on us for leads and sales cues

I'm writing to remind you that we in Customer Service are a great source of leads and a clearing house for customer issues and concerns. We're here to help you by serving as another link to your customers.

We invite you to check in with us on a regular basis.

———

Date:

To: *(Name)*, Sales
From: *(Name)*, Customer Service
Re: We're here to help you sell

Much of our work involves advising customers on the purchase of upgrades, accessories, and new products. We will communicate all resulting leads directly to you as quickly as possible. Feel free to call us, too—especially during slack sales periods. Often, we can heat things up.

———

Date:

To: *(Name)*, Sales
From: *(Name)*, Customer Service
Re: We're part of the product

We always try to work closely with Sales, but sometimes we forget to see the forest for the trees. Not only can we help you by transmitting leads and generating customer interest in accessories, new products, and upgrades, the fact is that Customer Service is actually part of the product you are selling.

Please: exploit us for all that we're worth. Sell the "customer Service" advantage. Consider these *specific* advantages:

   (list)

— Memos: What Customer Service Needs From You —

Date:

To: *(Name)*, Sales
From: *(Name)*, Customer Service
Re: Sharing copies of sell sheets

We want to make it easier for you to make sales. Accordingly, when the opportunity arises, we like to talk up what you are pushing with our customers. We think of this as presales preparation, and it would help us to focus our efforts in this area if we had copies of your monthly product sales goals. If we know what you are pushing, our presales conversations would mesh perfectly with your pitch and help you to close a sale more quickly.

Can you supply these on an ongoing basis?

Date:

To: *(Name)*, Sales
From: *(Name)*, Customer Service
Re: How can we offer more?

We've been urging and reminding you to sell the "Customer Service" advantage. It's a two-way street. Just as you tell Design and Marketing what it is your customers are asking for in hardware, please let us know what they want in service. What can we do better? What can we offer that we do not currently offer?

We'll endeavor to oblige.

— Memos: Communicating Customer Concerns/Comments —

Date:

To: *(Name)*, Sales
From: *(Name)*, Customer Service
Re: "High-pressure" tactics

I thought it a good idea to pass on three recent complaints from customers concerning what they all call "high-pressure" sales tactics. The comments are as follows:

   (comment 1)

   (comment 2)

   (comment 3)

To put this in perspective: during the period of *(date)* to *(date)*, when the first and last comments came in, Customer Service handled *(number)* calls. With that, I leave it to you to evaluate the significance of the comments.

––––––––––

Date:

To: *(Name)*, Sales
From: *(Name)*, Customer Service
Re: Negotiating

A number of current customers calling to inquire about related product lines have asked us about our policy on negotiating prices. We have informed them that the individual sales representative enjoys a varying amount of latitude, depending on product and quantity.

You should be aware that pricing flexibility seems to be emerging as a selling point for many customers, particularly the more experienced and sophisticated individuals. The trend for this kind of call has been upward, increasing at the compound annual rate of *(percent amount)* for the past *(number)* months.

Chapter
34

Interdepartmental
Positive Reinforcement

How to Do It

Leading the overall customer orientation means that Customer Service should foster and acknowledge positive customer-oriented trends or specific events throughout the company. Company-wide responsiveness requires effort from everyone, not just Customer Service, and, to drive the customer focus, that effort must be recognized and reinforced when it occurs.

Be especially attuned to those who make the system work, who bend or twist the existing rules, thereby formulating new and better rules for tomorrow. There are many exceptions to the rules and procedures. There are many who must use independent judgment to resolve unique problems. These folks are in engineering, production control, manufacturing, assembly, and shipping. In short, they are everywhere. Find these people and make them heroes. Ultimately, they are the ones building future profits through applied customer service.

Congratulations and positive memos are simple and pleasant to write. There are a few essential secrets to keep in mind. Number one is to be certain the praise is authentic and has real meaning. Napoleon said it almost two hundred years ago: "People will die for a ribbon." To complete that thought, people will die for a ribbon—*if* they believe in the cause. If your memo is not authentic, if you do not believe in the congratulatory position you are taking, if you are just saying nice things about the "little" people, then it is better to say nothing at all. Everyone, especially front-line people throughout the company struggling to make the system work will see through the phoniness in an instant.

The second simple secret is that to create authenticity, be certain the note relates to specific, tangible, measurable, and observable behavior. Comment precisely on what was done, achieved, or accomplished. Address the specific performance only, and offer congratulations for it. Never use patronizing (and infuriating) comments such as: "this new flexibility shows you've come a long way, but there is still plenty of room for improvement."

The third secret is to comment on behavior that is reproducible by all. Acknowledging the highly exceptional or one-in-a-million event is fine if you are also acknowledging a reasonable sample of the much smaller thousands, but still very important, moments of excellence that people produce every day.

Consider public channels with these memos. Send copies of the memo to managers, or perhaps even to the editor of the company newsletter. Don't overdo this, however, by putting *everything* in the newsletter. A solid *representative* selection of well-publicized recognition will go a long way in reinforcing the company-wide customer focus.

Remember to write from the perspective of a team member or colleague. Of course, you can also offer praise to an entire department as well.

— Congratulations on a Job Well Done —

Date:

To: *(Name)*, Advertising
From: *(Name)*, Customer Service
Re: *(Date)* ad for *(product)*

I wanted to follow up on the conversation we had on *(date)* concerning the ad modification. Because of your adjustment to the copy, the number of complaints we have received has plunged by *(percent amount)*, representing a savings of *($ amount)* per month. Not only are we saving money, customer satisfaction has to be improving. We in Customer Service appreciate the great work.

Date:

To: *(Name)*, Sales Manager
From: *(Name)*, Director of Customer Service
Re: Record for quarter

Do you recall that discussion we had on *(date)* about the incorrect spin on *(sales pitch)*? I just wanted you to know that because of your efforts, the complaint call rate has dropped by *(percent amount)*. This is representing a true savings of many dollars, to say nothing of positive P/R because our customers are no longer angry with us. Many thanks, and please extend my congratulations to the entire selling team.

––––––––––

Date:

To: *(Name)*, Design
From: *(Name)*, Customer Service
Re: *(Name)* Design Award

Congratulations on the *(Name)* Award. Not only do I think you deserve it, but, judging from the response to *(product)*, so do our customers. And that's a lot more important than what I think.

The word is out. *(Number)* customers have commented that they have heard about the award.

You've created a great product, and we're all proud to be associated with it.

––––––––––

Date:

To: *(Name)*, Shipping
From: *(Name)*, Customer Service
Re: Expedited shipment to *(Name)*

Thanks so much for getting that shipment out to *(Name)* so quickly. As you know, they're a very important account, and your extra effort made them very, very happy. You should also know that *(Name)* has referred us to *(Name 2)* in large part because of our response on the delivery problem.

— Transmitting Positive Customer Response —

Date:

To: *(Name)*, Sales
From: *(Name)*, Customer Service
Re: Happy customer

Too often, you hear from us only when we have a customer complaint to pass on. That's unfortunate, because most of the time, you do such a great job that our reward is blissful silence. But—sometimes—you make a customer so happy that he just has to tell someone.

On *(date)*, you sold a *(product)* to *(Name)*. On *(date)*, he called me. I assumed he was having an installation problem. No—he just wanted to tell the company how pleased he was with *(product)* and how "delightful and informative" the sales experience had been.

Congratulations on making a great sale and recruiting a very satisfied customer.

———————

Date:

To: *(Name)*, Design
From: *(Name)*, Customer Service
Re: Customer with good taste

We just got a special request from a customer who called in. She said, "Please tell your design department that they have done a very thoughtful job on the new *(product)*. We all love it."

Enough said!

———————

Date:

To: *(Name)*, Billing
From: *(Name)*, Customer Service
Re: Thanks for extra effort

All too often, I communicate with your department when there is some misunderstanding about an account. This time, however, the customer understands very well: You went the extra mile. *(Name)* needed back receipts for tax purposes, and you came through with the usual flying colors. She's very happy, and she sends her thanks.

— Acknowledging Improvement —

Date:

To: Quality Control staff
From: *(Name)*, Customer Service
Re: No more complaints!

I bet you were getting pretty tired of hearing from us last quarter. Well, don't reach for the aspirin this time.

I'm just dropping you a note to let you know that since you've begun the new quality control program, we have received no quality-related complaints about *(product)*. Complaints about *(product)* previously represented *(percent amount)* of our total load.

I think it's safe to conclude at this point that the measures your department took have had a tremendous effect on the quality of our product and the satisfaction of our customers.

Thanks for the great work.

———

Date:

To: *(Name)*, Shipping
From: *(Name)*, Customer Service
Re: Turnaround time

I've got at least one customer, *(Name)*, thrilled with the turnaround time on his orders. It's no wonder. You have done a splendid job of streamlining your operation and improving efficiency. I'm confident we'll be fielding a lot more calls like this one.

Date:

To: *(Name)*, Quality Control
From: *(Name)*, Customer Service
Re: *(Percent amount)* reduction in problem calls

If you want the proof that your new quality control procedures are having an effect, just compare this quarter's trouble call total with last quarter:

(provide figures)

The improvement speaks for itself. Congratulations!

— Reinforcing Improvement —

Date:

To: *(Name)*, Director of Sales
From: *(Name)*, Director of Customer Service
Re: Customer inquiry follow-up

Just the other day, I got one of those customer calls that you always hope for. It was a customer telling me how impressed he was with the prompt follow-up from your department. He had inquired on *(date)* about *(product)*, and within *(number)* hours, one of your staff called him with all the information.

The bottom line: You made the sale.

Not too long ago, the only calls our department received concerning follow-up were calls complaining that there wasn't any.

You are doing some great work.

Date:

To: *(Name)*, Shipping Manager
From: *(Name)*, Director of Customer Service
Re: Trend toward faster turnaround

I am delighted to see how quickly we're moving toward our improved turn-around goals. As you are well aware, fast turnaround is a real customer concern, and you're obviously working hard and well to give the folks what they want. Consider these statistics in your next report: The number of complaints about turnaround have dropped from *(number)* to *(number)*.

Congratulations.

— For Customer-Oriented Actions —

Date:

To: *(Name)* Head of Production
From: *(Name)* Director of Customer Service
Re: Customer-oriented action

Last week we had a serious breakdown at *(customer location)*. Ron Jones in your area was flexible enough to rush through a series of needed special parts. We shipped out the parts counter-to-counter, and our service technician managed to get the customer back on-line. Total downtime was less than 24 hours. More importantly, our super responsiveness saved our customer *($ amount)*.

And best of all, we are writing up this case and distributing it to our sales force, so that they can more effectively discuss our responsiveness with new prospects.

(Name), congratulations to Ron Jones and your entire production team. This kind of response clearly keeps us ahead of the competition.

Date:

To: *(Name)* Head of Production
From: *(Name)* Director of Customer Service
Re: Customer-oriented action

Last week we activated our new "customer-first" philosophy. As you know, the new policy established that a completely down system in the field, which is still under warranty, has priority over current shipments.

Of course, we never really want to be in this position. However, in this case, the only *(part)* available was already scheduled into final assembly for a shipment required within this period. Your people diverted the part from assembly to service parts.

Yes, our scheduled shipment had to be delayed. However, our warranty customer was up and in full production within 24 hours.

From the "customer" side, I just wanted to say thanks for your support. Missing a shipment is tough, no doubt. I will give you any support you need in defending your action.

Date:

To: *(Name)* Service Representative
From: *(Name)* Director of Customer Service
Re: Customer-oriented action

Dear *(Name)*:

I have been given a full report covering your extraordinary action last week at *(customer site)*. Even though you were blocked by our own internal procedures and regulations, using your personal initiative, you still found the resources you needed to bust through the procedural boundaries and keep the customer on-line.

You and I both know it: Rules and procedures are not designed to be arbitrarily disregarded. However, we also recognize that the organization must look at special circumstances when they arise. I appreciate your initiative.

Date:

To: *(Name)* Editor of company newsletter
From: *(Name)* Director of Customer Service
Re: Customer-oriented action

Last Sunday the plant was closed as usual. Jane Doe was in working overtime and heard our customer service line ringing as she walked by the office. She took the initiative and answered the phone.

What she found was a customer in desperate shape. *(Customer)* was late on a $250,000 shipment to *his* customer, who was literally standing by waiting for urgently needed product—remember, we're discussing fresh food here! Our production system was totally down.

Jane contacted our regional manager at home. *(Manager)* created a three-way conversation between the customer, a technician, and herself, and they determined what the problem had to be. Fortunately, the customer had spare parts on hand, and our technician talked him through a part exchange. *(Customer)* was up and running again within two hours. And to think, Jane could have walked by that ringing phone!

Let's do a story on this for the newsletter. It would benefit the entire company.

Date:

To: *(Name)* Director of Sales
From: *(Name)* Director of Customer Service
Re: Customer-oriented action

No one in sales likes to admit our system can at times go down. We don't like it, either.

Last week *(customer)* had a down machine, and we in service had no ability at all to get them up and running again. Parts just were not available.

(Name), our technician on site, called the local sales rep to see if she could help out, and help she did! She jumped on the problem, located another customer in the area with the same equipment, and managed to lease some production time from him. Thanks to *(salesperson)*, we maintained customer satisfaction.

Chapter 35

THE CORPORATE CUSTOMER SERVICE NEWSLETTER

HOW TO DO IT

We have observed several times that the mission of Customer Service is often misunderstood or understood incompletely by other departments. For this reason alone, a Customer Service interdepartmental newsletter can be highly valuable. As an ongoing definition of the department, the newsletter can facilitate cooperation and coordination between Customer Service and other departments. It also serves as a vehicle to publicize customer-oriented activity that occurs anywhere in the company.

Information and Education

The newsletter also serves two other important functions. It relates information—and coordinates action—on particular events. For example, if the company has launched a new product or project, the newsletter can be used to inform all departments of initial customer reaction to the launch. Dependent on the issues, the newsletter can be the place to update other departments on customer issues relating to the new product or project.

Finally, as Customer Service educates customers, so it can, through the newsletter, educate all employees and build the company-wide customer focus, particularly among those who have a significant degree of customer contact. The principles of effective customer service are not the sole province of the Customer Service Department. It is up to the department to see that such principles permeate and motivate the entire organization. The interdepartmental newsletter is an ideal classroom.

Something of Value

Just as you would not sit your customer down and threaten to "educate" him, you should not approach the newsletter as if it were a textbook. The more substantial "educational" articles should be offered as valuable information, a *sharing* of experience that will help your colleagues to function more effectively and creatively. These are "tips," and they should be presented as such.

Consistency of Organization

The newsletter should not degenerate into a catch-all of miscellaneous information, but like any other professional periodical, should be divided into regular "departments": perhaps beginning with news, then some "educational" features, then some procedural reminders (such as how and when to call Customer Service or now Customer Service can help). It is also highly effective to have the authors sign their articles. You don't want the departmental personality to overshadow the personalities of the individuals who make up the department. Further, be certain to include customer-oriented copy developed by those in other departments.

— *Service News:* Two Sample Issues —

1

CUSTOMER SERVICE HELPS LAUNCH 300 DPI COLOR DYE SUBLIMATION PRINTER
By *Kimmel E. Howard*

Now that the new 300 DPI Color Dye Sublimation Printer has been released, Customer Service is working to see that the launch is a great success.

We are providing leads to Sales

We are listening to customer response and communicating with Design, Engineering, and Marketing

We are helping our customers get the very most our unit has to offer

One feature our customers have picked up on is the photographic quality of the printer output. It is this above everything else that motivates most of our customers to invest their $9,000 in the unit. Our representatives have been very impressed by the level of sophistication among our customers and the degree to which they want to control every aspect of output: color, tint, intensity, contrast, and sharpness.

Customer support for this unit is proving to be a demanding, but very rewarding assignment, and we appreciate all the help we've gotten from Design and Engineering. For all those communicating with customers about the 300 DPI, be certain to stress how much control they have over output. Based on preliminary results, control is the hot-button issue.

A TIP FROM CUSTOMER SERVICE
By *Anne Franklin*

A big part of customer service is simply getting information and transmitting it to the right person. Any employee who takes a customer's call should do the following:

1. Note the time and date of the call.

2. Always get a phone number, even if the caller says the intended "callee" already has it.

3. Obtain a best time for the callee to reach the caller.

4. Get some specific information about the subject, so that the callee can do some preliminary work before returning the call.

5. Tell the caller you *will* deliver the message. (Then do so personally.)

WHAT IS A CUSTOMER?
By *Michael Ramundo*

Fighting everyday pressures and frustrations sometimes makes us lose perspective about the meaning of our jobs. Whether in a not-for-profit agency providing services, in a consumer products company manufacturing perfume, or in a hospital performing surgery, servicing the customer is why all jobs exist.

The customer is the person or entity writing the check.

In a high-tech computer manufacturing organization, positive customer servicing does not mean doing the minimum expected to keep the consumer from being upset with us; positive service means doing the maximum you can possibly afford to do.

The customer, the user of the service, is the most important person in the organization. She is not dependent on the organization; the organization is dependent upon her.

The customer is not an interruption; he is the purpose of all our work, and does us a favor when he calls. We are not doing him a favor by serving.

The customer is a partner in any business or service entity. He is not an outsider or a statistic; he is a flesh and blood human being with feelings and emotions just like our own.

The customer is not someone with whom to argue or match wits. She is a person who brings us her wants and needs; furthermore, she *pays* us to fulfill them.

The customer is deserving of the most courteous and attentive treatment we can give because he is the lifeblood of this and every other business, organization, or service.

GETTING IN TOUCH WITH CUSTOMER SERVICE

Just dial extension 2345, or drop by the third floor. We'd love to see you.

2

THINK OF US AS CUSTOMER EDUCATORS
By *Ellen Lowry*

If there is one thing our new line of software has demonstrated, it's that Customer Service is not just the "Complaint Department" anymore. Customer service representatives still handle problems, but increasingly, our time is spent educating and training customers. We spend less time fixing and more time teaching.

Training the customer does not stop with a one-time demonstration or a quick review of the technical manual. Prudent customer servicing means building on-going training into the total product sale and customer satisfaction process.

This is not a grim necessity, but a center of profit and a great selling point.

To continue to be competitive in this decade and in the coming century, selling the most advanced technology will be important. But it will not be enough. The successful company will sell the most advanced technology and the *application* of that technology as a single comprehensive product.

TIP FROM CUSTOMER SERVICE
By *Edgar Reiss*

Do you ever get a customer or client who drives you crazy?

Customers, bosses, and others do not "make" us angry. We *choose* to get angry. We can't always choose what happens to us, but we *can* choose our reaction to what happens to us. Here's a strategy for choice:

1. **Stop.** Notice that you are getting angry.

2. **Identify.** What aspect of the other's message is hooking you and why?

3. **Remember.** Anger is a secondary emotion. Focus on the feeling behind the anger.

Take time to dissipate energy. If you must respond, do so by sharing your feelings, using "I" messages: "I feel . . ."

What does it mean to lose your temper?

It means that you have given up on all other alternatives. It also means you may be very sorry later.

KEEP IN TOUCH

We're at extension 2345. We're here to serve customers—and to help *you* serve customers.

IF YOU PICK UP THE PHONE, YOU OWN THE CALL
By *Michael Ramundo*

As a customer, how many times have you played "runaround" on the phone with a vendor?

You know the scenario: you call the company and explain your situation to whomever answers. That person directs your call to the proper place. Once you are transferred, you explain the nature of your call again, only to be told that you've reached the wrong department. After the third transfer and subsequent explanation, you've finally reached the right department only to be told that the people you need are not available and could you please call back later? Yep! That's called creating dissatisfied customers.

This "runaround" wastes customers' time, and if there is anything at all consistent in customer satisfaction surveys, it is that customers *hate* to have their time wasted.

Runaround situations can be offset. However, because an attitude or culture change is called for, it does require a commitment and maybe someone or a department to champion the cause.

We in Customer Service devised the principle of "call ownership" to help CSRs (or anyone else, including managers) understand the runaround game and start killing it. Call ownership is a simple concept that does not increase corporate costs and takes very little effort. It goes a long way in creating customer satisfaction without adding a nickel to corporate costs. Try it in your department. We think you'll like it.

What does call ownership mean? Simply put, if you pick up a ringing phone, you *own* the problem either until it is resolved, or until you can sell it to someone else. You cannot delegate the problem; i.e., "It's not my job." You must sell it. Selling it means you must find someone who can take action or accept responsibility for the issue.

You say you don't have the time to accept call ownership today? Well, then don't pick up the phone. Or to state it another way: It's not fair for the customer to pay for our poor planning. Let's discuss what implementation of this philosophy really means given differing situations.

You pick up the call and can handle the problem—Super! This is the easy one. Deal with the issue right now, resolve it, and put it to bed forever. Incidentally, don't forget to follow up if follow-up is necessary. Try to find a way to eliminate the problem from recurring in the future.

You cannot handle the issue. The call is for your colleague who is currently unavailable—Well, you still own the call and simply listening to the issue and advising the caller that "Charlie will get back" wastes time and is not good enough; the customer will need to repeat later to Charlie what he just told you. Even if the call eventually gets to Charlie, if you understand that you own the call, then you must do some basic research work for

Charlie. Specifically, get key details covering basics such as name, number, callback time, and include in those details *what the caller wants*. In short, give Charlie a starting point. Send the message to Charlie, and be certain to follow up with Charlie to ensure that he did indeed return the call as promised.

You cannot handle the issue. The call is for another department—Well, you picked up the phone, and you still own the call! The customer took time educating you on the issue. Use your new education to educate someone else. Don't just transfer the call to the appropriate department. Put the customer on hold (be sure to give him an estimate of the amount of time he will be on hold) and call ahead. Brief whomever you get on the situation at hand and be sure to include the customer's name. Only transfer the call after you have "sold" the other department that they should be the new owners. If they are not the correct source, check elsewhere. Find the correct source before sending your call away.

After listening to the customer's issue, you have no idea who is qualified to handle the problem—Sorry, you picked up the phone, and you still own the call—no one ever said customer servicing was easy, or a job that does not require extensive professionalism. It's time for homework. Get the information, ask questions, and put the facts in writing. Explain to the customer what you do and do not know, explain when you or someone else will get back with her, then start digging. You own the call until you can find a solution. Talk to people. Someone in your company has to have a solution. When the solution is found, either you or the person you sold the call to must get back to the customer with the solution. Incidentally, be sure to get back at the agreed time even if you do not yet have the promised solution. To the customer, while a solution is required ultimately, progress reports are better than nothing at all.

So, all this will take you more time. We agree that each individual call will likely, on average, take a bit more time. However, positive customer serving is a corporate activity made up of *individual* activities. So, even though each individual call will take more time, the corporation as a whole will receive fewer calls because the game of runaround is being eliminated.

Does the system only work if everyone does it correctly? Yes. Individuals cause systems to change. The important questions are: When, where, and with whom do we start?

Part Five

Public Relations

Chapter 36

SAFETY ISSUES

HOW TO DO IT

Coordinating and transmitting safety information is one of the most important Customer Service functions. As with product recalls, communications regarding safety must be absolutely authoritative and take into account all possible liability issues. Customer Service representatives should not take it upon themselves to issue opinions regarding the safety of a procedure or product. All such statements should be founded in verifiable research confirmed by tested engineering and must be part and parcel of a consistent company-wide policy. Before any safety pronouncement is made—whether on a product label or as part of the information a Customer Service representative may share with customers—the appropriate in-house experts and out-of-house professionals should be consulted in the areas of technology and application as well as law and liability.

Letters Responding to Safety Issues

Letters are an ideal medium for responding to safety issues. They promote greater clarity than a phone conversation, and they set remarks (and warnings) down in writing. They also allow sufficient time to research an issue, to ensure that the response given is correct in every way. Further—and this is very important—letters provide a "paper trail," which is critical if the issue ends up in litigation.

All safety issues must be taken seriously. None should be dismissed as "silly." Be very careful to avoid a defensive tone. Instead, adopt the stance of an eagerness to cooperate with the correspondent to promote the safe and efficient use of the company's product. However, do not be afraid to take a firm stance when necessary. As a general rule, protecting the public safety will be more important than making the customer happy.

Press Releases

If the responsibility of issuing safety-related press releases falls to Customer Service, it is first necessary for the customer service professional to obtain all relevant documentation from various departments. Usually, a legal review is also appropriate, although the release should not be filled with legal jargon.

Safety memos should be approached, first and foremost, as efforts at public service education and, secondarily, as public relations and publicity opportunities. In explaining the safe use of your product, you should promote the inherent safety of the product as a product feature. To be sure, safety memos should not distort or disguise important safety information, but in showing how to use your product safely, you are not so much pointing out potential hazards as you are demonstrating that the product is so well made that it can be used effectively and safely.

Memos Conveying Public Concerns

Customer Service is an important set of eyes and ears for the company. Many times, it is a customer service representative who is the first to learn of important issues of concern to customers and public alike, including those related to safety. All significant safety-related issues raised by customers and others should be reported to the appropriate departments.

Memos reporting safety-related issues should be crystal clear:

1. State subject.

2. State source of information.

3. Provide context (customer calling about another issue mentioned the safety-related one; customer was injured; and so on).

4. Mention related calls. Has Customer Service received other calls on this issue?

Memos to Public Relations

It is not up to Customer Service to tell Public Relations how to treat a particular safety-related issue. However, Customer Service should attempt to present—and represent—to Public Relations the customer's point of view on issues of safety. This is the thrust of memos to that department.

— Letters to Concerned Individuals/Groups Regarding Products —

Dear *(Name)*:

Thank you for your letter of *(date)*, in which you express a very reasonable concern about the safety of our Model 54 Power Saw.

Concerning the Model 54, and all our power tools, two points must be kept in mind:

1. All power tools do a tremendous amount of work. However, their intended use is such that extreme care must always be taken to minimize the potential for personal injury.

2. We design our power tools to be the safest in the industry—and that very definitely includes the Model 54.

What this means *(Name)*, is that no matter which safety features we or any other manufacturer build into a unit like the Model 54, the key safety component is the extreme care that the user must always exercise. Our design facilitates safe, intelligent operation, but cannot absolutely prevent careless operation. Power tool safety is an equation with the equipment and benefits on one side and the user and safety practice on the other.

I *can* assure you that as far as engineering and materials are concerned, it is the safest power tool available.

Here are the special safety features of the Model 54 and what they do:

Special heavy-gauge construction—ensures structural integrity and prevents breakage.

Auto-stop clutch—stops the blade within one-quarter turn.

Fully adjustable finger guard—automatically adjusts blade depth to the thickness of the work.

Approved circuitry—maximum electrical safety with built-in secondary ground to protect operator.

Audible alignment indicator—emits a high-pitched whine if the blade is out of alignment.

In summary *(Name)*, used intelligently, the Model 54 is the safest portable power saw you can buy. However, it is a very powerful saw and must be treated with due respect. If used incorrectly, it can cause injury.

If you have any further questions, please contact me at *(phone number)*.

Sincerely,

Dear *(Name)*:

Thank you for your letter concerning the outdoor use of our Penetrator Cordless Drill.

Your question concerning safety is an easy one to answer: The Penetrator Cordless Drill is safe to use out of doors. Once it is detached from its recharging unit, the unit is a low-voltage appliance. It is also double insulated, so that most weather conditions will not affect operation.

While the Penetrator Cordless Drill is safe to use in all weather, it is a good idea to provide some protection in inclement weather. Frequent exposure to moisture or severe environmental conditions will shorten its life and reduce the efficiency of its batteries.

Sincerely,

Dear *(Name)*:

Thank you for your recent letter concerning the safety of our motorized toys.

At *(Name of company)*, your child's safety is our greatest concern. We protect your child by:

1. Labeling all our products for age appropriateness. Please note the package label.

2. Building for durability, using materials that will not create sharp edges or shatter.

3. Providing full instructions and safety documentation.

Of course, virtually any product can be abused to the point of creating a hazard. However, with normal use—and by "normal," we mean by a child of appropriate age (see package labeling)—our motorized toys are among the very safest in the industry.

You may buy them and let your child play with them with complete confidence after you have ensured that your child completely understands the safety documentation, which is enclosed with every toy.

Sincerely,

— Press Releases Concerning Product Safety: General —

Contact: James Smith, Director of Customer Service
(phone number)

FOR IMMEDIATE RELEASE
SUN LIGHTING BEGINS NEW PRODUCT SAFETY
ASSURANCE PROGRAM

Sun Valley, Idaho, May 15, 19__, Janice Hamilton, vice-president in charge of consumer affairs, Sun Lighting, today announced her company's new Product Safety Assurance Program, designed to bring lighting and lighting control devices to unprecedented levels of safety.

"Let's face it," Hamilton said, "few people give any thought to lighting safety. But the fact is that lighting-related accidents kill or injure ___ people each and every year. We cannot continue to take lighting safety for granted, and we owe it to our customers to make it a top-priority design and manufacturing issue."

Hamilton pointed out that Sun Lighting has a safety record unmatched in the industry. She also observed that all Sun Lighting products currently meet or *exceed* government safety standards.

"But meeting government standards isn't enough," Hamilton stated. "And exceeding them isn't enough either. We want to set all-new standards. Not just for Sun Lighting, but for the entire industry."

Hamilton announced that the first phase of the safety program would be conducted over a 12-month period and would concentrate on:

Insulation safety

Inert gas safety

Fire safety

Electrical shock hazard

Spontaneous bulb explosion hazards

Structural safety

She further stressed that all safety-related developments produced by the program would remain free of patent protection and would be made available industry-wide.

"Safety is more than a dollars-and-cents issue," Hamilton said. "But it is also true—thank goodness—that safety sells, and whatever promotes safety in our industry, promotes sales for Sun Lighting."

Contact: Joanne Duncan, Director of Customer Service
(phone number)

FOR IMMEDIATE RELEASE
VITAWORLD INTRODUCES NEW TAMPER-RESISTANT PACKAGING

(Place, Date) More Customers familiar with Vitaworld's famous red-and-gold bottle will find something new: a bright yellow safety-seal band.

"We decided to introduce the new safety seal to ensure freshness and to protect consumers against possible tampering," said company vice president for marketing J. K. Sprockett. "It's a major investment in peace of mind, and we are using it on all our vitamin products."

The new packaging will begin to appear in stores by *(date)* and will be universally available by *(date)*.

Contact: Eddie Langford, Director of Customer Service
(phone number)

<u>*FOR IMMEDIATE RELEASE*</u>

ANYTOWN PUBLIC SERVICE OFFERS ELECTRICAL SAFETY CLASSES

(Place, Date) Beginning *(date)*, Anytown Public Service Electric Company will offer special one-hour classes in electrical safety around the home. Classes will be offered on the following dates and at the following places:

(list)

Topics covered include:

How to recognize house wiring problems

How to recognize problems with appliances

What to do when the circuit breaker trips

What to do in an electrical emergency

Many other topics

"The electric power industry is obsessed with safety," said company president Harry Moore, "and that's the way it should be. But a concern for safety shouldn't end with delivery of power to the consumer. We have an obligation to share our safety knowledge with the public in their homes."

For further information on these free classes, call Anytown Public Service at *(phone number)*.

— Press Releases Concerning Product Safety: Specific Product —

Contact: Sarah Moran, Director of Customer Service
Super Solvent, Inc.
(phone number)

FOR IMMEDIATE RELEASE

SUPER SOLVENT ANNOUNCES NEW BIODEGRADABLE FORMULA

For 30 years, Super Solvent has been marketed as "The Solution" for industrial-strength solvent needs. One of the key features of Super Solvent has always been its relatively low level of toxicity—much less toxicity than any other comparable industrial solvent.

Now, after a 5-year research and development program, the Super Solvent formula not only features a low level of toxicity, it is completely biodegradable according to the latest EPA standards.

"This is an unprecedented development in high-performance industrial solvents," company president C. Fred Green stated. "And the really remarkable thing is that the new biodegradable formula actually *improves* Super Solvent's organic degreasing power." Green continued: "In every other way, Super Solvent is the same effective product it has always been."

The new biodegradable Super Solvent demonstrates the 30-year-old firm's commitment to excellence that includes user safety and environmental safety.

"Our commitment to these values will never diminish," company president Green concluded.

Contact: Sarah Ford Henley, Director of Customer Service
(phone number)

FOR IMMEDIATE RELEASE

ANYBANK INSTALLS 24-HOUR SURVEILLANCE AT ATM FACILITIES

(Place, Date) Anybank has installed sophisticated, centrally monitored video surveillance cameras at its 12 ATM (Automated Teller Machine) facilities throughout the metropolitan Anytown area.

"We are very fortunate to live in a generally safe community," bank president Gina Fowler said. "We've installed the new equipment to help keep it that way."

Fowler and other bank officials stressed that the installation is a preventive measure and not a response to a crime report.

"Why should we wait for an incident? Let's be proactive in this. Let's practice deterrence. Let's give our customers not only the convenience of ATMs, but an added dimension of security and peace of mind," Fowler remarked.

— Memos: Transmitting/Summarizing Public Concerns —

Date:

To: All Customer Service Representatives
From: *(Name)*, Director of Customer Service
Re: Public concern over small parts in *(Product name)* toy

Recent stories in the media concerning the choking hazards presented by toys with small parts have caused understandable alarm among many parents. It is possible that some of you will receive calls from individuals concerned about the safety of our toys.

1. Please treat all such calls with considerate and serious attention.

2. Advise the caller to pay careful attention to the age-appropriate labeling on all our toys. (A checklist is attached.)

3. Advise the caller to read and review all *Owner's Manual* directions with the child, and to be certain the child understands how the toy should be used.

4. Advise the caller that all our toys meet or exceed federal safety regulations and guidelines.

5. Advise the caller that safety is our highest priority and that our toys are engineered and manufactured with safety in mind.

Date:

To: All Customer Service Representatives
From: *(Name)*, Director of Customer Service
Re: Fire hazard with refinishing products

The public is very reasonably concerned about possible fire hazards when using the following refinishing products:

(list)

If you receive any calls concerning fire hazard issues and these products, please respond with the following information:

1. Yes, all of these products contain solvents that are volatile and therefore flammable. These products cannot perform their function without these petroleum-based flammable solvents.

2. *(Name of company)* provides extensive and explicit safety instructions on the packaging of each of these products. This safety information must be read and heeded or serious personal injury may result.

3. Adequate ventilation is the single most significant fire-prevention step users of these products must take.

4. These products must not be used within *(number)* feet of open flame or other heat source.

5. These products should not be applied while electrical heating appliances are in use anywhere in the area.

6. Avoid applying these products in areas there is the potential for electric spark.

7. Do not power-sand surfaces to which these products have been applied *until* those surfaces are completely dry. (Wait a minimum of *[number]* days before power sanding.)

8. Assure customers that our products meet or exceed all relevant fire safety labeling requirements.

9. End by emphasizing the necessity of following safety directions on the product packaging. Urge customers to *stop use* and *call you* if they have any additional questions concerning the safe use of these products.

———————

Date:

To: All Customer Service Representatives
From: *(Name)*, Director of Customer Service
Re: Ladder safety

A recent story on television's *"Heads Up!"* program about unsafe ladders has sparked a number of customer calls concerning our Extendo line of ladders. Here is some helpful information for use in responding to questions you may be asked:

1. Extendo ladders were *not* a subject of the program.

2. Extendo ladders are carefully designed, tested, and built in the U.S.A., using only high-quality materials.

3. Used according to directions, Extendo ladders are as safe as any ladders can be.

4. Like any other tool, ladders—even Extendo ladders—can be abused to the point of causing a hazard.

5. Follow safety directions attached to each Extendo ladder product.

— Memos: To Public Relations Department —

Date:

To: *(Name)*, Director of Public Relations
From: *(Name)*, Director of Customer Service
Re: Toy safety concerns

You should be aware that a number of our Customer Service representatives have received calls from parents concerned about the safety of our toy line for children under 3 years of age. This concern is apparently in response to recent stories in the media focusing on choking hazards.

We have alerted our representatives and have issued guidelines for responding to callers. A copy is attached. However, I believe the matter is of sufficient concern that your department should consider action. We need to be out in front on this issue. For example, during the past *(time period)*, we have logged *(number)* of calls, representing *(percent amount)* of total load, on this issue alone. This issue is currently consuming *($ amount)* of all available resources per month and shows signs of increasing in importance.

Date:

To: *(Name)*, Director of Public Relations
From: *(Name)*, Director of Customer Service
Re: Safety of *(product)*

In light of recent media reports on faulty *(products)*, it is important that we issue a press release demonstrating the safety of our line. Customer service representatives have been receiving safety-related calls concerning *(product)* at the rate of *(number)* per day. This type of call is consuming *(percent amount)* of all available resources and is increasing.

We need to act quickly and decisively.

Chapter 37

PRODUCT RECALLS

HOW TO DO IT

As is the case with all safety-related issues, careful consultation with in-house experts and out-of-house professionals must be completed before issuing a recall, whether safety-related or quality-related. It is crucial to ensure the safety of consumers and to understand and limit your company's liability exposure. This is no time for guesswork.

Press Releases

As was observed in connection with the recall and safety issues addressed in Chapter 11, a recall can be a public relations catastrophe or an opportunity to build or reinforce a positive corporate image by demonstrating honesty and an overriding concern for consumer safety and uncompromising product quality.

The recall press release should accomplish the following:

1. Make crystal clear what is being recalled and why.

2. Convey unmistakably that the company is master of the situation, that the recall is not a collective corporate *OOPS!* but a rational step in an ongoing program of quality control, responsiveness to consumers, and a clear sense of public responsibility and corporate accountability.

3. To the degree that it is possible to do so, the press release should present the recall as an opportunity to upgrade and improve the product. Stress *opportunity,* not avoidance of liability.

Letters Responding to Public and Customer Concerns

The same approach that governs recall-related press releases should also direct letters in response to various recall issues.

1. Take all questions seriously.

2. Provide the appropriate information as clearly as possible.

3. Without distortion, attempt to place the recall in the context of service—an opportunity for service, for product improvement, for instance—rather than as an irritating chore the customer must perform because of the company's error.

— Press Release for a Safety-Related Recall —
(NAME OF COMPANY) RECALLS *(PRODUCT)*

FOR RELEASE: *(date)*
RELEASE NUMBER: *(number)*
PRODUCT: *(description)*
PROBLEM: *(narrative description of hazard)*
WHAT TO DO: *(describe action consumers should take)*

Dateline—In cooperation with the U. S. Consumer Product Safety Commission (CPSC), *(Name of company)*, *(city, state, zip)*, is voluntarily recalling *(product)*. The *(product)* can present a *(describe hazard)*.

(Name of company) has received *(number)* reports of *(type of injuries, harm)* to users of the product. These incidents occurred when *(describe)*.

The *(products)* were sold nationwide *(in specific region, etc.)* from *(date)* to *(date)* in major retail stores *(or other outlets)*. Approximately *(number)* products are believed to be in use by consumers.

Consumers should stop use of affected products and should return them to *(Name of company)*. Consumers who need information can call 1–800–555–5555 toll free. *(Name of company)* will replace or repair the affected products free of charge.

Contact: *(Name)*, *(Name of company)* Customer Service

— Press Releases Announcing Quality-Related Recall —

FOR IMMEDIATE RELEASE
(NAME OF COMPANY) ANNOUNCES *(PRODUCT)* UPGRADE PROGRAM

(Date) In a bold move to assure the highest possible quality of its new *(product)*, *(Name of company)* announced a no-charge upgrade program for product owners.

According to *(Name)*, director of Quality Assurance for *(Name of company)*, "Tests in our ongoing quality-assurance program have indicated that the *(component name)* in a significant percentage of *(products)* does not perform up to our exacting specifications. We have earned and realize we must *keep* earning our reputation as the finest producer of *(products)* in the world. Therefore, we are asking our customers to take a few moments to bring their *(product)* to any authorized dealer before *(date)*. The dealer will install a new, upgraded *(component name)*."

In most cases, the replacement of *(component name)*, which is made at no cost to the consumer, can be performed in a matter of minutes. However, customers are urged to call their dealer before bringing the unit in.

(Name of company) has set up a special Customer Answer Line to handle any questions about this quality-related recall. Dial *(phone number)* during regular business hours.

Contact: *(Name)*, *(Name of company)* Customer Service

FOR IMMEDIATE RELEASE
(NAME OF COMPANY) INVITES *(PRODUCT)* OWNERS TO A
FREE QUALITY CHECK

(Place, Date) In response to scattered reports of quality-control problems with some of its *(products)*, *(Name of company)* extended an invitation to those *(product)* owners who feel it has not performed as expected to bring their units to any authorized dealer for a free quality check. If any problems are detected, they will be corrected free of charge.

"This is not a safety-related issue," company president *(Name)* remarked. "But we do want owners of our *(product)* to know we stand behind it. We want to assure owners that they are getting all of the reliability and durability designed into these units."

For a list of conveniently located authorized dealers, customers are advised to call *(phone number)*. This free program will continue for *(time period)*, after which time *(company)* will evaluate customer response.

— Letters: Responding to Safety-Related Recall Issues —

Dear *(Name)*:

Thank you for your letter concerning the recall of *(product)*.

We are recalling *only* those units manufactured between *(date)* and *(date)*, as only these units have the problem: *(describe problem)*. The manufacturing date is located on a metal plate behind the *(part)*. If the manufacture date of your unit does not fall within these dates, there is no need for the *(component)* to be replaced. If the manufacture date does fall within this span, we ask you to stop using the *(product)* and to please bring it immediately to *(location)* for service.

If you have any questions—or are unable to determine the date of manufacture—please call Customer Service at *(phone number)*.

Sincerely,

––––––––––

Dear *(Name)*:

Thank you for your letter concerning the recall of your *(product)*.

On *(date)*, *(Name of company)* announced a recall of all *(products)* manufactured between *(date)* and *(date)*. The reason for this recall is a possible defect in *(part)*.

(Name of company) urges you to bring your *(product)* to any authorized dealer for a free safety check. If *(part)* is found to be defective, it will be replaced free of charge.

This recall applies only to *(products)* manufactured between *(date)* and *(date)*; however, you may bring *any* *(product)* to an authorized dealer for a free safety check at this time.

Sincerely,

Dear *(Name)*:

Thank you for your letter of *(date)* inquiring about *(Name of company's)* announced recall of *(product)*.

I agree with you that having to bring your *(product)* to the dealer for replacement of *(component)* is a "hassle." However, *(Name of company)* must ask in the strongest terms that you do this as soon as possible. It is a fact that *(component)* has not tested up to specifications and that, therefore, premature failure of the part can be anticipated. We cannot tell you precisely *when* the component is likely to fail, but we believe the failure will occur. That is why we are recalling *(product)*.

Why not afford yourself the peace of mind that comes with knowing that your *(product)* is operating as safely and efficiently as it was designed to?

Sincerely,

Dear *(Name)*:

Thank you for your letter concerning our recall of *(product)*.

To answer your question: The recall was ordered by us and reported to the appropriate governmental agencies. We are obligated to protect the public safety. It is a company-initiated recall based on the results of our ongoing quality tests, which indicate that *(part)* may fail unexpectedly, possibly posing a personal injury hazard. We are reporting our concerns to the *(Name of government agency)*.

We urge you to comply with this recall request. The replacement of *(part)* is a simple matter and can be performed by your authorized dealer while you wait.

The authorized dealers closest to you are:

(list)

If you have any further questions, please call Customer Service at *(phone number)* or call your local dealer.

Sincerely,

Dear *(Name)*:

(Name of company) apologizes for the inconvenience caused by this recall, but we believe that in the interest of the continued safe operation of your *(product)*, a factory-authorized safety check is important at this time.

We have reason to believe that *(part)* in some units may be subject to structural failure. This possibility poses a safety hazard for users of the *(product)*.

We have reported our concerns to *(Name of government agency)*, and *(Name of company)* urges owners of *(product)* to stay on the safe side by allowing a factory-authorized representative to check out your unit.

You may take the unit to your local dealer—in your area, *(Name of dealer)* at *(address and phone)*. To assure prompt service, please call ahead before bringing the unit in.

Sincerely,

— Letters: Responding to Quality-Related Recall Issues —

Dear *(Name)*:

Thank you for your inquiry concerning our invitation to bring your *(product)* to an authorized service center for a complete quality recheck.

Our motivation in providing this invitation is to ensure that your *(product)* performs as you—and we—expect it to. Testing in our laboratories turned up a small percentage of *(products)* that did not perform up to specifications. Although small, the percentage was significant enough to prompt us to offer this quality recheck opportunity.

Whether or not you accept this invitation, your original warranty remains in force. Please note that to take advantage of this offer, you must bring your *(product)* in before the expiration of your original warranty.

Sincerely,

— Memos: Transmitting/Summarizing Customer Concerns —

Date:

To: All Customer Service Representatives
From: *(Name)*, Director of Customer Service
Re: Customer resistance to recall of *(product)*

The percentage of customers responding to our recent recall of *(product)* is quite low: *(percent amount)*. While this recall is quality related—and the *(product)* presents absolutely no hazard to users—*(Name of company)* deems customer compliance important to preserving the integrity of *(product)*. In short, we want all those units out there working exactly as they should.

Customers' main resistance to the recall is based on the inconvenience of having to make a trip to the dealer. Please impress on any callers who raise this issue that the opportunity *(Name of company)* is providing significantly outweighs any relatively minor inconvenience. Customers who have the upgrade performed will enjoy *(percent amount)* increased efficiency and can expect a significantly greater life from their *(product)*.

We will be sending another set of recall notices beginning on *(date)*. These will urge customers to call Customer Service if they have any questions. Please be prepared to encourage compliance with the recall.

———

Date:

To: All Customer Service Representatives
From: *(Name)*, Director of Customer Service
Re: Maintaining positive feelings about *(product)*

One of the dangers of a recall is that the customer loses faith in the product. Let's try to avert this by being very specific about the extent of the recall. Always refer to the action as a recall to replace *(part)*, not as a recall of a faulty or unsafe product. Make it clear that *(part)* has not tested consistently up to *our* standards; therefore, we have *chosen* to replace it in order to ensure that *(product)* meets the customer's expectations as well as our own.

———

Date:

To: All Customer Service Representatives
From: *(Name)*, Director of Customer Service
Re: Delay at dealers

Several customers have called complaining of dealer delays in completing the upgrade work required by the recall of *(product)*. Please advise any customers who call concerning the recall to (1) call the dealer before bringing the unit in, and (2) try to come in during nonpeak time periods: *(days and times)*.

Assure customers that we are doing our best to expedite the upgrade procedure.

— Memos: Transmitting/Summarizing Public Concerns —

Date:

To: All Customer Service Representatives
From: *(Name)*, Director of Customer Service
Re: Public perception of *(Name of company)*

A recall can be a public relations disaster—or an asset. And it is up to us to choose which it will be.

It is probable that you will receive calls not just from customers, but from the public—that is, *prospective customers*—concerning the recent recall of *(product)*. How you respond to these calls will, in large measure, determine whether this recall campaign shakes out as a disaster or an asset.

You do not want to project a defensive image or a reactive image. Instead, you want callers to feel that *(Name of company)* has taken a proactive step on its own initiative to ensure that its product is of the highest quality.

Please leave your caller feeling that this recall campaign is a bold and ethical action from a company that puts its customers before every other consideration.

Please leave your caller feeling our collective sense of commitment—our refusal to build something, sell it, then abandon it as "somebody else's problem." We're in for the long haul, not the quick sale, and we are responsible members of a business community.

Respond to your callers in this spirit, and you will make this recall what it is in reality: a positive step for the company and for the customer.

———

Date:

To: All Customer Service Representatives
From: *(Name)*, Director of Customer Service
Re: Public safety concerns

One of our representatives fielded a call recently from a concerned individual worried about owners of *(product)* who do not comply with our much-publicized safety recall.

While we cannot compel customers to comply with the recall program, we must urge compliance by fully explaining the hazard using the terms in our recall letter of *(date)*, a copy of which is attached.

— Memos: To Public Relations Department —

Date:

To: *(Name)*, Public Relations
From: *(Name)*, Director of Customer Service
Re: Customer response to safety-related recall of *(product)*

We in Customer Service are very gratified by the customer response to the recall of *(product)*. Customers are bringing their units in for retrofitting, and they are responding positively to the recall campaign as an opportunity to upgrade their *(product)* rather than as something they have to do to fix a mistake.

We suggest that you consider actually playing up this recall campaign, thanking customers for loyalty and cooperation, reiterating the critical safety importance of this recall, and assuring all concerned that this recall campaign is evidence of *(Name of company's)* commitment to quality and commitment to its customers.

———

Date:

To: All Customer Service Representatives
From: *(Name)*, Director of Customer Service
Re: Avoid term *recall* in referring to quality-related action

Please note that *(Name of company)* has deemed the quality-control action of *(date)* a product upgrade rather than a recall. Please use the term *upgrade* instead of *recall,* which has strong negative connotations and may also mislead the public into confusing this quality-motivated action with a safety-motivated one.

Chapter 38

Environmental Issues

How to Do It

Gone are the days when industry was the implacable enemy of the environment. It is not just that many businesses have learned to be responsible residents on planet earth, it is also that business has learned how profitable it can be to demonstrate a concern for the environment. People enjoy working with and buying from public-spirited, highly responsible companies. There was a time when the nation's auto makers insisted that they could not *sell* safety. Customers were interested in tail fins, not seat belts, let alone air bags. Nowadays, safety features are major selling points. The same trend holds true for the environment. People want to buy environmentally sound products from environmentally responsible companies.

Promoting Environmental Responsibility

If your company has a sound environmental policy, show it off proudly. Promote it as vigorously as you would promote any other positive product value. Emphasize that to do business with your company is to enter into a win-win transaction.

Responding to Particular Issues

As with safety and recall issues, it is important to respond with great care to customer queries concerning environmental policies or the environmental impact of particular programs and products. Make certain that there is a factual basis for any and all assertions. Always answer particular questions in the context of a greater corporate environmental policy. Make it clear that respect for the environment is a key element in how the company does business and manufactures goods.

It is possible that customer service representatives will be asked to respond to environmental issues that seem frivolous or "off the wall." These should not be dismissed. If it is impossible to respond in detail, point for point, to a question, respond with a general statement of corporate policy regarding the environment. The point is *to respond.*

Transmitting Customer and Public Concerns

Depending on the kind of business your company is in, the public may have prejudices and preconceptions about the impact your company has on the environment. Such preconceptions often produce unfounded fears and rumors to which, as one set of eyes and ears, Customer Service should endeavor to become sensitive. Any concerns that have a degree of substance should be conveyed to the appropriate departments.

— Press Releases Addressing General Policy —

Contact: *(Name)*, Director of Customer Service

FOR IMMEDIATE RELEASE

(NAME OF COMPANY) TO ACCEPT HOUSEHOLD
HAZARDOUS WASTE ON *(DATE)*

(Place, Date) (Name of company), one of the area's major chemical laboratories, announced today that on *(date)*, it will accept household hazardous waste for disposal. Residents of *(list communities)* are invited to bring the following waste to the *(Name of company)* disposal facility on *(date)*:

(list substances)

Please note that the following materials will not be accepted for disposal:

(list materials)

(Name 1), vice president for environmental affairs at *(Name of company)*, announced this special program in cooperation with the County Environmental Protection Agency.

"We are delighted to offer this service to our community," *(Name 1)* remarked. "We plan to provide this service annually."

(Name 2), county executive, praised the program. "The biggest source of soil and water pollution in our community is the home—especially careless disposal of such hazardous material as paint, paint thinner, cleaning supplies, and so on. *(Name of company's)* generosity in making its state-of-the-art disposal facilities available will go a long way toward reducing pollution."

For more information about this program, call *(phone number)*.

———————

Contact: *(Name)*, Customer Service

FOR IMMEDIATE RELEASE
(NAME OF COMPANY) BANS FOAM PEANUTS!

(Place, Date) (Name of company), a major supplier of *(product)*, announced today a major change in shipping policy. Effective immediately, *(Name of company)* Shipping Department will use only biodegradable products for shock absorbence rather than the more familiar "foam peanuts."

"As responsible members of this community—and residents of this planet, we want to do everything we can to ensure the safety of the environment," said company president *(Name)*.

"The best thing is that the new biodegradable shipping materials work every bit as well as the foam peanuts for low-weight shock absorption," said shipping manager *(Name)*.

Contact: *(Name)*, Director of Customer Service

FOR IMMEDIATE RELEASE

(NAME OF COMPANY) ANNOUNCES EMPLOYEE "FLEX TIME" AND TELECOMMUTING PROGRAM

(Place, date) *(Name)*, vice president for human resources at *(Name of company)*, announced a major flex time and telecommuting program for employees. Under the new program, *(Name of company)* staff will report to work at staggered intervals—or, in some cases, will not report to work at all.

Employees whose presence is required in the office will be given a range of starting times from 7:30 a.m. to 10:30, with corresponding quitting times. Approximately *(percent amount)* of the staff will work at least *(number)* days of each week at home, linked to the office by phone, fax, and computer modem.

Implementation of the program is expected to take *(number)* months.

"The benefits of this new policy are many," *(Name)* remarked. "Our staff can work more efficiently while they live more comfortably. Rush hour will become that much less congested, and if other firms follow suit, the environment and quality of life in our community will be improved."

— Press Releases Concerning Specific Products —

Contact: *(Name)*, Customer Service

FOR IMMEDIATE RELEASE

(NAME OF COMPANY) INTRODUCES NEW ULTRA QUIET LINE OF LAWN AND HEDGE CARE POWER TOOLS

(Place, Date) *(Name of company)*, long known for its optimum-quality line of mowers, edgers, and hedge trimmers, today announced a new line of "Ultra quiet" lawn and hedge care power tools.

"Anyone who has moved out to the suburbs hoping to escape the noise of the big city is soon disappointed," observed company president *(Name)*. "Come Saturday morning in spring and summer, the suburbs are very noisy places. The air is filled with the whine and roar of mowers, trimmers, and other power tools. It's bad for the environment. It's bad for our quality of life. And it's bad for our ears—and the ears of our children."

In an effort to reduce this major source of noise pollution, *(Name of company)* has developed a patented, super-advanced series of mufflers, which effectively reduce engine noise by *(percent)* amount without reducing effective power output or impacting fuel economy.

"We are very proud of this breakthrough achievement," said President *(Name)*.

Complete information on this new line of Ultra quiet power tools for lawn and garden is available by dialing *(phone number)*.

Contact: *(Name)*, Director of Customer Service

FOR IMMEDIATE RELEASE

(NAME OF COMPANY) ANNOUNCES RECYCLING PROGRAM
FOR BATTERIES

(Place, Date) Users of *(Name of company)* batteries need never throw another spent battery away. Instead, used batteries may be returned to the dealer for recycling.

Taking a cue from the glass bottle industry, *(Name of company)* will now include a modest deposit in the price of its batteries. Users who return spent cells will receive a refund of their deposit. More importantly, the environment will receive a new lease on life.

"The disposal of batteries of all kinds poses a serious environmental threat," *(Name of company)* president *(Name)* remarked today. "Heavy metals are not biodegradable. By recycling used batteries, everybody wins: The consumer wins, the manufacturer wins, and the environment wins. I am very excited about this new product and this new program."

The new batteries, which will cost on average *(percent amount)* more than conventional batteries plus a *(¢ amount)* refundable deposit, perform as well and last as long as the ordinary alkaline product. They will be available nationwide by *(date)*.

— Letters: Responding to Questions of General Policy —

Dear *(Name)*:

Thank you for your letter of *(date)* concerning *(Name of company's)* policy on using recycled materials in the manufacture of *(product)*.

As we state on our packaging, it is our policy to use at least *(percent)* amount recycled materials in the following products:

> *(list)*

As the technology becomes available, we intend to increase this percentage and also extend the use of recycled materials to such products as:

> *(list)*

At *(Name of company)*, we are committed to responsible behavior with respect to the environment, and we will continue to explore technologies that respect the environment while supplying our customers with the most cost-effective products we can create.

Sincerely yours,

Dear *(Name)*:

Thank you for your letter asking about our "telecommuting" policy.

At *(Name of company)*, approximately *(percent amount)* of our employees work at least *(number)* days a week from their homes. In an age of electronic communications and data transfer, the nature of their jobs does not require their physical presence in the office. The trend will increase over time.

What does this mean to them?

> Time spent commuting is now time spent working, or devoting more time to the family.
>
> Money spent on commuting can now be allocated elsewhere.

What does our policy mean to you?

The same efficient service as always.

A less congested rush hour. (Our cars are off the road.)

A less polluted environment.

(Name of company) is committed to our community and to our planet. We hope that other employers in *(place)* will experiment with programs similar to ours, and we have already met with several firms to share our experiences.

Sincerely,

———————

Dear *(Name):*

Thank you for your letter of *(date)* inquiring about our position on animal testing.

The answer to your question is an emphatic: No.

We do not test any of our products on animals, and we have not done so since *(year)*.

Furthermore, we endeavor to work exclusively with suppliers who use non-animal test methods only. At *(Name of company)*, we do not believe that it is necessary to hurt any living thing in order to make a fine product.

Sincerely,

———————

Dear *(Name):*

Many thanks for your recent suggestions about ways in which *(Name of company)* might minimize its packaging in order to conserve materials and protect the environment.

At *(Name of company)*, we are continually researching ways in which we can make our packaging more economical and less demanding on natural resources. In fact, since *(year)*, we have reduced use of nonrecycled packaging materials by *(percent)* amount. We have slashed use of non-biodegradable materials by *(percent amount)*.

And we're still working on doing even better—without, of course, compromising the quality of our packaging.

I have shared your suggestions with our Design, Engineering, and Shipping departments. Shipping in particular likes your suggestion concerning *(subject)*.

Once again, thanks.

Sincerely,

— Letters: Responding to Questions Concerning Specific Products —

Dear *(Name)*:

Thank you for your letter of *(date)* concerning disposal of used Super Solvent.

As with any petroleum-based substance, it is imperative for the protection of the environment that Super Solvent be disposed of properly at a registered household hazardous waste disposal site. Here is a list of such sites in your area:

> *(list)*

If you must store used Super Solvent, do so only in its original container, in a dry, well-ventilated area and keep from sources of heat or open flame.

Sincerely,

Dear *(Name)*:

Thank you for your inquiry concerning the environmental impact of our Brilliant Brand paints.

I have enclosed detailed Product Safety Data Sheets on these products, with particular emphasis on the quantity of gases released into the atmosphere under varying conditions. I'll let you study the figures and judge the environmental effects for yourself. However, I would like to highlight the following points:

1. *(point 1)*

2. *(point 2)*

3. *(point 3)*

4. *(point 4)*

I am confident you will agree that Brilliant Brand offers the best combination of beauty, durability of finish, and environmental safety of any paint available at present.

If you have any questions, please call Customer Service at *(phone number)*.

Sincerely,

— Memos: Promoting/Selling Environmental Responsibility —

Date:

To: All Customer Services Representatives
From: *(Name)*, Director of Customer Service
Re: Selling Environmental Responsibility

Back in the dark ages—that is, maybe five to ten years ago—too many manufacturers didn't much want to talk about the environment. Thank goodness, that's all changed.

(Name of company) is committed to maintaining environmentally sound policies. It's simple: People feel good doing business with a company that is a good neighbor and a good citizen, and our goal is to be both.

I urge you to promote our environmental policy, as appropriate, when you respond to customer questions and issues. Discuss the following list of specific milestones we have completed in the past year:

(list)

Date:

To: All Customer Service Representatives
From: *(Name)*, Director of Customer Service
Re: Promoting environmental features

Please be certain that you are aware, and that you make our customers aware, of the environmentally sound features of our new line of *(product)*.

These features include:

> *(list)*

(Name of company) believes that these product features are not only good for the environment, but good for business, too. Customers *want* to buy environmentally responsible products!

— Memos: Transmitting/Summarizing Customer Concerns —

Date:

To: All Customer Service Representatives
From: *(Name)*, Director of Customer Service
Re: Recycled materials

A number of us have been receiving questions from customers inquiring about *(Name of company's)* policy on manufacturing with recycled materials. Please convey to such customers the following information:

1. *(Name of company)* uses an average of *(percent)* amount recycled material in the manufacture of most products.

2. As the technology becomes available, we will use more recycled materials.

3. The recycled materials we use meet or exceed the specifications of all-new material.

Date:

To: All Customer Service Representatives
From: *(Name)*, Director of Customer Service
Re: Animal testing

One of our representatives responded recently to a call from an irate customer who was convinced that *(Name of company)* tests products on animals. Unfortunately, the representative did not have the facts at his fingertips and had to promise to get back to the caller.

Let's set the record straight now.

(Name of company) uses no animals to test products. This has been policy since *(year)*.

(Name of company) gives preference to suppliers who, likewise, do not perform animal tests. This has been policy since *(year)*.

Date:

To:	All Customer Service Representatives
From:	*(Name)*, Director of Customer Service
Re:	"Wasteful" packaging

A growing number of customers are concerned about how we—and other firms—package their products. There is growing resistance to nonrecycled, nonbiodegradable materials, especially styrofoam. Here is our current policy:

Wherever possible, we use recycled shock-absorbing materials.

We do not use foam "peanuts."

We do not use plastic bubble wrap.

We *do* use custom-molded styrofoam to cradle delicate merchandise. It affords maximum product protection. At present, there is no adequate substitute, but we are continually investigating biodegradable alternatives.

—Memos: Transmitting/Summarizing Public Concerns

Date:

To:	All Customer Service Representatives
From:	*(Name)*, Director of Customer Service
Re:	Pollution of *(Name of body of water)*

A number of *(Name of company)* employees have reported hearing a rumor that our company has discharged pollutants into *(Name of body of water)*.

Let's be clear about one thing: *(Name of company)* has not—and has never—discharged any pollutant of any kind into *(Name of body of water)*.

The source of this rumor is currently under investigation.

Since it is only a rumor, *(Name of company)* does not deem it appropriate to lend credibility to it by issuing a formal denial. However, it is possible that some of you may receive calls concerning this alleged situation. If you receive such a call, respond with this information:

1. *(Name of company)* has not, and has never discharged any pollutant of any kind into *(Name of body of water)*.

2. It is the policy and conviction of *(Name of company)* to respect the environment.

3. The procedures we use to check all discharge from the company are:

   (list)

4. We would appreciate any information you may have as to the source of the rumor.

Date:

To: All Customer Service Representatives
From: *(Name)*, Director of Customer Service
Re: Impact of new parking lot

Some of our residential neighbors are understandably concerned over the expansion of our parking facility. Should you receive calls from concerned individuals, please furnish the following information:

1. The parking lot is being built to blend into the community. It includes trees, shrubbery, and beautiful landscaping.

2. The expanded parking facility will not be used on weekends or on weekdays after *(time)* o'clock.

3. The expanded facility will have a very *positive* impact on the local street parking situation, freeing up approximately *(number)* spaces during weekdays—a *(percent amount)* increase in available parking spaces.

4. Because fewer of our employees' and clients' cars will be searching the neighborhood for parking, local traffic conditions should improve markedly.

5. In view of the above, our neighbors can expect the expanded parking facility to *improve* the quality of life in our community.

Chapter 39

Consumer Advice
and Product-Related Education

How to Do It

The communications in this chapter relate directly to the education and training role of the Customer Service Department. This role is not a customer service "frill," but rather, gets to the very heart of customer service as a *revenue-generating* function of the organization. Any effective program of education and training does the following:

1. Builds and reinforces a relationship between the customer and the company, enhancing customer loyalty by enhancing the customer's perception of the value of what she has purchased.

2. Enhances the perception of product performance by showing customers how to use the product most effectively and appropriately.

3. Provides an opportunity to promote the purchase of accessories and related products.

Public Service Bulletins

Public service bulletins promote a company and its products while educating the public in some significant way. These should not become disguised advertisements for the firm or its products. Customers readily see through such disguised ads and resent them, finding confirmation of a cynical view of corporate self-promotion tactics. The public service bulletin should provide a definite, no-strings-attached service with definable value. That alone will promote the company and its products.

Responding to Consumer Questions

Providing helpful information and advice is one of the strongest boosts to a company's image. It is also often an opportunity to promote a product or service that addresses the customer's question or issue directly. However, if you are writing in response to a consumer's question, make sure your primary focus is in answering that question. Clearly subordinate any product or service promotion to that primary purpose.

Suggestions for Responding to Consumer Questions

As the occasions arise, share your experience in responding to consumer questions. What kinds of questions might your colleagues (both within the department and in other departments) expect on current hot topics, products, or services? What kinds of responses have you found useful? To what resources might your colleagues direct customers?

— Product-Related Public Service Bulletins: Eight Samples —

1

IF YOU ANSWER YES TO THE FOLLOWING THREE QUESTIONS . . .

You may be eligible for up to *($ amount)* through the federal Earned Income Credit program!

1. Did you work at least part time during *(last year)*?

2. Did you earn less than *($ amount)* as a family in *(last year)*?

3. Did a child live with you for at least six months during *(last year)*?

If you answered yes to all three of the above, you are entitled to the Earned Income Credit (EIC), a tax benefit for working families.

If you owe federal income tax, the EIC will reduce the amount you owe. If you don't owe any federal income tax, the government will send you a check for the amount of your EIC benefit.

Here's what to do.

1. File a federal income tax return by April 15, 19__. Use Form 1040A or 1040, but *not* form 1040EZ.

2. Fill out a "Schedule EIC" and attach it to your tax return.

That's all there is to it.

2

AN IMPORTANT MESSAGE FROM ANY HEATING COMPANY

Do you know the warning signs of carbon monoxide poisoning?

Carbon monoxide poisoning is rare, but it can result when heating or water heating equipment is vented improperly.

Learn to recognize the warning signs.

1. Flu-like symptoms that disappear when you leave your home for a few hours.

2. Headaches, sleepiness, confusion.

3. Stinging, watery eyes.

4. Dizziness, weakness, nausea.

5. Ringing in the ears.

6. Shortness of breath.

7. Flushed skin.

If you experience any of these symptoms, seek fresh air immediately and call your gas company or Any Heating. Either of us will send out a representative to check out your heating and water heating equipment immediately.

Remember, carbon monoxide poisoning can be fatal. If you suspect a problem, let us—or your gas company—check it out. This is a free service.

3

WHAT MOTORISTS NEED TO KNOW IN (ANYTOWN)

Our community has a few motoring rules you may not be familiar with. *(Name)* Oil Company would like to pass on these reminders:

Right Turn on Red Permitted—Except where posted otherwise, right turns are permitted at red traffic signals *after* coming to a complete stop.

Overnight Parking Prohibited Except Where Posted—Overnight parking—after 3 A.M. and before 5 A.M.—is prohibited on many residential streets in *(Anytown)*. Exceptions are always posted.

Unattended Vehicles Must Be Locked—City ordinance 1234/5 specifies that all unattended vehicles on public property must be locked.

No Eating or Drinking While Driving—Drivers may not eat or drink (*any* beverage) while a vehicle is in motion or parked on public property.

In addition to these local ordinances, drivers must observe and obey all state laws, regulations, and ordinances.

4

(ANY) REALTY, INC. TIPS FOR MOVING WITH KIDS

In our country, one family in five moves annually, and some 9 million school-age children adapt to new homes and new schools.

At *(Any Realty)* we know that moving can be a trying time emotionally. It's hard enough on adults, and it can be stressful for kids.

Here are some ways to make the move easier on everybody:

1. Discuss the impending move with your kids. Tell them why you are moving. Give them something to look forward to. Let them share the excitement, but listen to their fears and anxieties.

2. Get your kids involved in the house-hunting process. Let them look around. Ask them what they like and don't like.

3. To the extent possible, let your kids choose their own rooms and special places in the new house.

4. If possible, take your children to their new neighborhood. Let them look around.

5. As soon as possible, visit the new school. Get a copy of the school handbook, newsletter, and yearbook.

6. Subscribe to local community newspapers.

7. When it comes time to move, let your children help with the packing, particularly of their own treasures. Let them mark their own boxes. You might ask the moving company to deliver these items first.

8. We know that settling in is hard. But don't get so bogged down with unpacking that you put off exploring the new area. Take your kids out into the new world as soon as possible. Discover your new neighborhood with them.

5

(ANY) MOVERS PRESENTS "HOW TO MOVE WITH PETS"

Let's face it, moving to a new place creates plenty of excitement, and plenty of anxiety, too. One thing you worry about is how those other members of your family—your dogs, cats, birds, and fish—will adapt.

Here's some tips to make moving with pets easier.

1. Identify your pets. Any collar worn should provide your new address and phone number. Take pictures of your pets.

2. Obtain all appropriate veterinary records, including rabies and other vaccination certificates.

3. If you are traveling by air, be sure to check out all special procedures with the airline. Feed your pets no less than five hours before flight time. Purchase a "travel kennel" (available in most pet shops) that is equipped with a stationary plastic cup you fill with ice cubes to quench your pet's thirst.

4. If you are traveling by car, make sure you have a roomy, comfortable pet carrier. Bring sufficient food, and provide small amounts every day. Offer water several times a day. Make frequent rest and exercise stops. Assign one family member the responsibility of looking after the pet during these stops.

5. If your pet tends to get sick during long trips, obtain medication from your veterinarian.

6. Plan your trip. Make reservations in motels that allow pets.

7. Never, *never* leave pets in a closed car during warm weather!

8. Transport fish in large, sealable plastic bags half-filled with water from their aquarium. Place the bag(s) in a foam picnic container to stabilize temperature. Never put the container in the car trunk! Open the bags several times during the day to replenish oxygen.

9. Transport small pets (hamsters, birds, mice) in their own cages. Cover the cage to reduce nervousness. Give water at frequent intervals. Do not transport these animals in the trunk!

10. Once you have arrived at your new home, it is best to confine the animals to the house for a week to ten days. Some dogs and cats will try to return to their old homes.

11. Find out about the new community's pet ordinances promptly, including licensing, leash laws, and clean-up regulations.

6

THE (ANY) LAND COMPANY BULLETIN ON:
SHOPPING FOR RECREATIONAL PROPERTY

Having a place of your own to "get away from it all" is great, and finding just the right place can be a wonderful experience too, if you follow a few do's and don'ts:

DO

1. Buy your vacation property for enjoyment, not for investment.

2. Try out your vacation locale by renting before buying.

3. Ask yourself: Could I retire here?

4. Inspect your vacation home as thoroughly and thoughtfully as you would inspect a home purchased as a primary residence.

5. Try shopping in the "off-season" for the best prices.

6. Find others in the area. Talk to them before you buy.

7. Let yourself get excited. But cool off before you sign on the dotted line.

8. Check the developer's credentials with the local resort association, Better Business Bureau, or the American Resort and Residential Developers Association.

DON'T

1. Buy in an area you are visiting for the first time even if you are carried away by it.

2. Buy in an area you rarely visit even if the property seems like a real bargain.

3. Expect a hefty rental income.

4. Buy a fixer-upper if you can't be present to supervise contractors.

7

(ANY) WATERPROOFING COMPANY—ASKS YOU TO GO DOWN TO THE BASEMENT

Psychologists call it "denial."

"Oh, sometimes the basement just gets wet."

"What do you expect when you live in a rainy climate?"

"Well, it's only a little water."

A house inspector would call it "disaster." At *(Any)* Waterproofing, we call it "fixable."

Please, take a look in your basement, and ask yourself: Is it chronically wet?

If the honest answer is yes, read on.

A wet basement usually results from poor drainage around the house. If water has no place to go, it will seep into the soil, then through your foundation, and into your basement. Or if your drainage is adequate, a wet basement may be the result of deteriorating support walls.

Either way, don't ignore it.

Call a qualified contractor in to inspect your drainage conditions and the structural integrity of your foundation support walls.

We'll perform these services free of charge, and there is never any obligation.

Except, of course, to your house.

8

A FEW WORDS ABOUT FIRE SAFETY FROM (ANY) INSURANCE COMPANY

There are two steps you can take right now to help ensure your family's safety in case of fire.

First—Put smoke detectors on every level of your house. Test them monthly. Make sure the batteries are fresh.

Second—Draw a floor plan of your home.

Make sure you show the exits from each room. It is safest to show *two* exits for each room.

Hold a discussion on family emergency procedures that includes the following:

1. Know which doors to close.

2. Have two escape routes from each room.

3. In a fire, test doors. If the door feels hot to the touch, take an alternate escape route.

4. Stay low: Crawl and hold your breath.

5. Escape fast. Don't stop to pack.

6. Meet at a predesignated *outdoor* location.

7. Call the fire department from a neighbor's house.

8. Do not go back into a burning building.

— Letters: Responding to Consumer Questions —

Dear *(Name)*:

I am responding to your questions about how to choose a personal computer.

I have an easy answer, and it's a very good answer, although you may not find it very helpful. The easy answer is this: The right personal computer is the one that is right for you. (That's why they're called "personal.")

Now, how do you decide what's right for you?

The best way is to ask yourself some questions.

1. What will I use the computer for? Word processing? Spreadsheets? Graphics? Communications? Games? All of these?

2. How much do I want to spend?

3. Am I comfortable with technology?

Armed with the answers to this self-exam, look through the brochures I've enclosed. They make recommendations about what's best for word processing, graphics, and so on. They also give complete price information. And finally, they will give you a good idea of what is provided with varying levels of technical sophistication.

I hope you find this information helpful.

Sincerely,

Dear *(Name)*:

Thank you for your inquiry concerning the use of our latex caulking for patching cracks in wood.

What your friend told you is perfectly true. Our latex caulk is very good for patching wood cracks. The beauty of it is that the latex is flexible and will expand and contract along with the wood. This is not the case with such conventional wood fillers as spackle or wood putty.

The caulking gun, by the way, makes it particularly easy to fill long cracks.

Sincerely,

— Memos: Suggestions for Responding to Customer Questions —

Date:

To: All Customer Service Representatives
From: *(Name)*, Director of Customer Service
Re: "Why does yours cost more?"

It's a fair question. And you are going to hear it a lot.

Why does the *(Name of company)* *(product)* cost more than the *(product)* offered by our competition?

The first part of the answer is threefold:

1. Quality

2. Flexibility

3. Customer service

We use higher-quality components, which are pretested in a series of shake-downs, including the following:

> *(list)*

Our *(product)* can be expanded and upgraded. All of our upgrades have been proven compatable with the installed base.

Everyone promises to support their product. Consider these specific support channels we maintain:

> *(list)*

All of these are part of total value received for the purchase price.

Now there is a second part to the answer.

It begins with a question: What does the customer mean by "cost"?

If he means initial purchase price, then, yes, our *(product)* does cost more. However, if he means total value received, ours costs less, because total cost includes backup support. And there is even more. You don't buy a *(product)* today and discard it tomorrow. You use it for months and for years. Over that long haul, our *(product)* actually costs *less* than the competition by providing longer useful life. Refer your customer to the attached maintenance cost and durability chart, and send him one. Cost is measured in time as well as cash.

Date:

To: All Customer Service Representatives
From: *(Name)*, Customer Service Representative
Re: Useful books

Here is a list of books I've found useful—and I believe our customers will find useful—dealing with *(subject)*:

(list)

I've read or at least dipped into all of them myself, and I feel confident in recommending them.

––––––––––

Date:

To: All Customer Service Representatives
From: *(Name)*, Director of Customer Service
Re: Technical bulletin #1234

I want to urge all customer service representatives to familiarize themselves with Tech bulletin #1234, which contains new ambient temperature recommendations for our Endurall Adhesive. I don't believe this bulletin has been widely distributed, and the information is quite important!

About the Author

Michael Ramundo is CEO of MCR Marketing, Inc., Cincinnati, Ohio, a training and consulting company specializing in service, sales, sales support and leadership development. The company also conducts research and publishes material about training, leadership, marketing, customer service and sales.

Michael has trained thousands of customer service, sales and management professionals since 1971. He has helped both large and small clients from diverse industries. His clients include the IRS, Digital Equipment Corporation, Cincinnati Milacron, Procter & Gamble, 3M Corporation, General Electric, Abbott Laboratories, DuPont, Cincinnati Bell, ADP, Minolta, Fuji, FTD and hundreds of others.

His career includes more than twenty-five years of corporate management experience at Vulcan Engineering, Food Management, Inc., and Cincinnati Milacron, a world-wide manufacturer of high-technology manufacturing machinery. Michael has managed servicing operations which produced more than 120,000 hours of technical training annually. As a product manager, he also managed marketing and new design developments for a $100 million product line.

Michael has served as adjunct faculty at Northern Kentucky University, the University of Cincinnati, Xavier University and the University of Syracuse. He currently serves as adjunct faculty with the University of Wisconsin and the American Management Association. He holds degrees from Miami University and the University of Oklahoma.

Index